THE RIVAL WIDOW.

MW01041729

Elizabeth Cooper's *The Rival Widows, or Fair Libertine* provides a unique opportunity to restore to scholarly and pedagogical attention a neglected female writer and a play with broad and significant implications for studies of eighteenth-century history, culture and gender. Following the adventures of Lady Bellair, a "glowing, joyous young Widow," the storyline regenders standard expectations about desire, marriage, libertinism and sentiment. The play has not been reprinted since 1735; therefore this old-spelling edition gives scholars access to an important but neglected resource for studies of women writers and eighteenth-century theatre.

In an original and extensive introduction, Tiffany Potter presents cultural and historical information that highlights the scholarly implications of this newly available play. She offers a brief biographical sketch of the playwright; a summary of sources for specific elements of the play; an overview of the theatrical climate of the time (with particular focus on the conditions leading to the Licensing Act of 1737); a discussion of the place of women in eighteenth-century society; a summary of symbiotic cultural discourses of libertinism and sensibility in the early eighteenth century; and a discussion of the general cultural significance of Cooper's demonstration of the malleability of prescriptive gender roles.

Further value is added to this edition through its appendices, which reproduce documents relating to the playwright Elizabeth Cooper and to the Licensing Act of 1737 (including the text of the Act itself).

Tiffany Potter teaches in the Department of English at the University of British Columbia.

The Early Modern Englishwoman 1500–1750: Contemporary Editions

Series Editors: Betty S. Travitsky and Anne Lake Prescrott

Designed to complement *The Early Modern Englishwoman: A Facsimile Library of Essential Works, Contemporary Editions* presents both modernized and old-spelling editions of texts not only by women but also for and about women. Contents of a volume can range from a single text to an anthology depending on the subject and the audience. Introductions to the editions are written with the general reader as well as the specialist in mind. They are designed to provide an introduction not only to the edited text itself but also to the larger historical discourses expressed through the text.

Other titles in the series:

Genre and Women's Life Writing in Early Modern England
Edited by Michelle M. Dowd and Julie A. Eckerle

Lives of Spirit
English Carmelite Self-Writing of the Early Modern Period
Nicky Hallett

Women's Letters Across Europe, 1400–1700
Form and Persuasion
Edited by Jane Couchman and Ann Crabb

Autobiographical Writings by Early Quaker Women
David Booy

The Rival Widows, or Fair Libertine (1735)

Mrs Elizabeth Cooper

Edited by Tiffany Potter

UNIVERSITY OF TORONTO PRESS
Toronto Buffalo London

Published in cloth by Ashgate Publishing Ltd, 2007
ISBN 978-0-7546-5478-0
Available at www.ashgate.com

ISBN 978-1-4426-1545-8 (paper)

Library and Archives Canada Cataloguing in Publication

Cooper, Mrs. (Elizabeth), fl. 1737
The rival widows, or, Fair libertine (1735) / Elizabeth Cooper ; edited by Tiffany
Potter.

Includes bibliographical references and index.
ISBN 978-1-4426-1545-8

I. Potter, Tiffany, 1967-   II. Title.   III. Title: Fair libertine.   IV. Title: Rival
widows.

PR3369.C17R58 2013   822'.5   C2012-907324-5

University of Toronto Press acknowledges the financial assistance to its publishing
program of the Canada Council for the Arts and the Ontario Arts Council.

 Canada Council Conseil des Arts
for the Arts du Canada

University of Toronto Press acknowledges the financial support of the
Government of Canada through the Canada Book Fund for its publishing
activities.

Contents

General Editors' Preface

Foregrounding women and gender has created a genuine revolution in the way we construct the early-modern period, and the aim of *Contemporary Editions* (like its sister series, *The Early-Modern Englishwoman, 1500–1750: A Facsimile Library of Essential Works*) is to encourage and perpetuate this revolution by making available the texts that in so many ways have generated it.

Contemporary Editions shares with the facsimile series a desire to recover neglected or unknown texts as well as to make more readily available texts that the feminist rereading of the period has now brought to light. Apart from the inherent differences in editorial methodology between the two series, the format of the new series permits a fuller response to the wide range of writings of and about women. *Contemporary Editions* is designed to provide distinguished editions, in both modernized and old-spelling format, of writings not only by but also for and about early-modern women. Volumes include long, interpretive essays and range widely in format from anthologies to single texts.

We hope that this series will capture the energy of the many scholars who are engaged in the reinterpretation of the early modern period, and that *Contemporary Editions* will in time become, like its sister project, 'a library of essential works' for the study of early modern women and gender.

List of Illustrations

Acknowledgements

This edition is the result of many colliding and colluding influences, and I would like to offer my thanks to the many institutions and individuals who have contributed to its production. My own sense of the cultural importance and the inherent pleasure of Elizabeth Cooper's play has been confirmed over several years of teaching it to students who have tolerated photocopied texts and eighteenth-century fonts long enough. I owe a debt of gratitude to every student in my classes in eighteenth-century drama and in libertine culture at the University of British Columbia, and particularly to the following students, each of whom contributed an original annotation to this edition: Jennifer Caine, Laura Dosanjh, Nina Nadkarni and Tiffany Sloan. Even greater thanks are due to Kina Cavacchioli, a brilliant research assistant and scholar in her own right who worked tirelessly and cheerfully throughout this project.

At Ashgate Press, I am grateful to Erika Gaffney, my endlessly helpful commissioning editor, and to Betty Travitsky and Anne Prescott, the series editors, for their constant stream of good advice and for their progressive action to increase the availability of texts by women writers for scholars, teachers and students. Thanks too to desk editor Meredith Coeyman for all of her suggestions. I owe thanks also to Jessica Munns and *Restoration and Eighteenth-Century Theatre Research* for publishing the first full article on *The Rival Widows*, and then for allowing me to include revised portions of it here.

Research for this edition was supported by the Social Sciences and Humanities Research Council of Canada, the American Society for Eighteenth-century Studies, the William Ready Special Collections at McMaster University and the William Andrews Clark Memorial Library at the University of California. I thank each of these organizations for their financial assistance and for their recognition of the importance of archival research as a discipline. In particular, I thank the staff at the William Ready Special Collections at McMaster University for providing the copy text for this edition and the title page images for reproduction. For permission to reproduce images from their collections, I thank the National Portrait Gallery in London, the British Museum, the House of Lords Record Office, and the Art Archive and the Garrick Club.

For their kind help in confirming the bibliographical consistency of the extant copies of the play, I thank the special collections librarians at Cambridge University, the University of Leeds, the Sutro Library in San Francisco, the University of

California at Los Angeles and Berkeley, Yale University, Syracuse University, the Huntington Library, the Folger Library, the Library of Congress, the Newberry Library, the University of Kentucky, the University of Michigan, Duke University, Rice University and the University of Texas at Austin.

Finally, I thank my husband, Ken Madden, and my daughter, Sloane Amelia Potter Madden, for their support, their love, and their patience in listening with apparently authentic curiosity to eternal titbits about the eighteenth century, no matter how arcane.

Tiffany Potter
University of British Columbia
2007

Introduction

Tiffany Potter

When Elizabeth Cooper is discussed at all in literary scholarship, it is very often in reference to her 1737 anthology of poetry, *The Muses Library*. Less widely recognized is Cooper's contribution to our understanding of gender and its determinative value in mid-eighteenth-century England, particularly with reference to the waning cultural vogue of libertinism and the waxing one of sentimentalism. Cooper's 1735 play *The Rival Widows, or Fair Libertine* not only re-genders the libertine dramatic hero (with all of the shocking action, witty thrills, and disruption of prescriptive gender this implies), but does so in a way that appropriates and manipulates the culture of sentiment so influential to the stage at the time. In its clever interplay between the often symbiotic roles of performative libertinism and spectatorial sentiment, *Rival Widows* encompasses two cultural discourses traditionally held to be oppositional. In her heroine, Lady Bellair, Cooper creates a female libertine who does not even think of reforming herself until the last lines of the play, at least in part because from the start she has combined libertinism and sentiment into a perfectable image of feminine desire, frank sexuality, social autonomy, razor wit, and unregretted pleasure, unified by a truly good nature and concern for the pains and happiness of others.

Elizabeth Cooper

According to Yvonne Noble, writing in the *Oxford Dictionary of National Biography*, Elizabeth Cooper lived between approximately 1698 and 1761. She was the daughter of Aubrey Price and Bridget Claypoole (daughter of the second wife of John Claypoole, who had earlier been married to Oliver Cromwell's daughter Elizabeth). Cooper was married to a Covent Garden auctioneer, John Cooper, from February of 1722 until his death in 1729, and bore him six children (one of whom died in its first year). After being widowed at a relatively young age, Cooper first tried her hand at performing on stage. In 1734, she was employed as an actor in the Company at Drury Lane, playing roles in James Ralph's *The Cornish Squire* and the pantomime *Cupid and Psyche, or Columbine Courtezan*. That same year she organized a benefit performance for herself, playing Lady Easy in a Lincoln's Inn Fields performance of Colley Cibber's *The Careless Husband*. She acknowledges in a letter to the *Grub-Street Journal* that the leading role might 'be thought too great an attempt, for, almost, a first tryal' (see appendix A). And perhaps it was, for Cooper seems to have given up acting that same season, turning instead to playwriting. The Covent Garden Theatre's staging of *Rival Widows* was her authorial debut. The play ran on February 22, 25 and 27, and March 1, 4 and 6 of 1735,[1] a six night run that would have been considered a success, especially for a new play by an unknown author. Cooper would have received the proceeds of her two benefit nights on the third and sixth performances. She chose to play the leading role of Bellair herself in those performances, much to the dismay of *The Prompter*, which ran an extended review of the play on March 7 expressing outrage that playwrights dare turn actors too (see appendix B). A much later review in David Baker's 1764 history of English theatre (*Biographia Dramatica*) notes that the play met 'with some success ... Allowing for the too common freedom of female dramatists, this is far from bad comedy' (III: 212–13). Although Cooper does not seem to have worked again as an actress, she did write a second play: *The Nobleman, or The Family Quarrell* ran on May 17, 18 and 19, 1736 at the Haymarket, but was never published, perhaps being overshadowed, as was so much else that season, by Henry Fielding's runaway hit *Pasquin*, which occupied the Haymarket stage for much of the year.

Given that her late husband had specialized in auctioning art, books and manuscript collections, it is not surprising that, after the Licensing Act put an end to her dramatic career, Cooper's next major project was *The Muses Library: or, a Series of English Poetry from the Saxons to the Reign of King Charles II*, published in 1737. The volume was the first of a projected series but did not sell well, and plans for subsequent volumes were abandoned. Despite its limited financial success at the time, *The Muses Library* is important; Elizabeth Eger calls it 'an early reclamation project' in which Cooper's almost 'antiquarian interest in the buried poems of the past' allowed '[a]uthors now considered firmly canonical, such as Gower and Langland, [to be] rescued from oblivion' (203–4). In creating the collection, Cooper borrowed books from the antiquary William Oldys and contacted poets' descendents in search of unpublished manuscripts; she also researched biographical information and offered concise but insightful critical commentaries on the literary material she rescued. Noble notes that modern scholars have said that the anthology was 'the model for Samuel Johnson's format in his *Lives of the Poets*' and 'the chief inspiration for Thomas Chatterton's antique style'. Although Cooper does not appear to have been widely praised during her life, Baker thought her a writer 'whom we must rank among the Female Geniusesof this Kingdom' (I: 148).

---

[1] Although the *Biographia Dramatica* lists the play as running for nine nights, I find more probability in John Genest's tally in *Some Account of the English Stage*, which also lists the plays that alternated nights with productions of the *Rival Widows*.

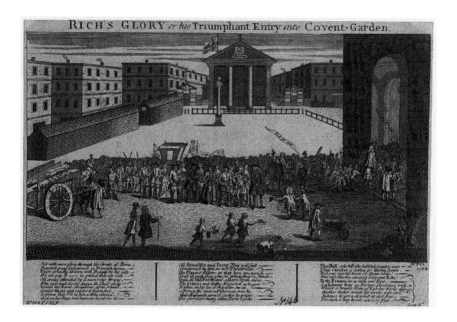

1 *Rich's Glory, or the Triumphant Entry into Covent Garden*, William Hogarth, 1732, British Museum

Hogarth's engraving represents John Rich crossing the piazza at the new Covent Garden Theatre, with St Paul's Church in the background. Though we might assume that Rich is the Harlequin (driving the carriage), the verse below indicates that he is 'proudly drawn with Beauty by his side,' which would locate him as the figure appearing as a dalmation (perhaps the performing dog that appeared in his production of *Perseus and Andromeda*). Lacy Ryan is also depicted here in Roman garb: 'The Players follow, as they here are nam'd. / Quinn th' Old Batch'lour, a Hero Ryan shows, / Who Stares and Stalks Majestick as he goes.'

Sources

The Rival Widows is a play of its own day, engaging and interrogating many expected narratives and types of scenes from both the libertine and sentimental traditions. It also, however, has at least two scenes that are notably similar to those in works by earlier playwrights. As John Genest notes in *Some Account of the English Stage* (1832), much of the lovers' proviso scene in Act III scene 12, including the negotiation of exemptions and Bellair's eventual promise not to love Freelove are 'copied from Hide Park act 2 scene the last'. Although 'copied' is an exaggeration, most of the exemptions and some phrasing are indeed borrowed from James Shirley's *Hyde Park* (1637). Genest also exaggerates when asserting that the 'two speeches of Modern, about the pleasures of the country [Act III, scene 9], are copied from Massinger's Guardian' (III: 462). Several details do carry over from Philip Massinger's *The Guardian* (1633)—most notably the phrase 'whorish air', breakfasting on nectar, and a reference to Echo—but the borrowing is primarily in the general tenor of the speeches.

There is also one plausible and interesting biographical source for the play's action: both Cooper's mother and grandmother appear to have had the misfortune to put their trust in the wrong men (see Noble). The grandmother, Blanche Claypoole, had brought a fortune of some £10,000 to her marriage, but Cooper's mother, Bridget—Blanche's only heir—was by the time of Elizabeth's birth already a widow and a pauper. Thus the restoration of the £10,000 of which Bellair is initially bilked by Lady Lurcher seems intriguingly like an imagined narrative of the life that might have been possible had Cooper's own mother's circumstances been different in her young widowhood.

Theatrical Environment

The wittily licentious and raucous environment of the Restoration theatre, both on-stage and off, is well known, but both stage and playhouse environments had been changing as the eighteenth century approached. By the end of the succession crises of the late seventeenth century, a less flippant and more socially grounded tone began to emerge in the plays that were staged. This was partly a response to the change in aristocratic mood as the reign of the libertine Charles II gave way first to the short and tense rule of his Roman Catholic brother, James II, and then to the firm Protestantism of William and Mary. At the same time, the growth of the middle class, together with that class's increased disposable income, led to a more intellectually and morally diverse audience. Because the audience also now included more women, argued such social critics as Jeremy Collier, the theatre should demand greater moral responsibility on the part of both playwrights and audiences. Collier voiced a widespread perception when he asserted that:

The Business of *Plays* is to recommend Vertue, and discountenance Vice; to shew the Uncertainty of Humane Greatness, the suddain turns of Fate, and the unhappy Conclusions of Violence and Injustice: 'Tis to expose the Singularities of Pride and Fancy, to make Folly and Falsehood contemptible, and to bring every Thing that is Ill under Infamy and Neglect ... [to stage immoral women before female audience members] is Violence to their Native Modesty, and a Misrepresentation of their Sex. For Modesty, as Mr. *Rapin* observes, is the *Character* of Women. To represent them without this Quality is to make Monsters of them (1.6).

Though both moralist and libertine plays continued to be produced during the first third of the new century, the trend was identifiably toward the conservative, both in the values of the heroic in the genre of bourgeois drama and in the increased appeal of emotion over wit in comedies. As Janet Todd puts it, the rise of sentimental comedy 'severed the tie of court and stage ... [because it was] associated with the parliamentarians, the supporters of the Protestant succession, the mercantile and less educated classes, with women, and those who held Whiggish sympathies' (33). The theatre-going experience, too, slowly became more decorous, and the physical theatre space reflected this shift with a growing separation of stage and audience, even if it was not until mid-century that David Garrick finally succeeded in ending the custom of allowing members of the audience on stage during the performance.

During the early eighteenth century, in relative proportion to more varied and larger audiences, the number of performance venues increased from the original two patent theatres up to twenty in the London area alone. The most important of the theatres were the Queen's Theatre opera house (made King's on George I's accession in 1714); the original patent theatres, Drury Lane and Lincoln's Inn Fields (replaced in 1732 by the Covent Garden Theatre); and the so-called illegitimate theatres, Goodman's Fields (opening in 1729) and the Little Theatre in the Haymarket (1720), which welcomed much of the politically-oriented and satirical material that would cause so much trouble.

It was perhaps the enormous success of John Gay's 1728 *The Beggar's Opera* at Lincoln's Inn Fields that opened the door to increased critical political commentary on stage, although Gay's use of the phrase 'great man' to link Prime Minister Robert Walpole to the highwayman Macheath and the stool-pigeon fence Peachum is mild compared to what followed. Henry Fielding was only one of several playwrights who worked political content into their plays, but he is certainly the best known, most prolific, and most successful of them, and was therefore long (if falsely) blamed for inviting governmental intervention in theatrical management. Though only a late handful of Fielding's more than twenty plays explicitly attack Walpole and his administration, those plays and others like them evoked outrage in powerful places. Fielding's *Don Quixote in England* (1734), *Pasquin* (1736), *Eurydice* (1737), *Eurydice Hissed* (1737) and *The Historical Register for 1736* (1737) all make explicit accusations of electoral corruption, drawing parallels between corrupt theatre managers and corrupt politicians, and parody bad theatre to point at what Fielding thought the appalling government of the 'Robinocracy'—a robbing government headed by Robert Walpole, who was frequently granted the pseudonym Robin in critical satires and political commentary.

For the authorities, the last straw was *The Vision of the Golden Rump*, which first appeared as an anti-Walpole essay in *Common Sense* (19 March 1737) and was reputedly dramatized for production at Goodman's Fields. The play was never staged, and no copy text survives; perhaps the dramatized version never existed at all, but was imagined for political purposes (and to avoid giving Fielding the satisfaction of having forced the government into action). In any case, by 20 May 1737 the Licensing Act had been introduced in Parliament, and despite brisk debate in the journals, only Lord Chesterfield offered effective parliamentary opposition. The measure received Royal Assent in June of 1737. Both the text of the act and arguments supporting or opposing it are printed as appendices in this volume, but in brief, the Licensing Act required that scripts for all new productions be approved by the Lord Chamberlain, and that dramatic performances be restricted to the two patent theatres, now Drury Lane and Covent Garden. Not least because the sudden narrowing of venues hugely increased profits for the surviving theatre managers, the number of new plays produced shrank precipitously. Nevertheless, creative minds endeavoured to slip through loopholes in the Act. Musical productions were not regulated, for example, and so a concert with a free dramatic performance during the interlude might easily go unchallenged. Similarly, performances without an admission fee were also excluded from the Act, which led to subterfuges such as selling food or drink to go with the 'free' dramatic entertainment. Though rarely enforced after the eighteenth century, the Licensing Act was not formally rescinded until 1969.

Libertinism and Sensibility

In its broadest terms, eighteenth-century libertinism[2] was an ideology and a public identity assumed by a small but highly influential group of privileged young people—generally men—that allowed members of that group to demonstrate their status above the reach of social, religious, moral, or sexual regulation and to flaunt their challenge of social assumptions and prescriptive normative culture. That most of those called 'libertines' were male members of the established élite is the first of many paradoxes concerning libertine identity. As James Grantham Turner points out, 'libertines may be seen as secular antinomians, not simply above the law, but

---

[2] For detailed discussion of English libertinism's evolution into the eighteenth century proper, see Tiffany Potter's *Honest Sins*, chapter 1. For the most current work on seventeenth-century models of libertinism, see James Turner's *Libertines and Radicals*.

deeply in need of the law to guarantee their privileges and to fuel their emotional rebellion. They confirm in the very act of infraction' ('Properties' 81). It is this paradox that provides a critical distinction between the libertine and the merely ill-behaved: while the less privileged might well be derided or even imprisoned for blasphemy, illicit sexuality, violence or public subversion, both libertines and the wider society above which they position themselves know that the libertine is virtually never subject to such consequences. The essential quality of libertinism is difference; distinct from all others, the libertine embraces social privilege as the means to confirm the capacity to subvert the very cultural assumptions required for that distinction.

Even in such an environment of paradoxical privilege and disruption at the zenith of libertinism's cultural vogue in the Restoration, men like George Villiers, Second Duke of Buckingham and John Wilmot, Second Earl of Rochester (and their fictionalized representations in figures such as George Etherege's Dorimant and William Wycherley's Horner) resented the boundaries of acceptability drawn by parliament's regulation of public behaviour and the conservative-moralist tenor of public opinion. They demanded for the privileged individual the freedom to think and act according to his or her own judgement, without regard to convention or a socially constructed morality. This extravagant individualism and its attendant emphasis on originality together function as a second major characteristic of libertinism. And from this in turn emerge some more concrete and publicly performable subsidiary ones. In the Restoration these include the unapologetic atheism that performs a libertine rejection of established religious doctrine; the pursuit of absolute sexual freedom through sometimes cruel but clever means; and the consequent increase in the sexual independence of certain culturally, economically or artistically privileged women in games of wit, conquest and status. These activities and attitudes are in turn related to the libertine fascination with disguise (in masks, masquerades and appropriated identities), which, aside from providing amusement, allowed both men and women to pursue pleasure without the impediment of accountability. Deeds requiring acknowledgement, however, could be justified by adopting a Hobbesian view of humanity, by privileging the supposedly natural over socially-constructed limits, and by an anti-rationalism denying that morality can be based on a human capacity for reason. It is a supposedly natural Hobbesian honour, not a socially determined or moralistic honour to which the libertine subscribes:

> *Honourable* is whatsoever possession, action, or quality, is an argument and signe of Power ... Dominion, and Victory is Honourable; because acquired by Power; and Servitude, for need, or feare, is Dishonourable ... Riches, are Honourable; for they are Power. Poverty, Dishonourable ... Nor does it alter the case of Honour, whether an action (so it be great and difficult, and consequently a signe of much power,) be just or unjust; for Honour consisteth onely in the opinion of Power. (Hobbes 155–6)

Such distinct constructions of honour are likewise made clear in Ned Ward's satirical poem 'The Libertine's Choice: or, the Mistaken Happiness of the Fool in Fashion' (1704). This accusatory summary of libertine views of religion and social regulation confirms a widespread perception of links among sexual privilege, atheism, Hobbeseanism, and naturalism:

> Let holy Guides prevail on Tim'rous Fools,
> T'abridge their Pleasure, and conform to Rules
> Impos'd on Youth, by Hoary heads long since,
> When dwindl'd into Age and Impotence;
> Hating their Vig'rous Progeny should taste
> Those Lushious Joys, their own weak Loins were past,
> Who in their Strength did Nature's Will Obey,
> And ne'er grew Temp'rate till their Hairs grew Gray;
> ...
> Then to some Rakish Friends my course I'd steer,
> Strangers to Faith, and Enemies to Fear;
> There Ridicule with them the Canting Priest,
> And make *Religion* but our Common Jest;
> Raise up Dead *Hobs* to Justifie our Cause,
> And overth[r]ow Divine, by Natures Laws;
> Burlesque the Scriptures, and Asperse the Creed,
> Aw'd by no Musty Rules; Love, Drink and Feed.
> This is the Happy Life we Modish Rakes would lead. (1–8, 426–34)

Though the Restoration saw its most impressive cultural moment, libertinism continued well into the eighteenth century. Libertinism lost its ascendancy, even among aristocrats, with the death of Charles II, but such a powerful and creative mode of performative identity could not simply be relegated to memory by the emerging culture of sentiment and the rising status of the merchant class. The central elements of Restoration libertinism are still present in Georgian libertinism, although in forms that moderate somewhat the consuming egocentrism of the earlier mode. Challenges to dominant cultural assumptions remain, as do the pursuit of individualism, self-determination, and power over others so as to assert privilege. Distrust of traditional religious doctrine continues to be central, of course, but less often as outright atheism than as attacks on blind faith or the failures of institutionalized religion, and a preference for a selective faith that subscribes to those parts of a religion that serve individual desires while rejecting those that interfere with self-satisfaction or that threaten punishment.

In particular, eighteenth-century libertine thinkers endeavoured to reveal philosophical failures in religion and to condemn what they saw as the tendency of of the established Church to function primarily in service of political and economic expedience. Bernard Mandeville's 'Enquiry into the Origin of Moral Virtue' (1714), for example, notes that

The chief Thing, therefore, which Lawgivers and other Wise Men, that have laboured for the Establishment of Society, have endeavour'd, has been to make the People they were to govern, believe, that it was more beneficial for every body to conquer than indulge his Appetites, and much better to mind the Publick than what seem'd his private Interest ... they extoll'd the Excellency of our Nature above other Animals, and setting forth with unbounded Praises the Wonders of our Sagacity and vastness of Understanding, bestow'd a thousand Encomiums on the Rationality of our Souls, by the help of which we were capable of performing the most noble Atchievements ... the first Rudiments of Morality, broach'd by skilfull Politicians, to render Men useful to each other as well as tractable, were chiefly contriv'd; that the ambitious might reap the more Benefit from, and govern vast Numbers of them with the greater Ease and Security. (81–2, 85)

A less widely known example of libertine comment on religion comes from *An Essay upon Improving and Adding to the Strength of Great Britain and Ireland, by Fornication, Justifying the Same from Reason and Scripture* (1735). Now generally attributed to Daniel Maclaughlan, though ostensibly 'by a young Clergyman', the essay adopts views similar to those of Mandeville and other philosophical libertines who advocated naturalism and the Rule of Right, the notion promulgated by intellectualist deist thought that there exists a natural and eternal reason of things, such that morality can be made into a rational science entirely without the requirement of divine sanction. To encourage fornication, the author asserts the culturally constructed nature of human rationality and redirects the Christian belief in a benevolent God:

whatever action introduces more Pleasure than pain among such perceptive Beings as we are, must always be agreeable to what we call Reason, and worthy the Dignity of our Nature. This is the great Rule of Righteousness; and a hearty, sincere Endeavour to conform our Lives to it, is the only Thing that can entitle us to the Favour of that benevolent Being, who proposed to himself no other thing than our Happiness in bringing us to Being; and who is only pleased with such of our Actions as are productive of our own Welfare, and is only displeased with us when we do these Things that necessarily give us Pain, and tend to make us miserable. If any one, therefore (pretending to have a particular Power and Commission from Almighty God, to instruct mankind in the Exercise of Piety, Virtue, and Temperance) shall offer to prescribe any thing inconsistent with our temporal Interest, we may safely reject him as a false prophet. (6–7)[3]

---

[3] The more traditional view of fornication is summarized in a passage from 'A Discourse on Fornication: Shewing the Greatness of that Sin,' published in 1698 by John Turner, Vicar of Greenwich: 'by consequence [of fornication], upon the Want and Deprivation of this Spiritual Assistance, we must lose both our Inclinations and our Power of being Religious. We must become subject to our Bodies, Appetites, and Sensual Delights ... from the dire Effects of this deadly Sin, they must fall into Atheism, Profaneness, Blasphemy, and an Universal Scorn, and Contempt of God and Religion' (48–9).

The link between eighteenth-century religious and philosophical libertinism and its socially disruptive physical manifestations is noted succinctly by Thomas Keymer in his analysis of Samuel Richardson's mid-century libertine anti-hero Lovelace. Keymer cites Samuel Johnson's definitions of the libertine, which range from the neutral 'one unconfined; one at liberty' to the more ominous 'one who lives without restraint or law' and 'one who pays no regard to the precepts of religion' (158); he then explains that in 'Johnson's definition, the libertine's transgression of law is only the practical counterpart of a more dangerous ideological licentiousness, which works not only to disregard particular laws at particular times, but also to demolish their very basis, the religious and moral structures by which *all* law is underpinned' (163). Those offended by the libertine rejection of social values seem rarely to have perceived the paradox mentioned above: libertines needed a public morality against which to define themselves as socially superior to such social regulation. Though hindsight makes this paradox clear enough, eighteenth-century moralists tended to condemn what they thought a libertine threat without recognizing that gamesmanship, rather than revolution, informs the culture of libertine pleasure.

Both male and female libertines of the eighteenth century still privilege the natural over artificially constructed social limits, but now with the proviso (absent in earlier, more Hobbesian versions) that no other person be injured in one's own pursuit of pleasure. Ward's 'The Libertine's Choice' again communicates the position succinctly:

> Shall I, if I've an Appetite to Eat,
> For Roots and Herbs forsake much better Meat:
> Or if my Heart to *Hymen* does incline,
> Must I Drink *Water*, when I Lust for *Wine*?
> No, let dull Bigots with the Stream agree,
> *Bacchus* shall be the Jolly God for me.
> What if *Celinda's* Graces I admire,
> And her soft Charms should set my Breast on fire;
> Why should not we, if the kind Dame agrees,
> Our Loving selves, instead of others Please?
> In doing which, we mutually approve
> The *Works* of Heav'n in the Delights of *Love*. (107–118)

This good-natured form of libertinism carries the libertine ethos through the age of sentiment that is so often assumed to have replaced Restoration libertine culture. In any case, the cultures of libertinism and sentiment were not the binary that they are often perceived to be, particularly when it comes to the sexuality of women like those depicted in Cooper's play. G.J. Barker-Benfield, for example, makes much of the potentially disruptive implications of a sentimental culture that so relishes sensual response, and he argues that sentimental fiction's image of woman as a moral measure was a conscious or unconscious attempt to manipulate and suppress these implications. These conflicts between intent and effect help to clarify how, despite the traditional ideal of a virtuous, passive and pious femininity in eighteenth-century discourses of sensibility, the freedom to pursue emotional, intellectual and other stimulation remained available to women of high privilege. Links between women's quests for pleasure and the framing discourses of sensibility and libertinism provide what Barker-Benfield terms 'dramatic evidence of women's wishes for the individual pursuit of self-expression and hetero-social pleasure in a wider world, the unambiguous expression of which was epitomized by the figure of the rake. The expressive consciousness connoted by "sensibility" extended even so far as women's own sexual wishes' (xvi–xvii). Perversely, then, libertinism and sensibility promote some of the same ends: a space for feminine desire or play, and a sense of the privileged individual's power to foster and then manipulate these natural instincts.

The culture of sentiment, then, did not then simply replace a culture of libertinism, even among the narrow groups that could lay claim to libertinism in the first place. But there was indeed a shift in cultural self-perception as the first part of the eighteenth century progressed, a shift marked by social changes such as an increase in the percentage of the population with disposable income and relative respectability; an expansion of literacy and greater availability of printed texts through circulating libraries; an increased value put on the affectionate nuclear family (though the actual prevelance of companionate marriage is in dispute); greater stress on benevolence rather than on doctrine in religion; and a shift from a Hobbesian view of primitive human life as poor, nasty, brutish and short to a more Shaftesburian belief in humanity's intrinsic virtue and goodness. These myriad shifts are reflected in a movement that combined them in a perhaps illogical but very influential way; as Barker-Benfield puts it: 'While sensibility rested on essentially materialist assumptions, proponents of the cultivation of sensibility came to invest it with spiritual and moral values' (xvii).

Although the terms 'sentiment' and 'sensibility' are often used interchangeably, Janet Todd makes a useful observation when she notes that, for the time when Cooper was writing, 'sentiment' is more appropriate for the earlier part of the century, whereas 'sensibility' (both as a term then in recently increased use and as a modern critical concept) suits the mid-century. In brief, 'sentiment' is a moral reflection, usually linked to intellectual articulations of experience and morality; 'sensibility', on the other hand, more clearly relates physiological, bodily response to stimulation, and is linked to refined emotion and compassion for suffering. There is, however, continuity between the two, especially when represented on the stage, as witness, for example, Richard Steele's *Conscious Lovers* (1722), a play that meets Todd's criteria for sensibility: it 'reveals a belief in the appealing and aesthetic quality of virtue, displayed in a naughty world through a vague and potent distress. This distress is rarely deserved and it is somehow in the nature of things', creating archetypal victims of sentiment and sensibility: the 'chaste suffering woman, happily rewarded in marriage or elevated into redemptive death, and the sensitive, benevolent man whose feelings are too exquisite for the acquisitiveness, vulgarity and selfishness of his world' (3, 4). But rather than encourage a pure emotional response to their dilemmas, Steele's characters articulate the intellectual and philosophical implications behind human suffering and triumph. Sir John Bevil, for example, closes the play with this speech to his son and his beloved:

> Now ladies and gentlemen, you have set the world a fair example. Your happiness is owing to your constancy and merit, and the several difficulties you have struggled with evidently show
> Whate'er the generous mind itself denies,
> The secret care of Providence supplies. (V iii)

As Steele argues in the Preface to *The Conscious Lovers*, the goal of comedy should be not laughter at the expense of a character, but a 'joy too exquisite for laughter, that can have no spring but in delight'. This idea became central to sentimental culture.

The view of human nature and morality that informs the culture of sentiment early in the century is perhaps best articulated by Anthony Ashley Cooper, Third Earl of Shaftesbury, whose *Inquiry Concerning Virtue* (1711) posits that all human beings have an innate moral sense allowing them to gain pleasure from the pursuit of virtue and to be predisposed by nature to search for a moral and civilized life, one above the cares of politics and free from the poverty and violence that were seen—if at times problematically—as emblematic of vice. In the conclusion to his *Inquiry*, Shaftesbury argues that those who are vicious or ill-natured

> are plainly *unnatural* ... to be wicked or vitious, is to be miserable and unhappy
> And since every vitious action must in proportion, more or less, help toward this mischief, and *self-ill*; it must follow, That every vitious action must be self-injurious and ill.
> On the other side; *the happiness* and *good* of Virtue has been prov'd from the contrary effect of other affectations, such as are according to nature.
> Upon the whole: there is not, I presume, the least degree of certainty wanting, in what has been said concerning the preferableness of *the mental pleasures to the sensual;* and even *of the sensual, accompany'd with good affection, and under a temperate and right use*, to those which are *no ways restrain'd, nor supported by any thing social or affectionate.* (2:112–13)

As Todd so concisely notes, for Shaftesbury, 'Virtue was enjoyable as a spectacle in the self and in others. It needed no divine rewards and punishment as its support' (26).

Related to such philosophical understandings and particularly useful for reading *The Rival Widows* is the idea of 'the polite'. As Brean Hammond argues in *Professional Imaginative Writing*, 'politeness' can be read as the social embodiment of economic public life: 'politeness became an ideal of sociable conduct—a touchstone of civilised behaviour that could be invoked within many different situations or activities. It was the quality that validated an individual's engagement in "polite company"'. The 'terms and forms of that . . . gentility', he says, 'were also available to be employed by upper-class individuals, who could claim gentility through birth but sought to display the powerful alternative signs of civic virtue that were developing within the bourgeois sphere' (22). With fresh recognition that traditional markers of status are performable, with a higher value put on benevolence, and with more belief in the innate goodness of human nature, 'the polite body itself can be said to *perform* an act of civilisation' (Goring 24), and 'genuine aristocrats could be encouraged to covet possession of the polite codes as a more virtuous and ethical alternative to those, like duelling and hunting, into which they were born' (Hammond 151).

As Hammond argues, bodily performance of civility in polite society was both removed from and appropriated by the aristocracy, further underlining the malleability and constructedness of a supposed of human nature and the physiological response to emotional stimulus in the culture of sensibility. This recognition is of course shared with libertinism, which was often, as Turner notes, 'not so much a philosophy as a set of performances, and its defining "properties" … are better understood as theatrical props than as precise attributes' (*Radicals* x). In *The Rival Widows*, Cooper nicely recognizes the paradox that both libertinism and sentiment are built upon a founding discourse of naturalism but are themselves each fundamentally performative. As Bellair consciously plays the libertine for her own entertainment and for pleasure in the power of her beauty and sexuality, she spends the entire play making her lovers recognize the role playing that they have so unconsciously naturalized. In forcing Young Modern to exchange his false libertine identity for an equally false Puritan one, and in forcing Freelove to see the weakness and lack of masculinity in the idealized man of feeling he strives to embody, Bellair shows the nature of her own rebellion: the true individual must recognize that public identity is performance or risk losing the self.

Bellair, Sentiment, Libertinism, and Gender

What makes Bellair's character different from that of the libertine heroes in earlier plays is not only her gender but also her ability to transcend the anti-emotional and worldly irony of a Dorimant or a Horner. She can feel emotion and be good natured without allowing herself or the men with whom she is involved to descend into the over-feminized and passive sentimentalism of near contemporary plays such as Steele's *The Conscious Lovers*.

The Rival Widows is particularly important to our understanding of how identity was constructed for women of a certain class, for both libertine and sentimental generic expectations contribute to the struggle for dominance between

Bellair and Lurcher. Intriguingly, both the play and the broader constructions of libertinism and sentiment that it engages parallel changes in early eighteenth century society, both public and domestic, that have been outlined by such historians as Margaret Hunt and Lawrence Stone. Stone, for example, argues that in the sixteenth and seventeenth centuries, 'each individual thinks of himself as unique, and strives to impose his own will on others for his selfish ends. The result is a Hobbesian state of nature, the war of all against all, which can only be brought under control by the imposition of stern patriarchal power in both the family and the state'. By the eighteenth century, though, 'all human beings are [understood to be] unique. It is right and proper for each to pursue his own happiness, provided that he also respects the right of others to pursue theirs. With this important proviso, egotism becomes synonymous with public good' (Stone 258). While the broad sweep of Stone's simplified summary of complex cultural change and human nature is certainly somewhat problematic, his phrasing articulates felicitously the characterization of Bellair and its embodiment of the tension between egotism and public good in her conflation of libertinism and sentiment as a strategy for an empowered femininity. The transitional cultures that Cooper engages continued to evolve, so that by the time of *Rival Widows'* production, it seems possible for one who is 'good Nature[d]', 'wit[ty]', 'generous', and 'Well-bred' to be 'Libertine without Scandal.'

As one of the most intelligent, good-natured, and powerful heroines to grace the eighteenth-century stage, Bellair is able to turn her culture's assumptions concerning her womanly weakness and her desire for financial security in marriage to her advantage. Her rival widow, Lady Lurcher, presumes that a woman without money must marry the highest bidder, and she attempts to use this expectation of female powerlessness against Bellair to serve her own desire for Freelove. Bellair, however, is desperate neither for money nor for the social and economic stability of marriage. In other words, Bellair does not claim the economic privilege that sustains her libertine status only when she achieves her rightful inheritance at the end of the play; she assumes it from the beginning as her birthright, refusing to deny herself the pleasure that comes from her status, regardless of the wealth actually in her possession at a given moment. The creditors scene in Act II, for example—located in a way that would leave an audience of a sentimental drama expecting to witness the distress of a penniless and frightened heroine—confirms the informed intelligence of the libertine heroine, who knows the economic exchange value of her cultural status. As Double's apparent allusion to Bernard Mandeville immediately confirms, Bellair triumphs in this scene because 'we do very different Things from the same Principles.—'Twas her Pride to wear those Jewels, and her Pride to part with them'.[4] She embodies both libertine pride in

---

[4] To further their argument that private vices are public benefits, Mandeville's *Fable of the Bees* and its 'Enquiry into the Origin of Moral Virtue', both of which were widely

privilege and sentimental pride in being fair to subordinates. The play's male leads exhibit either old-style libertinism (Young Modern) or soul-deep sentimentalism (Freelove). Bellair, however, has the still greater privilege and pleasure deriving not from a prosaic balance of the two but from a recognition that the good-natured libertine wins privilege at all levels.

Bellair's libertine character is confirmed in the play's title, of course, and although her fifth-act reformation is possibly heartfelt, her character is drawn so as to encompass almost every recognizably libertine trait. She repeatedly makes decisions based on what is 'natural' rather than on what is socially expected, while Cooper's framing Preface also gives as Bellair's defining characteristics her 'thinking for herself, and acting on the Principles of Nature and Truth'. She therefore rejects the performance of religion as any sort of key to true goodness, which she imagines as a good nature. This good nature has much in common with that articulated by one of her contemporaries, the playwright and novelist Henry Fielding, whose youthful libertinism has been documented in Martin Battestin's standard biography, and whose work, as I have argued elsewhere, often engages the philosophical underpinnings of libertinism and its implications for moral character. Fielding argues in "On the Knowledge of the Characters of Men" and in other places that 'Good-nature is that benevolent and amiable Temper of Mind, which disposes us to feel the Misfortunes, and enjoy the Happiness of others; and consequently, pushes us on to promote the latter and prevent the former; and that without any abstract Contemplation on the Beauty of Virtue, and without the Allurements or Terrors of Religion' (Fielding 1743, 158). She declines the power gained through religious association, for example, in refusing a marriage proposal from the Lord Bishop some time before the beginning of the play because 'there are no Lady-Bishops ... and it may be against Canon to let a Woman be the Head of the Church.—Beside, I should be loath to kneel for a Blessing to him, who should think it a Blessing to kneel to me' (II vi). Bellair can think of nothing more ridiculous than a man who performs piety for gain, and so she tricks the libertine Young Modern, a would-be Rochester, into spending most of the play trying to appear a Puritan (in hopes that Bellair will secretly sleep with him once his public persona no longer puts her reputation at risk). Ridiculing both thoughtless libertinism and ignorant religion, the trick is a perfect device to show Bellair's independence and originality and to distinguish her stance from mere libertinism of faith or fashion.

Instead of meeting the expectation of either virtue or subversion, then, Bellair serves her own pleasure, from her mocking of established religion and ignorant libertines to her triumphs over sentimental romantic expectations. It is while Young Modern is being subjected to Bellair's mirth that he says, 'I know your Ladyship despises both [fraud and dissimulation] in your Heart, and that your real

---

thought libertine in the eighteenth century, claim that virtue and vice emerge from the same emotional and intellectual sources.

Principles are adapted to serve your Pleasures', but for once he is on the mark, and she replies, 'But then, Mr. *Modern*, my Pleasures always justify my Principles' (V iii). Young Modern has fallen victim to exactly the sort of female libertine his father warned him about (and indeed himself falls for in the play's closing scenes). Modern approves of a good bottle and a mistress for his son, 'only take this Caution with you; Tho' Women are necessary to your Pleasure, they are not to run away with your Reason: rather let them belong to you, than you to them ... and, if you once let a Woman know her Power, she'll be sure to abuse it' (I ii). Bellair, of course, never for a moment forgets the power she holds over almost every character she encounters, and such power is always used for good-natured pleasure rather than for more traditionally destructive libertine ends. Even in her irritated suspicion that Lady Lurcher is responsible for her financial difficulties, Bellair recognizes that 'Sorrow, or Resentment, are no Remedy for what's past, and 'twould be ridiculous to lose an Enjoyment in one's Power, for fear of a future Calamity' (II i). Her enjoyments are pleasurable both in how they manifest her natural wit, originality, power and seductive beauty, and in the promise they hold of sexual fulfilment. She refuses to be limited by ridiculous prescriptive social constructs such as modesty and fears for one's reputation. She rebukes her cousin's moralistic warnings with the clear-headed recognition that 'what you call Modesty, is but a monstrous Reverse of Nature, that breeds nothing but Uncharitableness and ill Humour ... When I am guilty, I will be asham'd—While I am innocent, I can have no Occasion' (II ii). Further, while all of her actions are based on enacting publicly the individualist privilege that drives her, she is entirely aware of the prerogative allowed to women of her social and marital status by those whose opinions matter—unlike the lowly sort regulated by mere need for public respectability: 'Lard, Cousin, the World is now become as fond of Liberty as I; all the brave and polite, I hope, will be my advocates, and, if they approve, I have nothing to wish, or fear' (II ii). As Lady Mary Wortley Montagu notes wryly in her letters, 'Beauty has a large Prerogative'; by 1723 she can report with minimal dismay that 'the Appellation of Rake is as genteel in a Woman as a Man of Quality' (3: 213, 2 :32).

Lady Bellair knows the cultural narrative in which she participates, and is confident throughout the play that she will win the contest for the male object of desire. The central conflict of the play, then, is neither of the romantic contests involving Lady Bellair and her two suitors, but rather the struggle for dominance between the rival widows of the title. As is true of Aphra Behn's *Rover* plays, the male leads are nearly incidental while the libertine women match wits, disguises, and devices of power, from wealth and servants to beauty and good nature. Both women genuinely desire Freelove and treat Young Modern as an object of derisive and entertaining manipulation; both seek the sexual and social freedoms that come with widowhood, a status outside the objectifying marriage market; both believe that public identity is a mere construct serving the private will; and both take reputation, virtue and the regulatory systems of official religion as mechanisms sustaining that construct. The different ways in which the two accept and enact these views are the crux of the play's revaluation of femininity.

The source of the two women's power is in many ways their widowhood, in which, Bellair explains, a woman might have 'a noble Jointure, rich Jewels, a pretty Chariot and Equipage, a Wardrobe, various as Fancy of Fashion can make it; your own Friends of either Sex, your own Talk at your Table, a trusty Confidant, a domestick Physician to make you sick, or well when you please ... Your Choice of Religions, or a Chaplain to save you without any at all' (II i). The pointed allusions to Lady Lurcher's ill-concealed affair with her doctor and her religious hypocrisy have an immediate context, but also refer to a liberty available more easily to a wealthy widow than to a woman of almost any other status. For Cooper's female libertine, however, the marriage so valued by the culture of sentiment could itself be a pleasure, if chosen from desire and genuine affection—as it must be to warrant the surrender of the other pleasures that Bellair catalogues.

In its depiction of women's power, *The Rival Widows* also demonstrates another of the paradoxes linking libertinism and sentiment in eighteenth-century culture. In his book on the culture of sensibility, Barker-Benfield notes that their supposed opposition may in fact be a symbiosis: 'The continuing attractiveness of this [libertine] style of manhood to women can also be explained by the apparent inadequacy of men of feeling or, rather, by the unfathomed question of their sexuality ... Presumably a gentler manhood could be compatible with the pleasurable difference of sex—including conflict. But the culture of sensibility generated a continuing spiral of hard but sexual rakes and sensitive but nonsexual men of feeling in reaction to them, both expressions of women's wishes' (340, 344). While I would challenge such a binary understanding of eighteenth-century masculinity and such a narrowing view of female tastes, Barker-Benfield's observation does illuminate Cooper's combination of the two masculine types in one female dramatic hero. Even in the 1730s, the old-style libertine and the hyper-emotive man of sentiment are objects of parody, but to combine the two into a single male hero risks pushing the comedy perilously close to traditional heroic drama, with a hero torn between public duty and domestic love. Instead, Cooper unites the two in a powerful, independent, but feeling libertine woman who uses the power generated by her beauty and intellectual independence to play the puppet master, revealing the ridiculousness of Young Modern by making him act the conservative 'Man of Sense' (II viii) and the over-nice sentimentality of Freelove by making him try to trick her into love. That Freelove and Bellair finally enter into a marriage determined primarily by libertine values maintains the tenor of the popular libertine comedy even as the play also inscribes a potentially reformative lesson worthy of sentimental comedy.[5]

---

[5] I use these terms advisedly, given the claim by John Loftis that '[t]here is no such genre as 'sentimental comedy'' (127) and by Robert D. Hume that the 'whole concept of sentimental comedy is in fact merely a distraction and a red herring' (224). More recently,

The play acknowledges the trend toward what George Winchester Stone, Jr. terms 'the appeal to sentiments of the heart rather than to the intellect, individualization of problems rather than universalization, interest in human nature rather than in manners, and a moral emphasis upon the goodness of man' (395). But it then queries the value of such qualities by finally subsuming them into a more pragmatic set of values dictated by the 'gay, roving, inconsiderate Libertine' Lady Bellair. Bellair explains that 'There's some Joy in having the Man you doat on for your Slave, but none for your Lord; I can now dispose of my Frowns, and Smiles, like an absolute Princess, to whom I please; can humble, exalt, undo, create again, to keep my Subjects in Obedience and exercise my Power ... [since] 'tis always my Way to strip Nature stark naked, and view her without the Disguise of Custom and Hypocrisy.—I think freely, and speak openly' (II ii). She consistently takes the wind from Freelove's most sentimental sails by reminding him of the reality behind his performative identity as the lover of feeling. Bellair controls the tone of every love scene as Freelove emotes his way through impassioned, but clichéd compliments and earnest declarations:

> *Freelove*: I have no Notion, Madam, that there is any Virtue you are not Mistress of.
> *Bellair*: Then you are much mistaken.—I insist upon all the Privileges of my Sex, and will go wrong whenever I have a mind to it. ...
> *Freelove*: I am sure Disdain agrees but ill with so much Beauty; and, while your Face has all that Sweetness, I must still adore it.
> *Bellair*: O! if 'tis my Face you are so fond of, you shall have Admission to my Picture every Day; and talk to it all the fine Things you can think of: I'll engage it shall not interrupt you.
> *Freelove*: I admire your face, Madam, but as the beauteous Index of your Mind.
> *Bellair*: Still more absurd! Why, I tell you, 'tis my Mind keeps my Body out of your Power.—As I love, this Love alters a Man strangely.—You us'd to look free, open, and disengaged, and now you blush and tremble, as if you were detected in a Robbery. (II vii)

Even when the two agree to marry, Bellair cuts off Freelove's expression of his sentiments with exasperation at his excess and tempers his grandiloquent emotionalism with a clear statement of the naturalist libertine philosophy behind her actions:

---

however, Frank H. Ellis has argued that the 'first and most obvious conclusion to be drawn from the foregoing evidence is that sentimental comedy exists,' although he acknowledges that 'the truth seems to be that sentimental comedy as such is morally neutral ... The sentimental attitudes are value judgments, not moral judgments' (117). Whether sentimental comedy is a genre in itself is less important here, however, as is Cooper's treatment of what was certainly a broadening cultural interest. Hume summarizes the dramatic trend, whatever one might call it: 'There is a tremendous swing [early in the century]—not from 'libertine' to 'sentimental' comedy but from light, satiric romance to solemn romance ... [W]riters turn to reform-oriented comedy which affirms the traditional status quo and papers over its problems. The earlier writers felt free to challenge, question, criticize' (206).

Freelove: O Extacy!

Bellair: Pshaw! I hate Raptures! You see I don't blush to own my Sentiments; and, if I
    have the Softness of my own Sex, I have at the same time the Courage of yours.—

Freelove: You are the Delight of our Sex, Madam, and the Glory of your own.

Bellair: No Flattery, dear *Freelove*, I despise it, tho' a Woman: My Actions are Meant
    to follow nature, not Applause.—I can by no means think Love a Crime in itself, or
    more so in us than you: Neither can I be persuaded, that 'tis any immodesty to
    confess its Power; or Virtue, to be, or seem insensible to it. (V vi)

Over and over again, Lady Bellair cites her philosophy so as to reject the values
that Cooper saw represented on the stage and to establish a revised understanding
of gender that sets independent thought and intellectual autonomy above platitudes
and formalized emotionalism. The idealism in *The Rival Widows* is not about the
sentimental 'communication of common feeling from sufferer or watcher to reader
or audience' (Todd 4), or about libertine domination by one privileged and
powerful individual; it is about the rejection of any sort of unconscious role-
playing. Cooper's play values the pleasures of the individual, transgressing the
prescriptive constructions of gender that would preclude the 'fair libertine' of the
title and rejecting the feminizing of men through the paradigms of sentimentality.
The play's hero cannot marry until he has relearned, at the elbow of a libertine
heroine, the masculine gamesmanship and wit needed to outplay the would-be
controller, Lady Lurcher. The period's now common plot in which the libertine
man is domesticated by the feeling woman is replaced by its reverse: masculinity is
remodelled by a disruptive, autonomous female who embodies a powerful but
feeling libertine femininity not unlike the masculinity of libertine heroes later in
the century, such as Richardson's Belford and Fielding's "good natured libertine"
Tom Jones (Fielding, *Tom Jones* 962).[6]

Bellair and the female libertines of the stage have much in common with such
later figures particularly in that it is the male libertine's very subversiveness and
self-positioning above the rest of society that enable him to emerge the hero: his
illicit knowledge allows him to understand seducers and defend the heroine against
them; his social connections help him illuminate ill-natured plans; and his capacity
to defend a heroine's honour through a duel or well-timed assertion is strengthened
by the same power he has earlier misused. In the same way, Bellair's revisionist
femininity depends on her ability to work with or around social regulatory
mechanisms. The stage heroine cannot simply sit meditating on her virtue, its
preservation, and its place at the centre of her heart. Whether deployed as a
didactic device for reformation or as a subversive agent of change, she must be
given an identity that convinces the audience that she *chooses* her future from a
position of knowledge and experience. In female-centred drama, neither
didacticism nor disruption works if the playwright has not given the main character

---

    [6] See Potter, *Honest Sins*, chapter 5 on *Tom Jones*, and 'A Certain Sign that He is One of
Us' on Richardson's complex and contradictory articulations of an evolving libertinism.

the ability to choose submission or subversion, in marriage or independence. Without such choice the play is merely a representation of parental force or domestic coercion, rather than an illustration of good or bad acts derived from true or false motivation, or from libertine or sentimental philosophy.

Cooper imagines a female libertine with the freedom to choose when to be cruel and when kind, one always driven by her good nature and steady in her wit, her privilege, her power, and her desire for her own happiness above all. The relative social liberty of widowhood allows Bellair to recreate herself not as a mere extension of a man, nor as a woman appropriating the privileges of masculinity, but as a model for a revised femininity that others might emulate. Even as she chooses the true man of sentiment for her husband, Cooper's fair libertine defeats challengers who, like Lady Lurcher and Young Modern, wear the values of sentiment as mere disguise. Both libertinism and sensibility win in this play, but only when they are genuine, original, and passionate, and in this balance Cooper's *Rival Widows* looks outside rigid binaries to locate a femininity that can integrate the competing value systems of eighteenth-century culture without sacrificing the individual woman's good natured privilege, intelligence or passion.

Editorial Method

This edition is based upon the first and only printing of *Rival Widows*, published in London by T. Woodward in 1735. ESTC currently lists 32 extant copies. To prepare this edition I reviewed the single copies held by the University of Pennsylvania, McMaster University, UCLA and the Clark Library, as well as the three copies held by Oxford University, all of which appear to be from the same print run. In correspondence with the extremely helpful librarians at the other holding institutions I have confirmed that all surviving copies share the same typographical errors, page breaks and graphic additions and hence seem to be from the same print run. McMaster University provided the copytext for this edition.

Because I believe that a scholarly edition of a largely unavailable text should resemble the original as much as possible, thus allowing for all types of analysis, including comparisons of non-standard spellings and syntax, this edition replicates the McMaster copy as closely as I can manage. I have maintained old spellings and the eighteenth-century conventions for the capitalization of nouns (insofar as Cooper's printers follow them). I have maintained inconsistent spellings, which seem particularly significant because they appear in extended segments of the text, probably indicating the work of multiple hands in the typesetting rather than inconsistency in the composition. I have altered only obvious typographical errors, indicating these emendations and the original forms in the notes. This method seems particularly important for Cooper's play, given that her Preface claims a style of 'Regularity and Decorum' and explicitly takes on the expectation of immorality in female authors and the anticipation that the play's formal elements would reflect that immorality. The textual specifics need to be available so as to facilitate their comparison with Cooper's own claims and the work of other female playwrights.

A major editorial problem concerns Cooper's use of the dash. Cooper clearly employs it as a standard punctuation mark, but in its elongated form it is also apparently a directorial marker indicating a pause. These elongated dashes, moreover, may parallel those of writers such as the novelist Eliza Haywood, who uses dashes of varying lengths to convey breathlessness, passion, and powerful emotion. Despite their unconventionality in modern typography, therefore, the long dashes have been replicated exactly in this edition. In order to ensure accuracy in representing the dashes, the 1735 text was first scanned from photocopy into an electronic form, after which the usual editing process continued.

THE
RIVAL WIDOWS:
OR,
FAIR LIBERTINE.
A
COMEDY.
As it is Acted
At the THEATRE-ROYAL, in *Covent-Garden*

By Mrs. *COOPER.*

This was an Off'ring to the sex design'd.
CONGR[1].

LONDON:

Printed for T. WOODWARD, at the *Half-Moon,*
between the *Temple Gates,* in *Fleet-Street.* 1735.

---

[1] The closing line of the epilogue of William Congreve's *The Mourning Bride* (1697), addressing the play to the sympathies of its female audience members.

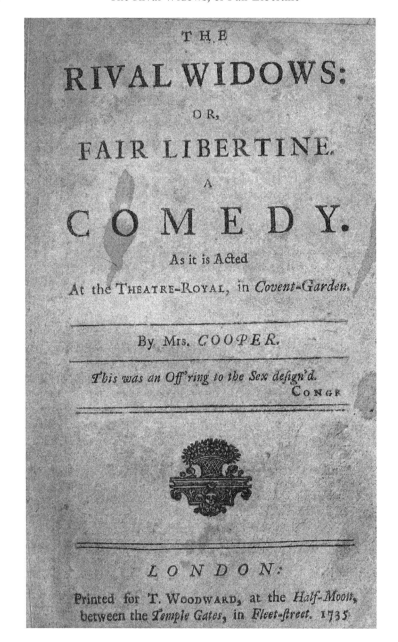

2   Title Page, *The Rival Widows, or Fair Libertine.* 1735.
William R. Ready Division of Archives and Research Collections
McMaster University

Her Grace the Dutchess of Marlborough.

3 *Sarah Churchill, Duchess of Marlborough after Kneller*, John Smith, ca 1700. National Portrait Gallery, London

To Her GRACE the

Dutchess-Dowager of MARLBOROUGH.[2]

MADAM,

IN Addresses of this Nature, Men of any Genius, and Politeness, have ever chosen such Patrons as were the most obvious Subjects of Panegyrick; such as the Voice of the Publick distinguish'd, where Praise was Truth, and Flattery almost impossible: Hence it was that the late Duke of *Marlborough*'s Name[3] did Honour to the most elegant Pens of our Nation, who thought it Prudence, as well as Justice, to make his Glory the Foundation of their own.

'Tis on the same Principles, Madam, that I presume to take this Liberty with your Grace: Like them, I would not be at the Pains of imagining Qualities I could not find; but had rather be thought an honest Historian, than a flattering Orator. Little Characters are not incompatible with great Titles; and to applaud a Person who does not deserve it, is like making a beautiful Portrait after an ugly Face, and turns the intended Compliment into real Satire.

This is a Danger, Madam, I am wholly secure from, in presenting this Trifle to your Grace: Were it of Consequence enough to deserve the noblest Patronage, I could not make a more judicious Choice; and I have no other Fear, but that I do myself too much Honour on the Occasion.

My Sincerity, I am sure, will not be call'd in Question; for I publickly declare, I have no other Motive in making this Address to your Grace, but my Zeal to publish the Acknowledgement of a whole People, who universally allow your Grace the singular Happiness, to have conquer'd the Malice of Envy, Prejudice, and Misrepresentation, by a Series of such humane and publick-spirited Actions, as

---

[2] Sarah Churchill, Duchess Marlborough (1660–1744), wife of the great military leader John Churchill, Duke of Marlborough (1650–1722), and one of Queen Anne's closest advisors both before and during her reign. After a falling out with the Queen (possibly over Sarah's assumption of intellectual superiority and Anne's sense of her lack of investment in the personal friendship), Sarah was removed from her government posts in January 1711. She was a prominent Whig for much of her life, but vehemently disliked Sir Robert Walpole (once her husband's clerk) and spent substantial sums of her great wealth supporting anti-Walpole politics. She is remembered as one of the first publicly political women in England.

[3] John Churchill, Duke of Marlborough (1650–1722), a highly successful military leader, tactician, and statesman, notably as the allied commander-in-chief during the War of the Spanish Succession. He was also remarkably good at obtaining and maintaining the social and fiscal rewards of royal favour, including that of James II, William III, Anne, and George I. Marlborough was briefly discredited as a corrupt war profiteer in documents like Jonathan Swift's 1711 *Conduct of the Allies*, but was restored to reputation after the Hanoverian King George I came to the English throne in 1714.

make a greater Distinction in Souls, than Wealth, or Titles in Precedency and Fortune. I am, with the most unfeign'd Respect,

May it please Your GRACE,

Your GRACE's *most Obedient,*

and most Humble Servant,

E. COOPER.

PREFACE

THERE have been so many unsuccessful Attempts made in Comedy, *that young Authors are sure to be heard with Prejudice, and must undergo the Weight of other People's Faults, as well as their own. What therefore have I to apprehend, who set out with so many Disadvantages? sure to be suspected of Dulness, before I am read, and in Danger of being condemn'd for Self-sufficiency afterwards, – For making so difficult a Task the first publick Tryal of my Muse.[4] – Perhaps, there may be much Reason for both; and I, tho' most concern'd, may be the last Person to find it out. I have, however, taken some Pains to be able to justify myself; whether I have succeeded or no, the World must judge. – I have chosen a Tale that is not very barren of Incidents, neither are those Incidents, I hope, forc'd or unnatural, ill-tim'd or superfluous: Some of the Characters are meant to be new; and the Rest, not mere Copies, or void of Entertainment. – I have endeavour'd to contrast them too, and shew them by each other's Light: One I have labour'd to make Principal, to be the Soul of the Piece, and to be seen, or referred to, almost thro' the whole Action; it happens, indeed, to be a Woman, and I flatter myself I shall have no Apology to make to the Ladies, for having drawn her capable of thinking for herself, and acting on the Principles of Nature and Truth. – The Title, perhaps, may give the Narrow and Precise an Alarm, but no Offence to the Innocent and Virtuous. – As to the rest, I have been bold enough to deviate from the Authority of many of the* English *Writers, and aim at Regularity[5] and Decorum.[6] 'Tis what we Women-Authors, in particular, have been thought greatly deficient in; and I shou'd be concerned to find it an Objection not to be remov'd. – It has been my Endeavour to preserve what the Criticks call the Unities;[7] unless the Scene being laid in one House, during the first Act, and in another, during the other four, shou'd be thought any Violation; the Time is little longer than the Representation, and the Action, as far as I can judge, single and intire. – The Stage too is never vacant, and every Scene is intended naturally, and consistently to*

---

[4] Muse generally refers to the nine Muses of Greek mythology, the patron goddesses of humanity's intellectual and creative endeavors, but possibly also an allusion to Cooper's work on *The Muses Library*, published in 1737.

[5] Both formally correct and observant of broader social rules of conduct. The printed play further emphasizes formal regularity in its use of the classical principle of scene division according to the entrance or exit of any character.

[6] Both in the general definition of propriety of behaviour and the precept of dramatic theory that characters should act and speak according to the expectations of their particular class, sex and social position.

[7] The classical unities are of time, place and action, such that events on stage should not absorb notably more fictional time than real; the action should take place in a single location, or ones that characters could reasonably move between in the staged time; and elements of plot should not diverge fundamentally in tone or subject. See appendix 2 for a contemporary contradiction of Cooper's claims to unity and regularity.

produce or make Room for the next; no Person enters or goes out without a manifest Reason, either as to Intention, or to answer the Purpose of the Scene; and the Business is so divided, that neither of the Acts can be spar'd, not even the last; which is often as superfluous as the Rhimes at the End of it.[8] *The Dialogue is mostly copied from the Life, and the Phrases such as are us'd in common Conversation; the Manners, I presume, are the Growth of the Age, and the Stage was meant to be a Looking-Glass for the Times. If I have made any Reflections too free, they are general, and none but those, who feel them, will complain.*

---

[8] Particularly in plays about libertine heroes who reform just in time to be happily married in the end, fifth-act conversions were notoriously unconvincing (leading to plays like Sir John Vanbrugh's *The Relapse* [1696]). This blunt recognition of the often extraneous quality of fifth acts is particularly intriguing here, given that Bellair's ostensible reformation takes place in the last scene of the last act, and is most directly asserted by the play's closing couplet.

PROLOGUE.

YOUR Veteran Bards, long-wedded to Renown,
Bully in Prologues, and defy the Town;
Assert their high Prerogative in Wit,
And scorn the Factions, which disturb the Pit;
Arraign their Judges, lash the sing-song Age,
And call for Penal Laws to purge the Stage.[9]
But our Initiate[10] *modestly declares,*
That no such Dread Authority is her's;
That Britons *shou'd in all Respects be free,*
And all the Sister-Arts,[11] *like Friends agree:*
If Faranelli[12] *warbles Airs divine,*
Her Praises in the general Chorus join:
Nor dares she hint one Judge of Musick here,
Is void of Sense, because he has an Ear.
A Bard, you lov'd, already has confest,
Musick has Charms to sooth a Savage Breast:[13]
Can it be then the least Degree of Fame,
That Wits[14] *are wild, when Savages are tame?*
But, when this due Applause to Musick's given,
And Earth's allow'd, so near to copy Heaven,
Leave not our native Muses quite forlorn!
Nor plead the Mode to treat their Scenes with Scorn!
Wit[15] *is a Plant that thrives as kindly here,*
When nurs'd by you, as in a Foreign Air;
It flourish'd in your great Fore-father's Smile;

---

[9] A reference to the efforts leading up to the passing of the Licensing Act of 1737, which declared anyone associated with theatrical productions unapproved by the Lord Chamberlain a rogue and vagrant, subject to penal law. See 'Introduction' pages 4–6 and appendices C, D and E.

[10] A novice, as this is Cooper's first play.

[11] Traditionally, painting and poetry (a term that usually encompassed drama in the eighteenth century), though Cooper broadens the reference here to include musical performance.

[12] The stage name of Italian castrato singer Carlo Broschi, who was in tremendous vogue in London between 1734 and 1737, performing primarily at the Haymarket Theatre.

[13] From the opening scene of Congreve's *The Mourning Bride* (1697).

[14] Generally upper-class young men who were or wished to be recognized as clever.

[15] In the eighteenth century, a contested term incorporating intelligence, verbal cleverness and ingenuity. Perhaps most concisely defined by Alexander Pope in his 'An Essay on Criticism' (1711) as 'Nature to advantage dress'd, / What oft was thought, but ne'er so well express'd' (ll 297–8).

And, if some blasted Years have starv'd the Soil,[16]
When the same genial Warmth again is known,
We too may boast a Harvest of our own.
Let then this Night's rude Essay first receive
The happy Omen, that the stage shall live!
Fame is too vast a Growth at once to raise,
You first must pardon, if you hope to praise.

---

[16] Cooper suggests that the time has come for the wit that dominated the stage in previous generations such as the Restoration to return to the stage after an extended vogue for emotional sentimental comedy on the English stage.

4   *John Hippisley*, Artist Unknown (once attributed to William Hogarth).
The Art Archive/Garrick Club, London

5 *The Theatrical Contest*, Artist Unknown, 1743. © Copyright The Trustees of the British Museum

No formal portraits have survived of Lacy Ryan, the actor who played Freelove in the 1735 performances of *The Rival Widows*. However, according to Frederick George Stephens' *Catalogue of Political and Persnal Satires*, Figure M here is an image of Ryan. The figure is supported by bladders imprinted with 'Macduff', 'Hamlet' and 'Edgar', all roles that Ryan had played during the 1743 season. Ryan is also a background figure in Hogarth's 'Rich's Glory' (see page 3).

Persons Represented.

Sir *William Freelove,*	Mr. *Hippisley.*[1]
Modern,	Mr. *Bridgwater.*[2]
Freelove,	Mr. *Ryan.*[3]
Young *Modern,*	Mr. *Chapman.*[4]
Lady *Bellair,*	Mrs. *Horton.*[5]
Lady *Lurcher,*	Mrs. *Hallam.*[6]
Double,	Mrs. *Stephens.*[7]

Creditors, Servant.

---

[1] John Hippisley (1696–1748) acted at the Covent Garden Theatre from 1732 to 1748, and was famed particularly for comic roles as women and aged men. He had facial scarring from a childhood burn that was said by Samuel Foote to make 'the left corner of his Mouth, and the Extremity of his Chin … very near Neighbours" (*Roman and English Comedy Compared*, 1747).

[2] Roger Bridgwater (d. 1754) moved from Drury Lane to the Covent Garden Theatre in 1734, where, after his first seasons, he began to move away from comedic roles and to appear more consistently in tragedies and history plays.

[3] Lacy Ryan (1694–1760), a handsome actor known for his performances as villains and lovers in tragedies and fine gentlemen in comedy. On 15 March 1735, nine days after the final performance of *Rival Widows*, he was shot in the face and lost four teeth, but continued on stage until 1760 in different types of roles.

[4] Thomas Chapman (1638–1747), noted for playing comedic clowns, fops, and would-be wits.

[5] Christiana Horton (1698–1756), a very popular actress who was noted for her beauty and was particularly successful in coquette roles. In the 1735–36 season, she earned an enormous salary of £250 at the Covent Garden Theatre.

[6] Anne Hallam (1696–1740) also appeared on stage under the names of Mrs. Joseph Berriman, Mrs. Lewis Parker, and Mrs. William Hallam. She acted at Covent Garden from its opening in 1732, and was one of the 22 prominent performers to sign an unsuccessful petition to Parliament against pending regulation of the theatres.

[7] Mrs. Stevens (or Stephens) was a stage name for Priscilla Wilford (c1713–83), who acted at Covent Garden from 1732 until she became the third wife of manager John Rich in 1744. As Priscilla Rich, she was a mostly silent but equal partner in the management of the Covent Garden Theatre after the death of her husband in 1761. She is depicted as a religious tyrant in Tobias Smollett's *Roderick Random*.

THE

RIVAL WIDOWS

OR,

The *Fair Libertine.*

ACT 1. SCENE I.

Sir William Freelove *and* Modern.

Modern: TALK to me of his Expences! Pray, Sir *William Freelove*, has my Nephew ever sent his Tradesmen or their Bills to you? Let him spend what he will, 'tis his own.

Sir William: Don't be so warm, Mr. *Modern.*

Modern: 'Slife![8] if a Guinea[9] would save his Soul, you would not give it him, tho' he's your own Sister's Son.

Sir William: You are my Friend, and I am concern'd for your Interest.[10]

Modern: Interest! I despise it, and so shall he, or he's no Relation of mine.

Sir William: If you would but hearken to me, he should not cost you half the Money.

Modern: Half! no, nor the Moiety of that: You would have me reduce him to a sneaking, pitiful Hundred Pound Annuity,[11] with the Run of my Kitchen[12] to keep him, and his Valet from starving, till the Quarter[13] came round.

---

[8] An exclamation, considered a mild swear, derived from 'By God's/His Life'.

[9] A gold coin, nominally worth 20 shillings, but fixed at 21 shillings in 1717.

[10] Sir William implies interest to mean Modern's good or safety, but Modern interprets the word fiscally, the need to earn interest from his wealth (and to be concerned with such low things).

[11] A popular form of investment among the upper classes in the eighteenth century, by which the grantor would purchase a hundred pound share of the state Tontine (a group annuity) and in return would receive an annual sum of money during the life of their nominated person (usually a child or young relative). As the grantor and nominees died, the annuity would grow larger until there were no nominees left.

[12] Free access to the kitchen and its contents.

[13] Annuity payments were made quarterly.

Sir William: And, believe me, a plentiful Allowance too! 'Tis as much as I afford my Son.

Modern: It may be so, and That you grudge him into the Bargain. I know what you would be at, tho' you are asham'd to own it.

Sir William: Asham'd, Sir!

Modern: Aye, you are afraid my Liberality should reflect on your Avarice. But let it! I won't make myself scandalous, to be a Screen for you.

Sir William: I'd have you to know, Sir, I never wanted a Screen in my Life.

Modern: Your Betters have, Sir.

Sir William: Come, come, don't stand so much upon your Credit! I can assure you, Sir, it suffers greatly, for giving such an unbounded Licence to your Nephew, in the Opinion of all the wise Men of your Acquaintance.

Modern: Wise Men! Misers! Wretches! who hoard what they never design to spend, and possess what is not in their Power to enjoy. I scorn their Opinions, Sir, and would not have them in my Favour if I might.

Sir William: But, my dear Friend, you set all the young Fellows madding,[14] about the Town; and my Wilding,[15] among the rest, is ever plaguing me to undo myself, by your Example.

Modern: Do you think I'll train up my Heir like a Merchant's youngest 'Prentice, or some little sneaking Attorney's Clerk, to please you? Do you think I'll oblige him to keep such Company now, as he'll afterwards be asham'd of, for want of Money to introduce him to better? Or force him to throw away his Youth, and Vigour, on some old Dowager, to earn, by the Sweat of his Brows, the Subsistance I deny him. – No, no, 'tis only for such as you, to breed up their Children in Dirt and Frugality; I am above it, and resolve my Nephew shall take up a Life of Pleasure where I leave it off.

Sir William: Bless me! But will you indulge him in Midnight Riots, profuse Entertainments –

---

[14] Running mad.
[15] Wild young man.

Modern: Yes, Sir, Taverns, Horses, Gaming, Women, any thing in Reason.

Sir William: In Reason, quotha! is this a reasonable Catalogue!

Modern: Aye, and necessary too, to Men of Spirit and Fire, such as I was thirty Years ago, and he is now. – There's no Pleasure inexcusable in a young Fellow of Fortune, if he keep within the Bounds of Decorum.[16] – In a Word, Sir, except Avarice, Cowardice, and Hypocrisy, I can forgive him any thing.

Sir William: Why then, Sir, you oblige me to tell you, you are –

Modern: What, Sir? no Indecency at your Peril.

Sir William: Nay, don't be in such a Passion! let me tell you, Sir, at these Years 'tis not becoming.

Modern: Sense and Courage, Sir, are becoming at any Time, and I can soon convince you I am still in the *May* of my Life, tho' you have starv'd yourself into the *December* of yours: I can as ill bear with Affronts now as ever.

Sir William: Well, your Servant, Sir, your Servant; next to Extravagance I abhor a Quarrel. – Well, since he won't follow my Example, I must contrive the cheapest Way I can to follow his. [*Aside.*

SCENE II.

Modern, *and Young* Modern.

Young Modern: You seem angry, Sir.

Modern: I am so – an impertinent old Busy-Body!

Young Modern: If 'tis a Quarrel, Sir, I hope in Gad[17] —— to have no Share in it. [*Aside.*

---

[16] Behaviour suitable to one's position and status. Here, Modern assumes that the status of wealthy young man of spirit requires certain types of behaviour that would be considered undecorous by many.

[17] A minor swearing exclamation, derivative of 'God'.

Modern: No, no, I'll take my Revenge another Way. – I think, Nephew, 'tis 600 *l.* a Year I have settled upon you.

Young Modern: Yes, Sir, I hope you don't repent your Generosity.

Modern: Some time To-day I'll give you a standing Order on my Steward[18] for 400 *l.* more.[19] – I shall be revenged on the old Hypocrite! – Let me see – you shall set up a new Chariot,[20] add another Footman to your Equipage,[21] and lace your Liveries.[22] – This will break his Heart!

Young Modern: 'Slife, Sir, how shall I be able to shew my Gratitude enough.

Modern: By spending it, that's all I require of you. – If I know you have a Shilling at the Year's End, you'll not only forfeit this, but all Pretensions to my future Favour. —Come with his frugal Projects to me!

Young Modern: Egad, you need not fear me, Sir. I would venture to hold Ten thousand Pounds a Year by the same Tenure.

Modern: Bravely said! 'Tis the best Way to deserve it. – But spend it like a Gentleman, d'ye hear? and don't let me be asham'd of my Generosity.

Young Modern: You shall have no Occasion, Sir, if Dress, Taste, and so forth, will merit your Approbation.

Modern: I shall not take upon me to dictate, Nephew – But don't squander it all in Trifles! Lay out some to prove yourself a Man of Sense and Humanity, and establish a Character,[23] that wise and good Men may honour you. – Tho' I love Pleasure, I am never the less a Friend to Virtue;[24] and the more Merit you have, the

---

[18] The member of the household staff responsible for the supervision of domestic staff and the administration of household expenses.

[19] The eventual £1000 per year settlement would be worth approximately £114,000 in current funds.

[20] In the eighteenth century, specifically a light four-wheeled carriage with only back seats (differing from the post-chaise in having an enclosed seat for the driver).

[21] In this usage, a chariot or coach and the attendant servants.

[22] Modern proposes to add expensive ornamental braid to the likely already fashionably elaborate uniform worn by Young Modern's servants.

[23] Public identity or reputation.

[24] Traditionally defined as purity of thought and action in pursuit of human good. Contemporary thinkers such as Henry Fielding, Sir William Temple, and the Earl of Chesterfield, however, agreed with Modern's more fluid sense of the term. Fielding, for

more you will reflect on me; the only Interest I require of you for the Use of my Fortune.

Young Modern: Oh, dear Sir, I shall study all Methods to please you.

Modern: To please me will be the Way to serve yourself, Nephew. – No Man is a Loser by his good Behaviour, and 'tis as much his Interest to indulge his Reason, as his Passion.

Young Modern: S'Death,[25] Sir, you will not call on my Reason, to set aside a Mistress, or a boon Companion.

Modern: No, not at all; I love to be gay and good humour'd myself; and a Friend and a Bottle, moderately taken, are full half the Enjoyments of Life.

Young Modern: But a Mistress, Sir?

Modern: As many as you please, provided you encroach not on another's Property,[26] or sacrifice your own Quiet. Women are made on Purpose for our Happiness; and those sour, rigid Pedants fly in the Face of Nature, who describe them as the forbidden Fruit, and threaten that whoever tastes shall die.

Young Modern: Gad, Sir, with these Indulgences, I believe I shall not want any Security for my good Behaviour.

Modern: Nor do I ask for any; only take this Caution with you; Tho' Women are necessary to your Pleasure, they are not to run away with your Reason: Rather let them belong to you, than you to them. – *Hercules* made but a scurvy Figure under the Discipline of a Distaff,[27] – and, if you once let a Woman know her Power, she'll be sure to abuse it.

Young Modern: Never fear me, Sir; by the Lard,[28] I'm not easily enslaved.

---

example, argues that 'Virtue forbids not the satisfying our appetites, virtue forbids us only to glut and destroy them' (*The Champion* 24 January 1739/40).

[25] A mild swearing oath, derived from 'God's/His Death'.

[26] Most women were still legally chattel in the eighteenth century, either of husband or father. William Blackstone's codifying of English law notes that 'in marriage, husband and wife are one person, and that person is the husband'.

[27] According to Greek myth, in penance for the murder of Iphitus and the attempted theft of the Delphic tripod, Hercules serves Omphale, Queen of Lydia, for three years. Though they eventually became lovers, Omphale required that Hercules pursue traditionally female tasks, including spinning yarn with a distaff and at times dressing as a woman.

[28] A milder version of 'Lord'.

Modern: I tell you, Sir, Women made a Fool of *Solomon*[29] himself, and I'm afraid you are not above half so wise. – In short, I would not have you either a Tyrant or a Cully,[30] a Stoick[31] or a Debauchee.[32] – But of this you may reflect at Leisure: At present, I would have you think of nothing but breaking old *Freelove*'s Heart, for the Benefit of his Heir: I'll send for your Tradesmen myself, and hasten your Equipage,[33] that he may go off the sooner.

Young Modern: Gad a Mercy, Uncle; there's many an old Fellow that has ten times thy Religion, but not half thy Honesty.

Enter Servant.

Servant: Lady *Lurcher*, Sir, presents her Service, and will wait on you instantly.

SCENE III.

Young Modern *solus.*

Lady *Lurcher* do me the Honour of a Visit! The prudish, rigid Lady *Lurcher*! Is it possible? ⸺ Had it been her Cousin *Bellair*, a gay, roving, inconsiderate Libertine,[34] such a Freedom had been but natural, and I'm sure it had given me ten times the Pleasure. O Gad! There's a wide Difference between a glowing, joyous young Widow, and a notable experienc'd old one; more than half in the Wane of her Beauty, tho' in the Full of her Desires. ⸺ What can she want with me I wonder! ⸺ I wish to the Lard she was come. ⸺ Then how the Devil to employ myself till she does ⸺ Well, they may talk what they will of the Value of Time, but I'm positive 'tis the most impertinent Thing in Nature; for, when I want most to get rid of it, it sticks the longest on my Hands, and, when I would make the best of it, it slips the fastest away. – Then the Trouble of Thinking is insupportable! – and, in Company, one has no Occasion for it at all. ⸺ But,

---

[29] According to the Bible, in old age King Solomon allowed his feelings for his wives to turn his heart away from God and toward gods of other belief systems (I Kings 11).

[30] A dupe.

[31] One linked to the philosophical school of Stoicism, with its stern morality and expectation of natural virtue. Stoicism is an ascetic system, demanding rejection of the external world of the senses.

[32] One who indulges excessively in sensual pleasures.

[33] In this usage, the gathering of all necessary equipment (traditionally, as for a journey or battle).

[34] One characterized by habitual disregard of moral law, religion and sexual regulation in constant pursuit of power and individual pleasure.

hark, she comes! and, to prevent Scandal, with *Double*, her Woman,[35] too: As fit a Guard for Virtue, as a knavish Lawyer for an Orphan Heir.

SCENE IV.

Young Modern, *Lady* Lurcher, *and* Double.

Young *Modern:* Dear Lady *Lurcher*, this is such a Favour——

Lady Lurcher: O fie, Sir, Favours[36] to a young Fellow! You quite confound me: I would not have such a thing imagin'd of me for the World.

Double: O dear, Madam, 'tis impossible; as the Numbers that die daily for your Ladyship sufficiently evidence.

Young *Modern:* I vow to Gad, Madam, I only meant –

Lady Lurcher: Nay, I would not have you think my Virtue's the Result of Necessity neither; for I admit of Lovers, on Purpose to convince the world I can refuse them.

Young *Modern:* You may be sure, Madam——

Lady Lurcher: And yet I have known the most delicious Extasies of Love; nay, with Ardour too enjoy'd them. —— But now that luscious Time is over, I can deny my Heart its Longings, and see, without a Wish, the most alluring of Temptations.

Double: Aye, there's for you, Sir. —— Alas! 'tis nothing for an innocent Girl, who has never tasted the Honeycomb of Pleasure, to forbear it —— But for one that has rifled all its Sweets, and has the full Relish yet tickling on her Palate. —— Humh!

Young *Modern:* How her Mouth waters at the very Imagination? [*Aside.*] But, Madam, if I might have the Honour of knowing your Ladyship's Commands ——

---

[35] Her maid or personal attendant.
[36] Acts done out of good will toward the recipient, with passing reference of the colloquialism of the 'last favour', for the granting of sexual consent.

Lady Lurcher: I vow, Sir, you have put me in such Confusion; and one's Character is so tender – But, however, to the Point. —— Can you keep a Secret! For you must know, I should die to be quoted on such an occasion.

Young Modern: Lard, Madam, I'll out-swear the Returning Officer for a Borough,[37] if you require it.

Double: By no means, Sir; my Lady always swoons at an Oath.

Lady Lurcher: 'Tis my Infirmity, Sir. – Your Word and Honour are enough.

Young Modern: As you please, Madam. —— But, Egad, I had rather give you half a Score Oaths.

Lady Lurcher: And now, Sir, what think you of my Cousin *Bellair*?

Young Modern: Gad, Madam, as a new Fashion that all the Beau Monde[38] would follow, and I myself the first; or a new Opera that All admire, tho' Few can understand. —— She's as much in Request, as a Place at Court,[39] and never slighted but when out of Reach. ——Your Ladyship has fired me with your very Name; and, if there can be Harmony in any thing *English*, —— 'tis in *Bellair*, let me perish!

Lady Lurcher: With what a Zeal he praises her? I could almost burst with Spleen,[40] tho' it suits my own Designs he should do so. [*Aside.*] Well then, this courted, charming, fashionable Idol, that every Body follows, inclines to no Body but you.

Double: Yes, indeed, Sir, she is always talking of you, wishing for you, and extolling you to the very skies; and, if you don't make a proper Use of this Hint —— ——

Young Modern: May I never be trusted with Reputation more!

---

[37] Returning officers preside over elections, including the ability to administer an oath to affirm a voter's identity. In England, a borough is a town having municipal corporation and self-government.

[38] Fashionable society.

[39] A remunerative appointment in the service of the crown (such as Gentleman Usher or Keeper of the Stole), also implying a place of belonging in the high-ranking community surrounding royalty.

[40] Melancholy or irritability (presumed at the time to be physically located in the spleen).

Double: Or lose your own, when it concerns you most to establish it for ever.

Young *Modern:* Pshaw! never fear me! I am us'd to these Affairs every Day.

Lady Lurcher: Indeed, Sir, if I had not the sincerest Regard for my Cousin, and the highest Opinion of your Gallantry,[41] I would not have trespassed so far upon Form. – But, as I know her Caprice in Love-Affairs, and how fond she is of teazing her Admirers, even tho' it hurts herself, I thought I could not do either of you a greater Service, than by making this Discovery. – Beside, I am greatly concern'd for her Fortunes. – Her late Husband Sir *Jeremy*, indulg'd her extravagant Temper to his own Ruin; and she again gave up her Jointure,[42] in a Fit of foolish Gratitude, for his Affection; so that, when he died, he left her scarce enough to carry her thro' the modish Varieties of a first Mourning.[43] —— Thanks to my dextrous Management! [*Aside.*

Young *Modern:* So much the better! she'll be the easier won. —— Distress is the best Bawd[44] in the World. [*Aside.*

Lady Lurcher: Aye! But will you marry her?

Young *Modern:* Humph!

Double: Nay, my Life on't, she'll never ask you!

Lady Lurcher: Beside, you may settle that among yourselves. —— 'Tis no Concern of mine. —— But don't be discourag'd, if she should persist in her affected Indifference for a while. ——'Tis impossible she should fly into your Arms at once.

Young *Modern:* O Lard, Madam, I have a certain Way with me, that few Ladies can withstand.

---

[41] Usually devotion and service to ladies, but in the eighteenth century, also amorous intrigue or adultery.

[42] A legal arrangement usually made at the time of marriage, establishing the property and wealth that will be jointly held by husband and wife, but will pass to the wife for her sole provision in the event of her husband's death.

[43] First or heavy mourning could last a year and six weeks after the death of a spouse, during which time a widow was expected to wear black mourning dress, often in heavy and expensive silks and crepes.

[44] One who creates or manages prostitutes.

Lady Lurcher: 'Twill not be amiss, tho', to send her a tender Billet,[45] to clear the Way. —— I'll be your Messenger myself, and, take care to Time it exactly.

Young *Modern:* You oblige me infinitely, Madam; your Ladyship shall have one in half a Second.

Double: Then, I suppose, you write Short Hand,[46] Sir.

Young *Modern:* No, I have only the Direction to add. – There – 'tis done flying. – Rot me!

Lady Lurcher: Perhaps this was in your Head before, and you had provided one for the Purpose.

Young *Modern:* One, Madam! I have Dozens always by me, against every Emergency, sign'd, seal'd, and ready to deliver at a Moment's Warning. – I keep a Secretary[47] for no other Business.

Lady Lurcher: I see you are very adroit at these Affairs, and you shall find me no bad Second.[48] – To Day I'll make an Entertainment, that you may have all the Opportunity you can wish, to come to an Explanation. ——Your Uncle shall be invited too, to prevent Suspicion; and, for some private Reasons, Sir *William Freelove* and his Son. —— I'll both take Care they shall neither of them interfere with you, – nor any little Family-Ceremonies cramp our Designs.

Young *Modern:* Excellent! all this can never fail.

Lady Lurcher: Come, don't be too confident neither! —— Young *Freelove*, you know, is your Rival, and he's gay, handsome, witty, well-bred,[49] generous ——

Young *Modern:* And poor as the Devil! – 'Tis true, the Fellow has some Accomplishments that are well enough. –But, where I am favour'd, Madam. – Alack-a-day[50] ——

---

[45] A letter or love letter, from the French billet-doux.

[46] A method of writing quickly, using contractions and symbols for words.

[47] One employed to assist with correspondence and keep personal records. Given his lack of work or literary productivity, Young Modern's secretary is another affectation.

[48] One who supports another in a task, as in a man who serves as a second in a duel, acting as the representative of the duelist, preparing the site and weapons.

[49] Displaying the fine manners assumed to mark one's being of good family. Contemporary playwright Henry Fielding's 'Essay on Conversation' defines good breeding as not mere fashionableness, but 'the art of pleasing, or contributing as much as possible to the ease and happiness of those with whom you converse'.

[50] An expression of surprise from 'alas, the day', and here a smug sound of confidence in Young Modern's amorous expectations.

Lady Lurcher: But he that plays the Game well, would have his Eye on the Chances which are against him, as well as those in his Favour.

Double: Beside, Sir, can't you address yourself to his Wants, and bribe him off? Mine's a State-Creed[51] and I look upon Gold as more infallible than the Pope,[52] and more seducing than the Devil.

Young *Modern:* Faith, I believe so too! He's to be here this Morning by Appointment, – and I'll lay my Life Money is the Business: I'll find a Way to manage him, I warrant you.

Enter a Servant.

Servant: Mr. *Freelove*, Sir.

Lady Lurcher: O Heavens! I would not have him see me here for the *Indias.*[53] – My Reputation! my dear Reputation!

Young *Modern:* You need not be under any Concern for that, Madam. – Only step into my Dressing Room, and you are safe.

Lady Lurcher: This Moment then, dear Sir, – and I have one thing more to communicate, that will do my Cousin's business, I believe, and make her your's the sooner.

Young *Modern:* Desire Mr. *Freelove* to walk up, and tell him I'll wait upon him instantly.

Servant: [to *Freelove*, entering] Sir, my Master will wait on you instantly.

---

[51] Double's belief system revolves not around church, but her own state of well-being and prosperity.

[52] The doctrine of papal infallibility was not established until 1870, so Double likely refers instead to a recent crisis that had created doubt in the papacy even among Roman Catholics. In 1713, Pope Clement XI issued a papal Bull that among other things rejected the idea that everyone should be permitted to read the Bible, and appeared to limit the Church to the predestined only. The Bull sparked outrage across Catholic Europe and fostered debate as to the limits of papal authority.

[53] A reference to the great wealth held in and being imported from the Indian subcontinent.

SCENE V.

Freelove *solus.*

Love, I find, is as good a Receipt[54] to make a Philosopher, as Reason and Reflection. – I have forgot all my Wants and Misfortunes, to ruminate on my dear *Bellair*'s, and, to remove them, would gladly double my own. —— How to compass it indeed, is, at present, as much out of my Power, as to give Generosity to my Father, or Avarice to myself. —— Some young Fellows, in my Condition, would make a bold Stroke[55] at Lady *Lurcher*; Spite of her Prudery, I know she may be won; but that would be jumping into a bottomless Gulph, like *Curtius*,[56] and losing one's-self in the Experiment: If I apply to my Father, he disinherits me; if to young *Modern*, he'll answer like one of the World, that to lend Money is to lose one's Friend. No! I can never do it, tho' I came on Purpose; and so I must e'en let Fortune shuffle the Cards, and turn up what Trump[57] she pleases.

SCENE VI.

Freelove, and *Young* Modern

Young *Modern:* My dear *Freelove*, I beg a thousand Pardons. —— But a little Engagement.

Freelove: Not Business, *Frank*, I am sure. – 'Thy brave, generous, honest Uncle, takes all that Trouble off thy Hands. —— As I live, thou art one of the happiest Fellows under the Sun: Thou hast Money enough, and Liberty to spend it how thou wilt. —— Time and Fortune are thy Vassals;[58] and, as to Thought and Reflection, they are none of thy Acquaintance.

---

[54] Recipe.

[55] An aggressive attempt to marry, but likely also an allusion to fellow female playwright Susanna Centlivre's very successful play *A Bold Stroke for a Wife* (1718), still in repertory performance.

[56] The legend of Marcus Curtius dates back to the early Roman republic: when the ground opened in the middle of the Forum. After attempts to fill the chasm failed, an oracle foretold that the only way to close the chasm was to cast into it Rome's most prized possessions. Believing that Rome's young soldiers were its most important asset, Curtius donned his armour and rode his horse into the chasm, which then closed over him.

[57] In various card games, including bridge and ombre, a suit (i.e., spades) which for a portion of the game ranks above the others and can thus overmatch any card of other suits.

[58] Servants.

Young *Modern:* Faith, *Harry*, those who think as to little Purpose as I do, may as well save themselves the Labour. —— Let those study who are to live by it: A Gentleman should employ his Time to more Advantage.

Freelove: For my Part, if I could live by my Study, I should not be asham'd of the Occupation —— 'To say Truth, nothing is esteem'd scandalous but Necessity, and, if my Sword or Pen could remove it, I would not be long idle.

Young *Modern:* For Gad's Sake, no Military Exploit in Time of Peace! It may be dangerous. —— I think, of the two, you had better turn Author, and write a Play.

Freelove: No, no, there are too many on the high Road of Wit already; and I don't care to be damn'd in such Company: Beside, there's Action abroad;[59] where, Death or Preferment may be earn'd with Honour; and I am too much a Lover of my Country, to wish it may ever come home.

Young *Modern:* Spoke like a Hero, sink me! —— But, a Word in your Ear; a Man would make but a bad Soldier who left his Heart behind: And, if all the Trumpets of an Army were to summon you to the Field,[60] a Whisper from Lady *Bellair* would call you back. —— Come, come, 'tis she puts these Romantick Notions into your Head; and, let me tell you, so indiscreet a Passion is yet more to be condemn'd than the Enthusiasm of Fighting, or leaving Peace and Safety to be knock'd o'the Head with Honour.

Freelove: Prithee, what has Discretion to do with Love? or who can condemn a Passion when she is the Object? Why, 'tis Merit to admire her, and Reason to defend it, tho' Ruin should be the Consequence. —— I love her, because she deserves to be lov'd; and my want of Fortune shall never make me asham'd of my Understanding.

Young *Modern:* Hark you, my Dear, what are the mighty Charms that ——

Freelove: Charms! A Rose at fairest, neither a Bud nor too full blown, is but a faint Emblem of her Beauty. – The Painters need no other Model for a living

---

[59] England was involved in military skirmishes in Europe throughout the eighteenth century, but most notable for the immediate context of the play were the ongoing battles with Spain, including the War of the Spanish Succession (1702–13) and a second war from 1720–29. The War of the Polish Succession (1733–35) would also have been a topic of contemporary discussion, as Prime Minister Robert Walpole rejected the desire of Hanoverian King George II to go to war to support Austria and Poland against France and Spain.

[60] Battlefield.

Venus;[61] and Nature form'd her as a Mould for smiling *Cupids*,[62] to propagate a Race of Beauties, to insnare another Age. —— Then she has Wit enough to supply the present Dearth of it on the Stage,[63] and good Nature[64] to make that Wit agreeable even at Court. In short, she's Gay without Levity, Libertine without Scandal, Generous without Design, and Well-bred without Affectation.

Young *Modern:* Let me blush, my Dear, if she has not turn'd your Brain. Why, Fortune now a-days is the Parent of Love; and Passion, without it, nothing but Lunacy and Distraction: If you was as rich now, as a Stock-Jobber[65] in the Secret, or a Sharper[66] that had dealt in extravagant Heirs, till they were wise and poor together, something might be said in your Excuse. —— Tho' then you would not be able to cheat half so fast as she could squander. –But as the Case is ——

Freelove: I have little or nothing to fear for myself, but her Denial; and rather than hurt her, I'll die a Martyr to my own Desires.

Young *Modern:* But consider ——

Freelove: 'Tis to no Purpose; I would out-watch a Chymist[67] in his Pursuit of the Grand Elixir,[68] if any good could follow. —— But, as you yourself say, there can be none in Prospect, why should I look forward? – I had rather shut my Eyes, and be undone, without the Pain of apprehending it. – I know she's a Woman of Expence; but then she enjoys her Fortune with so much Elegance and Spirit, that I can't help being charm'd with it. – In most People Extravagance is a Vice, but in her 'tis OEconomy; she lays out her Money to its full Value, and has her Account in Pleasure, for what she diminishes in Fortune.

---

[61] Roman goddess of love and fertility, usually represented as the epitome of female beauty.

[62] Roman god of love, usually depicted as a cherubic baby or small child.

[63] Early eighteenth-century sentimental comedy endeavoured to appeal to the heart and virtuous emotions rather than the cynical intellect that was the emphasis of the Restoration preference for comedy of wit. Cooper's prologue notes the same absence of wit.

[64] Natural goodness of character, though Fielding's 1743 definition in 'On the Knowledge of the Characters of Men' seems especially informative for a description of Bellair: 'Good-nature is that benevolent and amiable Temper of Mind, which disposes us to feel the Misfortune, and enjoy the Happiness of others; and consequently, pushes us on to promote the latter and prevent the former; and that without any abstract Contemplation on the Beauty of Virtue, and without the Allurements or Terrors of Religion'.

[65] Pejorative term for one who deals in stocks either fraudulently or to his own benefit.

[66] Card sharp or cheat.

[67] From alchemist, a chemist who mixes medicines.

[68] A medication whose elusive formula was believed capable of curing all disease and extending life eternally.

Young *Modern:* S'Death! what signifies her Grace in lavishing, when 'tis out of your Power to supply her? You may undo yourself, if you please, to prove the Truth of your Affection; but, as I apprehend, that will do no Service to any thing but her Pride. —— Whereas, if you will hearken to me, and lay aside this infatuating Amour ——

Freelove: Not for your whole Wonder-working Fortune. – I would lay aside my Being as soon.

Young *Modern:* Why then, by the Lard, I'll declare myself thy Rival in stark Friendship, and try to wean you from her, by wooing her myself.

Freelove: You are welcome, with all my Soul.

Young *Modern:* I have your free Leave then?

Freelove: You have.

Young *Modern:* And it gives you no Alarm?

Freelove: No.

Young *Modern:* You are sure of her, perhaps?

Freelove: Very far from it.

Young *Modern:* And you will not be angry if I succeed?

Freelove: Not, if you give me fair Play.

Young *Modern:* Why then let us start together.

Freelove: With all my Heart.

Young *Modern:* Done! and he that is in first, shall make a Signal for the other to pull up.

Freelove: That shall be at the Rider's Discretion.

Young *Modern:* Be it so; and, if I don't mortify your Confidence ——

Freelove: You'll never presume to be vain again.

Young *Modern:* And now, if you'll step to the Chocolate-house,[69] I'll speak but one Word, and follow you in a Moment; after which we will adjourn to the Ladies, and make our Addresses in Concert.[70]

Freelove: Agreed!

SCENE VII.

Young Modern, *Lady* Lurcher, *and* Double

Young *Modern:* Egad, Madam, he's quite a Hero in his Passion. —— There's no removing it.—— All I could do was to declare myself his Rival; and that too gave him no more Concern than the taking a Pinch of Snuff.[71]

Lady Lurcher: So I heard; but I would not have you stay to debate about it now. – But make good your Appointment directly, and we'll compare Notes again by-and-by. —— I'll only stay a Minute or two, for fear he should see me go out, and be ready to receive you at home in an Instant.

Young *Modern:* Till when I kiss your Hands. —— Who's there! —— my People!

SCENE VIII.

Lady Lurcher, *and* Double.

Lady Lurcher: Now, *Double*, mind what I say! you know all my Cousin's Creditors![72] send a Messenger to them on the Wing; tell them she has Money, and, if they don't insist on it now, they'll never be paid. —— This will pinch her to the Soul; and, as her Pride will not suffer her to apply to me, nor my Prudence assist

---

[69] Similar to coffee houses of the period, chocolate houses served as a form of gentlemen's club, where men met, gambled, gossiped, and consumed exotic and expensive cocoa.

[70] Together.

[71] Powdered tobacco, consumed by inserting small amounts into the nose with the fingers.

[72] Those to whom one owes money.

her if she did; she has nothing for it, but to listen to the first Proposal that shall be laid in her Way.

Double: But, with Submission, Madam, What has she done to make your Ladyship so much her Enemy?

Lady Lurcher: Done! bless thee! What a Question is there? Why, I have hated her almost from her Cradle; and Increase of Years, has only increased my Aversion. — — In her very Childhood, tho' I had many Years the Start of her, she was eternally in my Way, and eclips'd me in every Body's Eyes, but my own; She was the Subject of every one's Praise, the Object of every one's Admiration; She never appear'd, but to be distinguish'd, and I only to be her Foil to set her off. —— As she grew up, she was the only Toast,[73] and more courted, without a Fortune, than I with a very considerable one. —— When she was married, her Servants were best manag'd, her Entertainments most elegant, her Taste the most follow'd; and she was esteem'd a better Wife to an old Husband, than I to a young one: In a Word, her Genius is above me still, and, whenever the two Widows are mention'd, she is sure to ingross the Conversation, and I am dropt as soon as nam'd.

Double: This is very hard, indeed, Madam! – But, then, why have you made her your Guest, and lodg'd her, as it were, in your Bosom?

Lady Lurcher: To answer two very good Ends. —— Get a Reputation of Humanity, and by pretending Friendship to her, get her more effectually into my Power.

Double: But how can your Ladyship reconcile this to your Endeavours to marry her to Mr. *Modern?*

Lady Lurcher: Marry her! poor *Double!* Thy Cunning, I see, is Second-hand, like thy Cloaths.[74] – No, no, *Modern* has no such thing in his Head now, and I'll engage he never shall. – He's one of those vain Coxcombs,[75] that fancy every Woman is in Love with them; and by doating on themselves, can never be very fond of any Body else. – Profuse in the Pursuit of Pleasure, but never generous enough to reward the Person who bestows it. In short, she wants Money, and he can supply her; and, when the Necessity and the Offer meet, 'tis easy to guess the Consequence.

---

[73] A lady to whom a group of drinkers is invited to raise their glasses in a toast.

[74] High-ranking servants like a lady's maid often inherited their mistresses' dresses after they ceased to be fashionable.

[75] A foolish man known for overconfidence and often over-elaborate dress.

Double: This is pure, indeed!

Lady Lurcher: Pshaw! this is but a Part of the Plot. – *Freelove*, thou knowest, is Fool enough to doat upon her, and 'tis my Curse to be as fond of him. —— Now, some way or other, that Affair must be broke off; and I have always found jealousy the surest Method of doing Mischief, on those Occasions.

Double: Oh, I conceive you now, Madam; and so, as the Affair advances between Mr. *Modern* and her, you'll betray it to Mr. *Freelove?*

Lady Lurcher: Yes, or invent Circumstances that will answer as well.

Double: But, pray Madam, have you ever let Mr. *Freelove* into the Secret of your Heart?

Lady Lurcher: Only by remote Hints, which he did not, or would not, understand.

Double: Why then, Madam, if your Ladyship will let me have the Honour of preparing the Way, I'll answer for your Success.

Lady Lurcher: O dear, *Double*, you don't know how strongly he is attach'd to her.

Double: Don't be afraid, Madam, your Ladyship knows I have brought about as difficult Jobs as this before now. – There was the tall Captain, and your present Favorite the handsome Doctor, and both owing to my Management.

Lady Lurcher: Lard! they are quite different Creatures.

Double: No matter for that, Madam, – leave it to me! and I warrant I'll set him on Fire.[76] – I am Mistress of my Trade, I can assure your Ladyship. —— I can both set the Snare, and secure the Game; can look like a Natural,[77] and cousin[78] all the while like a Devil. – I can hear and be deaf, see and be blind, swear and equivocate, have a Hand in every thing, betray nothing, and be ready with a Lie for all Things.

Lady Lurcher: I don't question thy Abilities. – But still it makes me blush, to think I must stoop to court him.

---

[76] Raise his romantic desires.
[77] One who is straightforward or even simple.
[78] Cozen, or cheat.

Double: Blush, Madam! —— Do something to deserve it, and blush afterwards; why 'tis natural as Food or Sleep, and necessary as Physick[79] when the Body's out of Order. —— A Lover is a Widow's Privilege,[80] and, if you give it up, you'll incur the Resentment of the whole Order.

Lady Lurcher: Well then, I don't care to give Offence to any Body. —— If you win him, I am happy, and, if not, I must practice something upon his Father, to make myself Amends for the Disappointment: He's not over and above wise, and any thing, in the Appearance of Interest, will win his very Soul.

Double: Suppose tho', your Cousin should, by any Accident, discover your Designs?

Lady Lurcher: Impossible! with all her mighty Sense, there's no Body more easily deceiv'd.

Double: That's so much the better, indeed: But I am afraid your Ladyship has sometimes been too open to her; and, if she should be provok'd, it may be in her Power to be reveng'd.

Lady Lurcher: 'Tis true, to convince her that she was not the only admir'd Creature in the World, I have let her see that my Cabinet has its Love Secrets too.

Double: After this then, does your Ladyship think she can imagine you only take Physick of the Doctor?

Lady Lurcher: Let her imagine what she will, I care not; nay, if she could ruin me, so I could have the Pleasure to see her fall before me, I should be contented.

Double: But has your Ladyship no Returns of Pity, for a Relation, a Friend, and Intimate of so long Standing?

Lady Lurcher: Pity! no, 'tis the Child of Folly, and I have turn'd it out of Doors to starve with Charity, its twin Sister, long ago. – They, that understand the World, love none but themselves; seek their own Pleasure only, insensible of what Pain it may give to others. – If thou wouldst thrive, *Double*, dissemble[81] as much

---

[79] Medicine.

[80] Privilege here connotes an exemption from regulation that is denied to the majority. Double implies a tacit social recognition of the sexuality of widows, the only class of respectable women unregulated by parent, guardian or husband. Sexually free widows were a fixture of amatory fiction and salacious literature of the time.

[81] Conceal or disguise one's true beliefs, motivations, or character.

Goodness as ever you can, but never be what you seem! For to cheat, or be cheated, is the whole Commerce of the World; and I had much rather be the Fox, than his Prey. —— As to Friendship and Affinity, they are very pretty Names to amuse the Vulgar; but, as they argue Weakness and Dependance, to be despised by those of a superior Turn, who can support themselves. —— In fine,

Let thy own Wishes, Passions, Views and Ends,
Like mine, be all thy Kindred, Lovers, Friends.

The END of the FIRST ACT.

ACT II. SCENE I.

Lady Bellair *sola.*

NOW would any other Creature, beside myself, be half out of their Wits, to see their Ruin so near, and so little hope to avoid it! – But, either I am insensible of Misfortunes, or so us'd to Pleasure, that I can think of nothing else. – Not even the Want of Money can make me regret the parting with it; and, if my Creditors would be easy without it, I'm sure I should. —— I can bear my own Distresses very well; but I must own it gives me some Pain to hurt others. – It does not please me neither, to lie at the Mercy of my Cousin; and, I am much mistaken, if I am not oblig'd to her Artifices for my present Difficulties: If 'tis as I suspect, the little Conveniencies of her House and Table, are but poor Amends for the Injury. —— But Sorrow, or Resentment, are no Remedy for what's past, and 'twould be ridiculous to lose an Enjoyment in one's Power, for fear of a future Calamity.

SCENE II.

Lady Bellair, *Lady* Lurcher, *and* Double.

Lady Lurcher: 'Morrow, my Dear! What alone? not a Lover, or Billet, or Copy of Verses, to entertain you? This is a Rarity indeed!

Lady Bellair: O, I love Rarities prodigiously, my Dear.

Double: Aye, Madam, you may very easily say so now, when your Ladyship's Apartment so often swarms with Admirers, as if it was Love's Exchange;[82] and when you are glutted with the fine Things they say —— but, if a Scarcity should follow ——

Lady Bellair: If it should, *Double!* I don't think I shall complain of it, like an old Maid, that lost more by her Pride in her Youth, than she could recover by her Humility ever after?

Lady Lurcher: Come, come, Cousin, I must not have you trifle with your Beauty any longer. – Remember 'tis all you have left to retrieve your Fortunes; and I am too much your Friend to let it fade upon your Hands.

Lady Bellair: That is to say, you would have me marry to mend my Circumstances. – Ridiculous! Why, you may as well bid me jump into a River, to avoid a Shower.

Lady Lurcher: I am sure a Husband is not of half the Importance to me; and yet there's something so comfortable in Marriage, that I'm resolv'd to have one very speedily to shew you the Way.

Lady Bellair: Impossible sure! What, are you weary of your Liberty? Have you too much Money, that you are impatient to throw both away? You have now a noble Jointure, rich Jewels, a pretty Chariot and Equipage, a Wardrobe, various as Fancy or Fashion can make it; your own Friends of either Sex, your own Talk at your Table, a trusty Confidant, a domestick Physician[83] to make you sick, or well when you please ——

Double: There she touch'd her to the Quick.

Lady Bellair: Your Choice of Religions, or a Chaplain[84] to save you without any at all.

Lady Lurcher: No trifling with Holy Things, I beseech you!

---

[82] The Exchange was the center of London commodities trading, the precursor to the London Stock Exchange. Double compares Bellair's apartments to the Exchange, but with romantic admiration as the primary commodity.

[83] A house doctor, though the term tends to refer to a physician of homeopathic or alternative remedies. Lady Lurcher, of course, is also sexually involved with her physician in a different sort of domestic relationship.

[84] A clergyman who conducts religious service in the private chapel of a wealthy family. Because their positions were at the whim of their employer, chaplains might be expected to be less spiritually demanding than other religious figures.

Lady Bellair: Lard, my Dear, I was only talking of Marriage – But would you exchange all these pretty things for a Husband? Men only buy their Slaves, but Women their Masters; – and I hate Fetters,[85] tho' of Gold. —— I have had one Husband, and lov'd him well enough, both to keep him and myself in good Humour; but I had rather have twenty Lovers, than be troubled with another, for all that; There's some joy in having the Man you doat on for your Slave, but none for your Lord; I can now dispose of my Frowns, and Smiles, like an absolute Princess, to whom I please; can humble, exalt, undo, create again, to keep my Subjects in Obedience, and exercise my Power.

Lady Lurcher: Lard, Child! Do you think your Raillery[86] will satisfy me instead of a Husband?

Lady Bellair: Nay, if you are so obstinate, may your first Husband's Ghost rise, at your Bed's-Foot, on your Wedding-Night, and frighten you from –

Lady Lurcher: Hold! Bless me, Cousin.

Lady Bellair: Closing your Eyes when you are sleepy.

Lady Lurcher: O! if that's all, 'tis well enough: I was terribly afraid of some Indecorum.

Lady Bellair: Indecorum! ha! ha! ha! Why, Cousin, we can talk of Murder, Theft and Treason, without blushing; and surely there's nothing a-kin to Love that's half so wicked as either. ——'Tis always my Way to strip Nature stark naked, and view her without the Disguise of Custom[87] and Hypocrisy. —— I think freely, and speak openly and the same honest Frankness, that obliges me to speak what I think, will oblige me to think is right.

Lady Lurcher: This Freedom may do very well among the Men, my Dear; but Modesty is the most becoming Virtue in a Woman.

Lady Bellair: Idle! Idle! Virtue is of neither Sex, but the same in both;[88] – a Deity full of Sweetness, tho' abounding with Majesty, —— and what you call Modesty, is but a monstrous Reverse of Nature, that breeds nothing but Uncharitableness and ill Humour.

---

[85] Restraints.

[86] Good-humoured banter.

[87] Social expectation.

[88] Bellair challenges the conservative assertion that virtue is intrinsically different in men and women, as exemplified in *The Tatler* 172 (May 1710), which argues in detail that 'The virtues have respectively a masculine and feminine cast'.

Lady Lurcher: Why, o'my Conscience, at this rate you would see the filthy, Anatomical Wax-work by open Day-light?[89]

Lady Bellair: Aye, and with all my Lovers about me. ——When I am guilty, I will be asham'd. – While I am innocent, I can have no Occasion.

Lady Lurcher: But still I must insist upon it, 'tis wrong to make a Jest of Modesty and Marriage.

Lady Bellair: Modesty and Marriage! I tell you, my Dear, they are no more a-kin than a Man and his Horse. ——Indeed Modesty often rides upon Marriage, and manages the Beast very well; but still they are very far from being of a Piece. – For Marriage is very often without Modesty, and Modesty yet oftner without Marriage.

Lady Lurcher: But, what do you think the World will say of you for such wild Opinions as these?

Lady Bellair: Lard, Cousin, the World is now become as fond of Liberty as I; all the brave and polite, I hope, will be my Advocates, and, if they approve, I have nothing to wish, or fear.

Lady Lurcher: Well, well, my Dear, whatever your Notions are, you must study your Interest now. – You talk as if you did not feel your Distresses; but I am afraid they will make you sensible too soon. —— 'Tis time to look about you, I am sure; your own Purse is exhausted, and no Friend can supply you, without being undone too: Then your Creditors are grown quite impatient, and I am afraid will stand upon Ceremonies[90] no longer.

Double: No, indeed will they not, Madam! – They are all below already; a compleat Representative of all the Trades-People in *London* Hark! o'my Conscience they are coming up in a full Body; and you may as well stop the Tide at *Gravesend*,[91] as keep 'em out.

---

[89] There was a vogue for wax models in eighteenth-century London. Among the most scandalous were the waxworks depicting human anatomy. French entrepreneur Guillaume Desnoües brought his collection of anatomical waxworks to London in 1727 and then displayed them again in Pall Mall from 1730–39. Another possible identification is a waxwork of a woman chained to a table as if dissected alive, displayed by surgeon Abraham Chovet, which was advertised in December 1733. With admission at five shillings, these attractions were marketed to an upper class audience.

[90] Observe conventional forms of deference or respect.

[91] Gravesend, on the south bank of the Thames, was the point at which ships had to wait for correct tidal conditions to continue a journey to or from London.

Lady Lurcher: Nay then, Cousin, I must leave you till they are gone; I can't bear to see a Misfortune I can't redress.

SCENE III.

Lady Bellair, Double, *and* Creditors.

Double: Pray stay without there, till you are sent for! Where did you learn this Rudeness to Persons of Distinction?

Creditor: Don't talk to us of Rudeness! we'll be put off no longer.

Lady Bellair: Let 'em come in! I am more afraid of their Bills than their Company. —— Chairs,[92] *Double!* as these good People have done me the Honour of a Visit, I ought to entertain them. – This is a very unexpected Favour – but, the less Ceremony, the more I am obliged.

I*st Creditor:* She's very complaisant methinks! But fine Speeches will not balance Accounts. – My Blood rises at her Again. ——You must know, Neighbours, that very Suit on her Back is not paid for; and my Fool of a Husband would present her with half a Dozen more, on the same Terms, if I would give him Leave.

Lady Bellair: I am afraid your Husband is not well, Mrs. *Lustring*,[93] that you have given yourself this Trouble.

I*st Creditor:* I knew she had rather deal with him. —— For, instead of paying him any Money, she always gets twenty Pounds more in his Debt.

2*d Creditor:* If your Ladyship pleases to remember –

Lady Bellair: I have remember'd you, Mr. *Remnant*,[94] and some Ladies of my Acquaintance, are so taken up with my last Gown, that they design you shall make for them.

3*d Creditor:* But, Madam ——

---

[92] Bellair's invitation for her creditors to sit surprises them, as convention dictated that persons of lower status would stand before their social superiors.

[93] A gauzy silk fabric.

[94] A term used by drapiers and clothiers for the part of a piece of fabric that remains after the garment has been produced.

Lady Bellair: Well, Mr. *Fringe*,[95] what new Laces[96] are lately come over? I should be glad to see some Patterns.

4th Creditor: I have your Ladyship's Promise –

Lady Bellair: You have so, Mr. *Gause*,[97] and you may depend upon my Business, as long as you continue so obliging.

4th Creditor: That's not the thing, Madam.

1st Creditor: No, indeed is it not, Madam. – My Husband sent in his Bill three Months ago.

Lady Bellair: I believe he did, now I think on't. – You need not make any Apology. – I know People in Trade are often forc'd to do, what they might as well let alone.

1st Creditor: An Apology, Madam! —— Your Ladyship is very much mistaken! – —— I expect my Money.

Lady Bellair: Your Money! Indeed, Mrs. *Lustring*, you must bear with me a little longer. – I am so taken with your Company – that I must have the Pleasure of seeing you again. ——Why, if you were to converse at this End of the Town,[98] – you would soon be taken for one of us. —— You have really a very good Presence of Mind already, and that's a chief Qualification.

1st Creditor: Your Ladyship may banter as much as you please, but I shan't stir without my Money.

Lady Bellair: Bless me! How can a Woman of your Figure talk in such a Strain?

2d Creditor: We are all of the same Mind, Madam.

3d Creditor: Aye, aye, Madam, Times are hard.

4th Creditor: Trading dead.

---

[95] A decorative fabric border.

[96] Decorative fabrics. The most valued laces were imported from the continent, including Brussels lace and Flanders lace.

[97] Thin transparent fabric of cotton, silk, or linen.

[98] Eighteenth-century London was firmly geographically divided, with the west being the fashionable end of town.

5th Creditor: No Money stirring.

6th Creditor: And Taxes must be paid.

Lady Bellair: I protest you are very unconscionable People. – Why, if the Times are so hard, and no Money stirring, how do you think I shall be able to pay you?

5th Creditor: Why really, Madam, that's true: but you should have thought of that before; and we must have Money, or Security,[99] notwithstanding.

Lady Bellair: Security! why that implies Friends, and Friends are harder to be found than Money.

2d Creditor: I protest 'twould do me more good, than if 'twas given me at another time.

3d Creditor: 'Slife, Madam, I must shut up Shop, and go to Prison[100] by *Saturday* Night, if your Ladyship does not pay me.

Lady Bellair: Not on my Account, Sir. —— If these jewels will make you easy, *Double* shall send for my Goldsmith to value them, and what they produce, I believe will satisfy you all. – I designed to put them to this Use before; and, if you had not been quite so pressing, you had succeeded as well. —— I can forego my Splendor at any time to do Justice, and barter Ornament for Ease and Quiet.

SCENE IV.

Double, *and* Creditors.

3d Creditor: 'Slife, Neighbours, is this like a Person of Quality?

---

[99] A promise from another to pay a debt if the original debtor cannot, or property deposited with a third party to ensure payment.

[100] Debtor's prison, which was in theory not intended to punish debtors, but hold them until they had paid. In fact, of course, being held in prison did little to allow one to raise money, and by 1770, half of the prison population were debtors. Lady Bellair is also a debtor, of course, but to call for a lady of rank to be imprisoned would be a violation of decorum that would cost a merchant a great deal of future business.

5th Creditor: I am sure 'tis not like a Citizen; for our Ladies would as soon part with their Honours as their Trinkets.

3d Creditor: As I have a Soul to be sav'd, it goes against my Conscience.

1st Creditor: Suppose we should restore them. – Who knows but she may marry again to Advantage?

3d Creditor: Nay, then 'tis our Interest.

1st Creditor: Oh! if 'tis our Interest, I can relent at any time.

Double: What the deux[101] do the Fools mean?   [*Aside.*

3d Creditor: Hark you, Mrs. *Double*, we have thought better on't.

Double: Pshaw, 'tis too late now. —— Do you think, when you have made so free with her Ladyship already, she has no more Spirit than to put herself into your Power again!

3d Creditor: So. —— We have made a pretty Piece of Business on't.

2d Creditor: Aye, so we have truly. —— But we must comfort ourselves with what we have got by her Custom[102] already.

1st Creditor: And selling the Jewels to the best Advantage.

Double: Not forgetting Poundage[103] to me tho', by the way.

4th Creditor: No, no, we understand Business better than that comes to.

---

[101] A euphemism for 'the devil' in mild swearing.
[102] Her business.
[103] A commission of so much per pound sterling upon the amount of financial transaction.

SCENE V.

Double *sola*.

Upon my Conscience she's come off with flying Colours! Who could have thought it? But, to be sure, we do very different Things from the same Principles. —— T'was her Pride to wear those Jewels, and her Pride to part with them. —— Well, my Mind misgives me; she'll slip thro' our Fingers at last. —— O! the Ladies are join'd again! and now for some new Hypocrisy, to make good the Damages in the old.

SCENE VI.

Lady Bellair, *Lady* Lurcher, *and* Double.

Lady Lurcher: And so, my Dear, you have parted with your Jewels?

Lady Bellair: As you see. – We are both satisfy'd; they to have them, and I to be without them.

Lady Lurcher: I grant you there's a Sort of Female Heroism in it. ——But would any one, beside yourself, dismiss such a Crowd of Lovers as you have done, when the worst of them all could have sav'd you from such a Perplexity ?

Lady Bellair: Yes, every one that either regarded their Husband's Happiness, or their own.——For I think there was scarce a reasonable Creature among them. – And there can be no true Friendship without an Equality.

Double: Dear Heart, Madam, what Objection had you to Colonel *Cockade?*

Lady Bellair: His Conversation! I don't like to hear always of Battles, Murder, and sudden Death. – I would as soon have married his Drum. – Beside, a Soldier has his Honour to serve, as well as his Wife; and two Mistresses are to the full as hard to please as two Masters.

Lady Lurcher: But there was Counsellor *Tangle* would have done any thing to please you.

Lady Bellair: No, my Dear, he would not have given me a Letter of Attorney for a Gallant.[104] – A Lawyer only enters upon the Premises to make good his Claim. – But, if I part with my Tenement, it shall be to one who would reside upon the Spot.[105]

Double: Then why, Madam, did you refuse my Lord Bishop?[106] they are obliged to visit, tho' not to reside.

Lady Bellair: Because there are no Lady-Bishops, *Double*, – and it may be against the Canon[107] to let a Woman be the Head of the Church. – Beside, I should be loth to kneel for a Blessing to him, who should think it a Blessing to kneel to me.

Lady Lurcher: I fancy by this time tho', my Dear, you would jump at Sir *Solomon Thrifty*, the rich Alderman?[108]

Lady Bellair: No, not to be Lady Mayoress, and Queen-it over Venison and Custards for Twelve Months of Mock-Majesty together.[109] —— You must know too, Cousin, if ever I marry, I design to be true to my Husband, —— and I should be loth to have him pointed at as a Monster, among his Brethren.

Double: 'Squire *Rustick* tho' ——

Lady Bellair: Is a Monster before Marriage, – bred up among his Hounds, and noisy as the whole Kennel; his Huntsman[110] and he are so alike, both in Dress and Manners, that there's no knowing 'em asunder; —— and, by some unlucky

---

[104] Power of attorney or legal authority to act. Bellair jests that she would have demanded legal documentation of her right to have a gallant.

[105] In English common law, tenement refers to ownership of property, but the term is also used here figuratively to refer to the body as the home of the soul. Thus Bellair will surrender body and soul in marriage only to one who will stay in her heart, whereas she asserts that a lawyer enters only to make claim of ownership and then moves on.

[106] The second-highest rank in the Church of England (after Archbishop), responsible for a specific diocese.

[107] Canon or religious law.

[108] Chief officer of a ward or district of London, ranking below the Lord Mayor.

[109] These menu items suggest the popular image of socially ambitious politicians imitating their betters. During the eighteenth century, the city of London developed corporate feasts to try to rival those held by aristocratic families. Custards were a feature of French cooking and of the French confectioners who were commonly hired by English aristocrats; they too suggest a pretension to style.

[110] One who manages the hounds for fox hunting.

Mistake or another, my eldest Son might have hollow'd[111] to the Field, as soon as he was born.

Lady Lurcher: Well, as you are fond of Power, pretty Mr. *Dangle* was just come out of the Nursery,[112] and might have been moulded into any Shape.

Lady Bellair: Lard, my Dear, do you think I am fond of a Baby still? —— Why, Breeches no more make a Man, than a Beard a Philosopher;[113] and, whatever you think of a Fool, a wise Man is easier govern'd.

Double: But, Madam, if you were in Love with Knowledge, Mr. *Formal*, the great Scholar, was Learning in Folio.

Lady Bellair: Yes, a walking Dictionary! Words in all Languages, and Sense in none.

Lady Lurcher: You are extreamly difficult; but I have a Lover in my Eye, that I am sure will please you, young, gay, rich, handsome; in a Word, Beau[114] *Modern.*

Lady Bellair: Fie, fie, Cousin, I hate a Man should lay aside his own Character, to take up ours; or make my Eyes a Looking-glass only to admire himself. – I should be apt to treat him like my Sister, make him a Confidant in my Amours, instead of listening to him as a Lover. – Had you nam'd *Harry Freelove*, indeed you had nam'd a Man, one who has Solidity enough to balance my Lightness; and, by an equal Mixture of Humour and Sense, make up the Difficiency of both; one who deserves to be distinguish'd ——

Lady Lurcher: For shame, my Dear! to distinguish a young Fellow, implies something like a Desire for him, and Desires are quite scandalous in us.

Lady Bellair: And yet you would have me distinguish another.

Lady Lurcher: Yes, to repair your Fortune, not to gratify your Desires. – Should you refuse such an Offer, give me leave to tell you, you'll be greatly your own

---

[111] To call to the hounds in hunting.

[112] Rooms where children are housed and educated.

[113] Greek philosophers were often depicted with long beards, though Bellair's doubt was widespread, most entertainingly in Desiderius Erasmus's *Praise of Folly* (1509), which was available in several editions in the eighteenth century: 'A beard [is] the symbol of philosophy, even though it's a symbol shared with goats'.

[114] A colloquial title indicating that a man is handsome and young, and often also foppish.

Enemy. —— He has broke his Mind to me already, and press'd me to give you this Letter in so moving and genteel a Manner, that I could not deny him.

Lady Bellair: Pray, are you acquainted with the Contents?

Lady Lurcher: No, but I would have you read it to oblige me.

Lady Bellair: [*reads*] – Hum. – The Stile's perfectly new. – Pray, Cousin, did you bring it in your Prayer Book?[115] —— So, so! more of the same! — Bless me! What a Rhapsody of Wickedness is here?

Lady Lurcher: What, in the Name of Goodness, has he wrote?

Double: Nothing like Goodness, I'll be sworn.

Lady Bellair: [*reads*] Prodigious! —— worse and worse! —— One would think he meant to raise the Devil.

Lady Lurcher: For Heaven's Sake! my Dear, what's the Matter?

Lady Bellair: Pray see yourself, 'twould blister my Tongue to repeat it. —— A Magazine[116] of Oaths, and Curses, – enough to stock a Regiment[117] in a Battle, or a Man of War[118] in a Storm.

Lady Lurcher: O monstrous! and make me the Messenger!

Lady Bellair: Towards the Conclusion, indeed, his Fury abates a little, and he ends cooly; Your's to the Centre, *Frank Modern.*

Lady Lurcher: I tremble at carrying such a Flame about me. —— Why, it roars like Thunder from End to End.

Lady Bellair: Yet this is a Lover of your recommending, Cousin.

Lady Lurcher: I must own he addresses a little oddly. – But, as long as he has Money, you'll be in the Wrong to refuse him notwithstanding.

---

[115] Probably the *Book of Common Prayer*, containing the traditional public liturgy of the Church of England.

[116] A general term for a storage area or receptacle, linked here specifically to its military meaning as storage for arms or ammunition.

[117] A military unit.

[118] A ship equipped for battle.

Lady Bellair: Would a Person of your strict Piety, have me marry an Atheist.

Lady Lurcher: An Atheist, Child! Why his very Oaths are a Proof of his Religion; or, if he is one, you may have the Merit of his Conversion. – Hark! I hear a Coach stop! 'tis he, I believe – I have invited him to Dinner To-day, with some more Company; and I'd have you entertain him by all means: 'Twill be easy for you either to punish, or forgive him, as you think proper: But, for my part, I am at present so provok'd at his Impiety, that I can't bear the Sight of him.

Lady Bellair: She did not use to be so concern'd for my Interest; and I dare be sworn she has some Design in it now.

SCENE VII.

Lady Bellair, Freelove *and Young* Modern.

Lady Bellair: Your Servant, Gentlemen – I protest, Mr. *Freelove,* you are a bold Man to introduce a Rival to your Mistress.

Freelove: A Lover, that could not bear a Rival, Madam, should not think of making his Addresses to your Ladyship. —— I am surprised tho', that you are acquainted already with his Devotion.

Lady Bellair: O he makes Love in State,[119] by his Ambassador,[120] and calls the Gods to Witness, in the Stile of the antient Heroes.[121]

Young *Modern:* Gad, Madam, I think 'tis as natural for a Lover to swear, as a Mistress to believe –

Lady Bellair: He makes no Secret of it, you see! you are his Master of the Ceremonies[122] then, I presume, and, now you have introduc'd him in Form, design to take your Leave.

---

[119] Courts a lady with high ceremony, as if from an office of high importance.

[120] Lady Lurcher has represented Modern's suit to Bellair.

[121] As in the classical tradition, wherein the gods watch over and participate in human life, as in Homer's *Iliad.*

[122] The one to preside over a formal event, introducing speakers or entertainers.

Freelove: I should be sorry, Madam, if you were to command it; because I don't know how to disobey you.

Lady Bellair: You don't consider what Joy it gives one to make a new Conquest. —— Why 'tis more than setting a new Fashion, or having the best fancy'd Suit on a Birth-Day.[123]

Freelove: Hardly to you, Madam, that make them every Moment.

Lady Bellair: But Mr. *Modern* is a very extraordinary one, —— and a Woman must have no Pride in her, that was not vain upon the Occasion.

Young *Modern:* Lard, Madam! —— She comes on rarely! [*Aside.*

Freelove: I hope, however, that your Favour to him, won't increase your Rigour to me.

Lady Bellair: Indeed I can't answer for myself; 'tis so effectual a Compliment to a new Lover, to use an old one ill, – that I'm afraid 'twill not be in my Power to help it.

Freelove: I have no Notion, Madam, that there is any Virtue you are not Mistress of.

Lady Bellair: Then you are much mistaken. —— I insist upon all the Privileges of my Sex, and will go wrong whenever I have a mind to it. – Beside, Cruelty to you is the Height of Kindness. – You make Love as if it hurt you, and I can't see any Body in Pain, without endeavouring to make 'em easy.

Freelove: But I am afraid, at this rate, you would rather kill than cure – I am sure Disdain agrees but ill with so much Beauty;[124] and, while your Face has all that Sweetness, I must still adore it.

Lady Bellair: O! if 'tis my Face you are so fond of, you shall have Admission to my Picture every Day; and talk to it all the fine Things you can think of: I'll engage it shall not interrupt you.

Freelove: I admire your Face, Madam, but as the beauteous Index of your Mind.

---

[123] Traditionally one wore one's finest clothes to celebrate the King's birthday each year.

[124] The ostensible science of physiognomy argued that beautiful features conveyed beautiful character.

Lady Bellair: Still more absurd! Why, I tell you, 'tis my Mind keeps my Body out of your Power – As I live, this Love alters a Man strangely. —— You us'd to look free, open, and disengag'd, and now you blush and tremble, as if you were detected in a Robbery. —— Bless me, were I a Man of your Merit, you see I hate Detraction, – Before I would make myself a Fool, to make my Mistress a Goddess, prefer her Smile to a Sun-beam, follow her like a Shadow, and have no Thought, Will, or Passion, but her's, I'd turn *Turk*, and make myself a Slave in the Seraglio for Life.[125]

Young *Modern:* Oh! How I love a Woman of Wit? Now is she at once exposing him, and instructing me. [*Aside.*

Freelove: Would you have us then, Madam, neglect the Sex intirely?

Lady Bellair: Much rather than yourselves! For shame, keep up your masculine Privilege! and, by knowing your own Value, teach us to treat you accordingly!

Young *Modern:* Right, Madam! it brings a Lady to Reason immediately.

Freelove: Henceforward then, I'll study to follow your Ladyship's Instructions.

Lady Bellair: I know you'd be glad to do it: But, alas! 'tis not in your Power, the Affectation[126] will be visible; and, tho' I like the Sentiment, I might condemn the Actor. —— In short, no one that has Eyes, will follow a blind Guide at all;[127] and you find Love is no better, since he has led you out of the Way.

Freelove: Is there no Method then to reach your Heart?

Lady Bellair: None that you'll find out, I'm afraid. – Take my Word for it, Women are either Fools, or very Wise: The Fools are not worth your Notice, and the Wise will take no Notice of you.

---

[125] Eighteenth-century England was fascinated with the cultural difference being encountered around the world, particularly that which seemed salacious, such as the Turkish seraglio, which was widely interpreted as a heavily sexualized environment (in fact, the seraglio was merely the living quarters reserved for women (wives and concubines) in polygamous Muslim households of the time). In this speech, Bellair argues that were she a man, she would become a sexual slave to multiple women before submitting to the emotional and intellectual control of a single mistress.

[126] The performance of an unnatural behavior, often in attempting to appear of higher class or greater intelligence.

[127] Likely an allusion to Matthew 15.14: 'If the blind lead the blind, both shall fall into the ditch.' The reference to love in the next line also links to Cupid, traditionally represented as blindfolded, as love is blind.

Freelove: I begin to think, Madam, your Scorn is Kindness indeed; and hope, at last, it will teach me to conquer a Passion, you are too cruel to favour.

Young *Modern:* Piqu'd by this Light! Piqu'd to Distraction! [*Aside.*

Lady Bellair: Why, what would you have one do now? 'Tis as little in my Power to love, as yours to hate.

Freelove: 'Tis in both our Powers to try – and I may be resolute, perhaps, tho' your Ladyship can't be grateful.

Lady Bellair: Nay, now you spoil all again. – I was in hopes you would have behav'd like a Man, and stood your Ground with Courage; but, if you grow angry, 'tis a certain Sign that you are conquer'd.

Freelove: Such Provocations are not to be borne.

Lady Bellair: Indeed but they are, and worse too. – I have seen many such Clouds as these end in a Shower. – When you quarrel next, I'd have you be more perfect in the Knack of it. – You have not half Confidence enough yet: There is scarce a Militia Captain,[128] who has not a better Face for it than you.

Freelove: Are you really as hard of Heart as you seem to be? or are you so fond of Affectation, that you'll put it on, in spite of Nature, to keep the Sex in Countenance?

Lady Bellair: Very pretty Reasoning, truly! I am hard-hearted, or hypocritical, because I love my own Happiness too well, to part with it in Pity of another's Sufferings. —— This now is the worst you can accuse me of, and surely Self-defence is Prudence, if not Virtue. —— Who knows but some of these pretty Pouts, and Humours of yours, may captivate me one Day or another, and then you'll have your Revenge in your own Power?

Freelove: I know, Madam, I have no Privilege to resent this Treatment; and Love, like Charity, will excuse a Multitude of Failings; but 'tis impossible not to feel it; and, rather than be made use of to please a Rival's Vanity – I'll tear, myself from your Presence for ever.

---

[128] Militias were domestic defense groups trained (often irregularly) for civil defense and supported by levies imposed upon each county. Officers were often drawn from the upper classes.

SCENE VIII.

Lady Bellair, *and Young* Modern.

Young *Modern:* Poor *Freelove!* Ha! ha! ha! Admirably perform'd, let me perish! Dear provoking Creature! Let me die, for a Man of Sense,[129] if I ever saw a poor Devil look more like an Ideot in my Life.

Lady Bellair: I thought you had pretended to be in Love yourself.

Young *Modern:* Terribly, deplorably, Madam. – My Heart is run quite thro' and thro', or may I be –

Lady Bellair: Hold, hold, Sir! no more Damns and Devils, I beseech you.

Young *Modern:* Your Ladyship will give one leave to express one's Passion.

Lady Bellair: Yes, among Bravoes and Ruffians,[130] in a Midnight Quarrel.

Young *Modern:* Gad, Madam, 'tis always my Way to come to the Point at once– and I had rather carry a Mistress by Storm, than wait the dull Formality of a Siege.

Lady Bellair: So that, upon the first Summons, you expect a Surrender of Course?

Young *Modern:* Why, what signifies dallying, when we know one another's Minds? I am for the *Spanish* Gallantry,[131] Madam, and taking Occasion by the Forelock.[132] —— A fine Creature, like your Ladyship, sets us all on Fire, and I can't help thinking that her Desires may be as troublesome as mine; and so, Madam. – Gad I shall carry her Sword in Hand.[133]

---

[129] Modern refers to the culture of sensibility (valuing the capacity for refined emotion even to the point of delicate sensitivity), though he also accidentally suggests his own lack of sense in the intellectual definition.

[130] Violent men of lower class.

[131] A peculiar form of gallantry that took root in Spain in the early eigheenth century by which nobles tacitly encouraged their wives to have a select male friend. This friend frequented the lady's house, performed gallantries, and was allowed to be alone with her. The relationship did not conventionally overstep the limits of platonic love, but the novelty of a woman so close to a man who was not her husband was widely seen as dangerous.

[132] A reference to the proverb 'Seize occasion by the forelock, for she is bald behind'. One must act decisively rather than wait cautiously and miss the chance to grasp passing opportunity.

[133] Often used in connection with the entry into a besieged city, the phrase means in readiness for battle.

Lady Bellair: Stay, stay a little, Sir. —— I am not in such Distress as you imagine, —— nor to be won like your Laundress, or Milliner,[134] with a Heap of passionate Nonsense. – You don't know me, I find. —— Impudent Coxcomb! [*Aside.*

Young *Modern:*   Faith, Madam, I am afraid not. – 'Slife, I was never so baulk'd[135] in my Life.   [*Aside.*

Lady Bellair: Why then I'll inform you better: – and, if you don't pay dear for your Experience, I shall much wonder. [*Aside*] – You must know then, that, tho' I don't wear my Virtue outwards, I have not left it off, as if 'twas out of Fashion, – and, tho' I often deviate from the common Road of Life in a Frolick, and indulge a Flow of Spirits,[136] as long as they will last me, I never trespass on my own Innocence, or injure any Body else. – Nay, I have some Plea even for my very Faults; for, if I am fond of Expence, 'tis because Money is of no Value till 'tis us'd: If I am thoughtless of To-morrow, 'tis because I would enjoy To-day; and, if I trespass on the narrow Limits that are prescrib'd to our Sex, 'tis because I am better pleased with the License that is indulg'd to your's. In a Word, tho' I would run thro' all the Refinements of Happiness, I would be able to justify myself in all.

Young *Modern:*   I could have granted your Ladyship all this in the Beginning: Love, Madam, Love was my Plea, and I don't yet perceive any Ingredients in your Character averse to it.

Lady Bellair: No, I'm free to own that Love is my favourite Passion; and Life hardly to be endur'd without it. —— But you see, I have some Reputation to preserve, and 'twould be absurd to trifle it away. – Tho' Opinion is but a Name, it, can hurt like a Reality; and I would not be uneasy even in a Dream, if I could avoid it.

Young *Modern:*   I am a Man of Honour, Madam, and, if you were a Vestal, I'd engage your Fire should not go out.[137] —— I have had many a Secret in my Hands before now.

Lady Bellair: Why, that's the thing, Sir. —— The only Objection I have to you.

---

[134] A laundress washes clothing and linens, and a milliner creates women's hats. Bellair assumes an ease in seducing women of lower class.

[135] Disappointed in expectations.

[136] A sudden impulse of cheerfulness of exhilaration.

[137] Vestals were ancient Roman priestesses, whose duty was to ensure that the sacred fire of Rome did not go out. The priestesses were required to be virgins.

Young *Modern:* Then your Ladyship differs extreamly from the whole Sex, – for I never knew a Woman in my Life, that did not always prefer the Man, who had been happiest with others.

Lady Bellair: I know 'tis a common Indiscretion, because few People in Love ever think of Consequences. —— But, alas! such Gallants as those carry a List of their Conquests in their Faces, look as if nothing could stand before them; and the poor Creature, they attack, thinks 'tis to no Purpose to defend herself; or, if she does, the World will conclude 'tis impossible she should hold out long, and so give her up to Scandal before her Time. – Now, I know you are one of those formidable Sparks;[138] nay, that you have taken Pains to be thought so; and, therefore, 'tis no Wonder I am afraid of you.

Young *Modern:* I vow to Gad, Madam, you utterly mistake me. —— If there's any Truth in Man, I'm a Maid[139] still.

Lady Bellair: Oh! this is only to impose upon me. Don't I know that from a Chamber-Maid to a Dutchess, no Creature escapes you? Don't I know that your Eyes have the same Quality with the Rattle-Snake's,[140] and that, as soon as you fix them upon us like the Squirrel, we drop into your Mouth?

Young *Modern:* As I have a Soul to be sav'd, Madam, 'tis all Vapour and Air. —— I'm a perfect Innocent, upon my Honour.

Lady Bellair: That's very strange, when so many Ladies have trusted you with their Secrets.

Young *Modern:* O, I ly'd, Madam, ly'd confoundedly! 'Tis what we Beaux[141] are forc'd to say every Day of our Lives, or we Dress, Powder, and Essence[142] to no Purpose. —— But, a lack-a-Day! there's no more Truth in our Amours, than a Secret-Service Man's No to a Bribe, or a Malcontent-Patriot's[143] to a Peerage.

Lady Bellair: But the Scandal will stick by you still; and whoever shews you the least Countenance, will be sure to share it. – As I live, I don't think it safe to let

---

[138] A generally deprecatory term for a young man of elegant or foppish character.

[139] Virgin.

[140] Rattlesnakes were believed to hypnotize their prey before attacking.

[141] Fashionable young men.

[142] Eighteenth-century fashion dictated that men's wigs be covered with white powder, and many men powdered their faces as well, for a paler, the thus presumptively more aristocratic complexion. Essence is perfume.

[143] During the first half of the eighteenth century, 'patriot' was often used as a derogatory term for those who claimed devotion to England but did not support the monarchy.

you lead me to my Chair, play with my Fan or, even bow to me in the Boxes. – 'Tis really pity, you are a very pretty Fellow. – I am sorry for you, —— but there's no help for it now.

Young *Modern:* Zoons,[144] I have made a fine Piece of Business on't. [*Aside.*

Lady Bellair: I vow you Men are strangely out in your Politicks; there's nothing you are more ambitious of, than to be esteem'd dangerous to the Ladies; whereas those, that would be well with us, should rather seem insensible of Passions than notorious for their Debauchery. – For the first we can favour, without being suspected, and the last we can't speak to without being condemn'd.

Young *Modern:* Gad, Madam, you're in the Right! What a Coxcomb was I not to see this before? But, rather than lose your Ladyship, I'll be a new Man in an Instant.

Lady Bellair: What do you mean, Sir?

Young *Modern:* To lay aside Lace and Embroidery, Frolick and Equipage, Masquerades and *New-Market.*[145]

Lady Bellair: Astonishing! But your Uncle ——

Young *Modern:* Lard! Madam, if I was to bid him take Orders,[146] he would sooner be damn'd than disoblige me ——

Lady Bellair: At your own Peril then ——

Young *Modern:* With all my Soul! Henceforward I'm a Rake in Masquerade, with the Face of a Cardinal, the Tongue of a Jesuit, and the Heart of a Debauchee.[147]

Lady Bellair: Then, if the Chaplain should be out of the Way at Dinner-time, which he seldom, is indeed, you may supply his Place.

Young *Modern:* With as good a Grace as he – sink me!

Lady Bellair: So! his own Folly will be his Punishment. [*Aside.*

---

[144] A mild swearing oath, derived from '– God's/His wounds'.

[145] A town in Sussex associated with horseracing and other forms of gambling.

[146] Become a member of the clergy.

[147] Modern will continue in his rakish ways, but will appear morally conservative. A rake is an immoral and licentious man; a cardinal is the second highest ranking in the Roman Catholic church, after the Pope; the Jesuits are members of the Society of Jesus, a group within the Catholic church known for intellectual and scholarly work.

SCENE IX.

Young Modern *solus.*

Let me see; a black Coat, a bob Whig without Powder, a Shirt without Ruffles, neither Sword nor Snuff-Box,[148] and I'm qualify'd to smoak with the Clergy,[149] sleep with a Bench of Justices, kill with a License among the Doctors,[150] or be happy, it seems, with the Ladies, without Suspicion. I see she loves me to the Soul, and 'twould be a Sin to let her languish. – Pox![151] What signifies a little Dissimulation? It costs a Man nothing, and is as natural to some People as to breathe. – Beside, 'tis the Custom of the World, and Tradesmen, Merchants, Lawyers, Poets, Statesmen, and Divines, set the Example to each other. – Then, if my Uncle should storm, as I expect he will, 'tis but to give him his Way, and he blows himself cool in a Moment.

SCENE X.

Young Modern, *and Lady* Lurcher.

Lady Lurcher: Oh! you may well sneak off, Sir!

Young *Modern:* I vow to Gad, I did not see you, Madam.

Lady Lurcher: Make a Person of my Character the Messenger of your Confound-me's, and Rot-me's, and Sink-me's! make me the Agent of your Oaths and Curses!

---

[148] Modern has costumed himself by rejecting all markers of fashion and status. The bob wig was the plainest and most natural-looking of contemporary styles, and was widely worn by professionals and clergy, but rarely by gentry, who still favoured the powdered tie-wig and other more elaborate styles.

[149] In 1724, Pope Benedict XIII had repealed papal Bulls against clerical smoking. Though this would not have affected the Puritan clergy that Modern imitates, his being without a fashionable snuff box leaves him able to consume tobacco only through smoking, widely considered a vice of the low and unfashionable, and often preached against from the pulpit.

[150] The negligent justice and the dangerously unskilled physician were widely recognized negative stereotypes of the day, as is the Dissenting clergyman as canting fool.

[151] A mild curse word signifying irritation, alluding to both smallpox and pox as a term for sexually transmitted disease.

Young *Modern:* Wou'd your Ladyship have me write to a Woman of Fashion, like a *London* 'Prentice to his first Sweet-heart? and begin with Hoping you are in good Health, and so on to Your's till Death. —— Ha! ha! ha!

Lady Lurcher: You may make a Jest of your Wickedness, if you please, —— but that won't make me Amends. – I protest I am afraid nothing I take in Hand will prosper after it.

Young *Modern:* So, so, she starts at an Oath, and yet is taking Pains to be a Bawd. [*Aside.*] By this Light, Madam, I meant no Harm.

Lady Lurcher: No Harm? Nay, then there's no Hopes of you; and I must wash my Hands of your Affairs.

Young *Modern:* For Gad-Sake, Madam, don't forget your Charity in your Zeal. – I am now riding Post[152] to Repentance, and, in Half an Hour's Time, shall be at my Journey's End.

Lady Lurcher: If this was true now ——

Young *Modern:* I vow to Gad, Madam ——

Lady Lurcher: O Mercy! talk of repenting, and trespass a-new with the same Breath!

Young *Modern:* The Devil take me then ——

Lady Lurcher: Again! prodigious! Your Servant, Sir. —— I see there's no Truth in you.

Young *Modern:* As I hope to be sav'd ——

Lady Lurcher: Oh!

Young *Modern:* Zoons, Madam! 'tis impossible to be a Saint at once; if you will give me but Time —

Lady Lurcher: How long do you require?

---

[152] Moving quickly toward, from the use of post horses to move from place to place. Post horses are hired from inns or stables, ridden to a specific destination, and then left for the owner to retrieve. Because of the constant changing to fresh horses, riding post was a faster way to travel than feeding and resting one's own horses at intervals.

Young *Modern:* Only till I shift my Cloaths. – When a Man's dress'd like a Gentleman, he must behave like one. – But, otherwise, I protest and vow; indeed and indeed, and such Sort of insipid Expletives, will do well enough.

Lady Lurcher: I don't understand you, Sir.

Young *Modern:* In a Word then, Madam; your Cousin has convinc'd me that a Man of Gallantry should never be thought so; and that a grave Look, and precise Manners, are the best Covers for an Intrigue.

Lady Lurcher: Aye, these Maxims she learn'd of me.

Young *Modern:* You know what this means, Madam; and Egad! I'll fit her Humour to a Hair.

Lady Lurcher: This is lucky, indeed! But has *Freelove* been here?

Young *Modern:* Yes, and she has us'd him like a Dog, in Complaisance to me.

Lady Lurcher: That's better still. —— I hope tho' he is not gone away in a Rage before Dinner?

Young *Modern:* No, no; he's only running mad in Heroicks[153] round the Garden, I suppose.

Lady Lurcher: Well then, if she should happen to put on any of her Coquet Airs,[154] and wheadle him to her Lure again; I have a little Practice to try on his Father, that will set them farther asunder than ever.

Young *Modern:* I need not wish your Ladyship Success for so much Piety, as yours deserves it.

---

[153] Referring to the style and language used in heroic poetry, grand and high flown. Modern assumes that Freelove must be making dramatic speeches in the agonies of lost heroic love.

[154] Flirtatious mannerisms.

SCENE XI.

Lady Lurcher, *and Sir* William.

Lady Lurcher: Oh, Sir *William*! I'm glad you are come. – I wanted to speak with you alone. – I have something to propose to you; but you must first promise to pardon me for meddling in your Family Affairs.

Sir William: With all my Heart, Madam. – My Family Affairs can't be in better Hands.

Lady Lurcher: You must know then, you have now an Opportunity of doing an Action that will distinguish you, as the most affectionate Parent of the Age. —— Your Son is in Love to Distraction.

Sir William: With a great Fortune then, I hope?

Lady Lurcher: No, no, he's above any such mercenary Views! 'tis with a great Beauty tho', and, if you'll give your Consent ——

Sir William: Oh, nothing more reasonable!

Lady Lurcher: Sure he is not in earnest [*Aside.*] Poor Souls! they were out of their Wits for fear of a Refusal.

Sir William: Why I do refuse it, Madam, and I will refuse it to my dying Day. A great Beauty, with a Pox! [*Aside.*]

Lady Lurcher: Why, 'tis my Cousin *Bellair*, Sir *William*.

Sir William: S'Death and Fury! I shall run mad – The most notorious She-Prodigal[155] in Town.

Lady Lurcher: You know she's undone too; and, with the Spirit of a Dutchess, must be expos'd to Misfortunes that will break her Heart.

Sir William: Aye, aye, the sooner the better.

Lady Lurcher: Consider, therefore, what a Compliment 'twill be to your Generosity!

---

[155] A woman who spends extravagantly, an allusion to the parable of the prodigal son (Luke 15:11–32).

Sir William: Madam, I hate Compliments mortally.

Lady Lurcher: To be the Instrument of retrieving her Affairs.

Sir William: I her instrument! I her Tool!

Lady Lurcher: Why every new Suit she wears, every new Equipage she appears in, every new jewel she buys, every Hundred Pound she loses at Play –

Sir William: Lord! Lord! what have I to do with her Extravagancies?

Lady Lurcher: I say all these, and ten times as many more Articles of Grandeur and Expence, will be so many constant Proofs of your Bounty and Compassion.

Sir William: Zoons, Madam, all the Bounty and Compassion in the World is not worth half the Money –

Lady Lurcher: Then again for your Fatherly Affection! To take such Pity of your Son's Passion, as to sacrifice all the Hopes of your Family to his Peace ——

Sir William: I'll see him dead first – Tell me of Fatherly Affection – I never knew a prudent Man that had any in his Life ——

Lady Lurcher: And this is your Resolution, Sir *William?*

Sir William: Positively! nor should all the great Beauties in the World persuade me out of it –

Lady Lurcher: Why then I applaud you for it; 'tis the only Way to save your Son from Ruin: what I said before was to try you, and I am glad to find you have his Welfare so much at Heart.

Sir William: You overjoy me, Madam, and, if you can carry your Kindness to him a little farther, you'll make us both happy at once.

Lady Lurcher: By what Means, Sir *William?*

Sir William: By marrying him yourself – 'Tis what I have long thought upon with much Pleasure.

Lady Lurcher: Is this a Motion of your own, or his?

Sir William: O, 'tis all my own, Madam.

Lady Lurcher: Suppose he shou'd decline it then?

Sir William: Let him if he dares! – 'Tis hard indeed if I can't command my own Son.

Lady Lurcher: Well, Sir *William* – I'll consider of it, and, if I do comply, I'd have you think, 'tis intirely in Regard to you, not the least sinister Views to myself.

Sir William: Your Ladyship is all Goodness – I'll find him out this Instant.

Lady Lurcher: He's now in the Garden, and I'll send some body to let him know you expect him – You see I'm quite impatient to oblige you – but not a Word that you have broke the Affair to me.

Sir William: Your Ladyship shall be obey'd most Punctually.
The END of the SECOND ACT.

ACT III. SCENE I.

Sir William *and* Modern.

Modern: 'TIS done, Sir, 'tis done.

Sir William: What's done, Sir?

Modern: That which will break your Heart, Sir.

Sir William: Sir, your humble Servant.

Modern: Pshaw! hang Ceremony! – you are welcome, and that's enough.

Sir William: 'Tis the greater Favour.

Modern: Not at all, Sir! I take a Pleasure in it – Beside, 'tis more for your Son's Sake than yours.

Sir William: Then you need not have given yourself the Trouble – He's in a fair Way of doing it without you.

Modern: Good! I like him the better for it —— He's a gallant young Fellow, and I honour his Spirit: How he came by it Heaven knows – I am afraid not very honestly, he's so little like his Father —— Hark you! I have given my Nephew a Thousand Pounds a Year.

Sir William: I am glad of it.

Modern: And have commanded him to spend it every Farthing.[156]

Sir William: You need not Fear his Obedience.

Modern: I have bespoke him a Chariot and Equipage, gay as a Bridegroom's.[157]

Sir William: And design to walk a-foot yourself.

Modern: Bid him look out for a Mistress, or two, and keep them[158] openly with Splendor.

Sir William: You must give him t'other Thousand then.

Modern: With all my Soul, and another to that.

Sir William: Ha! ha! ha!

Modern: You are merry, Sir.

Sir William: I have Reason —— you'll make yourself a Beggar to break my Heart.

Modern: A Beggar! S'Death! he does not feel it. [*Aside.*

Sir William: Aye! he that gives away his Estate in his Life-time deserves to be no other.

Modern: And he that does not, will never be thank'd for the Legacy when he dies.

Sir William: That will hardly give the Dead any Trouble.

---

[156] The smallest unit of coinage in the eighteenth century, valued at a quarter penny.

[157] A wedding day was expected to be one of lavish expenditure and celebration, including one's mode of transport. Cooper, with her anthologizing interest in lesser-known poetry, may have adapted this simile from Richard Blackmore's poem 'The Creation', which describes the sun as being 'gay as a bridegroom'.

[158] To maintain a lover through providing accommodation and living expenses.

Modern: But it may be a severe Reproach to the Living.

Sir William: You had better' guard against your own Prodigality, than reflect on my Prudence.

Modern: All the Town shall reflect on it as well as I – I know you are afraid of being detected in your Avarice; but I'll unmasque you, I'll expose you, in your proper Colours[159] – Henceforward your Son shall command my Purse, enjoy all the Pleasures you deny him, and the Credit of his Splendor, and Gallantry shall be mine.

Sir William: Do, do, I am easy as long as you pay for the Experiment. Ha! ha! ha!

SCENE II.

Sir William, *and* Freelove.

Sir William: Hark you, Sir; if Mr. *Modern*, or his Nephew, shou'd ever offer you any Favour – such as lending you Money, paying your Reckonings,[160] or so forth – I charge you, upon my Blessing, to refuse them.

Freelove: Suppose I shou'd want them, Sir? These are no Times to refuse Money in; and, if I shou'd ever be qualified to stand for a Borough, I may lose my Election, by fitting so bad an Example.[161]

Sir William: If you will learn to live as I did, when I was a young Fellow, you need not be oblig'd to any body – But you must wench, and game, and drink, and run in Debt, to prove yourself a fine Gentleman.[162]

Freelove: If 'tis the Fashion, Sir, how can I avoid it? – I don't care to be singular,[163] or make my Life a Satire upon my Acquaintance.[164]

---

[159] True self or true colours.

[160] Bills at taverns or inns.

[161] Freelove alludes to the practice of purchasing votes in elections, particularly in ridings known as pocket boroughs, where a small number of qualified voters means that deep enough pockets will virtually guarantee an electoral win.

[162] To wench is to have sexual relationships with women, particularly women of lower class; to game is to gamble. This argument on the flawed nature of the popular idea of the modern gentleman is articulated in very similar terms in Mary Davys's 1727 novel *The Accomplish'd Rake, or Modern Fine Gentleman.*

[163] Odd or unfashionable.

[164] Become an object of mockery among his peers.

Sir William: You may be frugal in your Pleasures tho' – But you are more inclin'd to dispute than obey.

Freelove: To dispute for Redress of Grievances, Sir, is the Liberty of the Subject.

Sir William: Nay, this is downright Rebellion.

Freelove: Only an humble Remonstrance, Sir, that's all.

Sir William: Well, Sir, on one Condition ——

Freelove: Any Condition.

Sir William: That you wou'd make your Addresses to Lady *Lurcher.*

Freelove: Confusion! [*Aside.*]

Sir William: What, don't you like the Proposal?

Freelove: 'Tis too soon to play the Fool, Sir, on this Side Thirty.

Sir William: And too late on t'other – Come, come, Sir, no Scruples! she has 30000 Pounds;[165] and, if you must live like the Prodigal Son,[166] it shall be at your own Expence, not mine.

Freelove: So it will indeed, Sir, on such desperate Terms.

Sir William: If you don't like them, Sir, I'll marry her myself.

Freelove: 'Tis very hard, Sir.

Sir William: What! to marry a fine Woman with 30000 Pounds?

Freelove: To be forc'd to marry any Woman at all; But, if I must comply, what will you advance me upon the Credit of my future Fortune?

---

[165] A substantial fortune, approximately £3.4 million in modern terms.

[166] A reference to the parable of the prodigal son in Luke 15:11–32, who leaves his family and spends all of his future inheritance on an illicit life. Apparently unlike Sir William, the father of the prodigal son welcomes his son home with a feast to celebrate his repentance and return to the fold.

Sir William: Let me see. —— Hum. —— Eight Hundred Pounds,[167] Sirrah![168] a most prodigious Sum! enough to eclipse Young *Modern* utterly. —— But I must have thy Bond, *Harry*, for 1000 *l.* to be paid on thy Wedding-Day.[169]

Freelove: If you insist upon it, Sir.

Sir William: Dutifully said! —— I'll order it for thee directly. – A most prodigious Sum indeed! —— I am too generous. —— 'Tis my Failing. – Perhaps tho' one Half of it will serve thee.

Freelove: Nay, Sir, no more Draw-backs,[170] I beseech you. —— I shall have no great Difficulty to get rid of such a Trifle as this.

Sir William: A Trifle! O monstrous! If I don't hasten the Contract, o'my Conscience he won't have a Guinea left to pay the Parson.

SCENE III.

Freelove solus.

So! There's 800 Pound secur'd however; and never Money came more critically, —— not for myself, but my dear *Bellair*. —— It went to my Heart, to hear she had parted with her jewels; and, tho' I have tacitly given her up in Complaisance[171] to my Father, 'twas only to have it in my Power to do her this little Service. —— No, cruel as she is, I can never be brib'd to forego my Hopes and yet, 'tis certain, I am undone if I pursue her. —— A Man of more Prudence, and less Passion tho', would know more of her Mind first; but, by what Means, would puzzle both him and I. —— I am sure I have but one Project for it left, and if that fails, I have nothing else to do, but despair, and die.

---

[167] Equivalent to approximately £91,000 in modern terms.

[168] Used to address men or boys with contempt.

[169] A promise to repay the £800 loan with £1000 on Freelove's wedding day. Sir William's initially generous gesture is weighted with a usurious interest rate of 25% for what would be a relatively brief period before the assumed wedding.

[170] An amount paid back from a sum previously paid, now more commonly 'claw-back'.

[171] A desire to please.

SCENE IV.

Freelove *and* Double.

Double: Sir! Sir! Mr. *Freelove.*

Freelove: Well, Child! What are your Commands with me?

Double: My Lady's, Sir! not mine.

Freelove: But which of your Ladies? my Curiosity's on the Rack[172] to know.

Double: Which of my Ladies! —— O'my Conscience, I believe you have no other Passion but Curiosity! – Grant me Patience! 'That ever I shou'd be so much mistaken in a Man! But alack! what's my Mistake to the Lady's that employ'd me? To be sure she thought, as well as I, that the accomplish'd Mr. *Freelove* had nothing of Winter in his Composition: That he was wanton as *April*, and warm as *Midsummer.* — But, as I have a Soul to be sav'd, she might as well have fallen in Love with a Picture, or made an Assignation with a Statue.

Freelove: A little Patience, good *Double* – I have not any Thing that's cold about me — But, when the Mind's wholly taken up with one Beauty ——

Double: Look you there again! one Beauty! Why is not Beauty the same thro' the whole Sex? and he, that doats on it in one, must love it in all. —— I am mad with myself for undertaking to animate such a Thing of Snow. —— I shall be utterly disgrac'd for ever.

Freelove: 'Sdeath what a Tongue she has? [*Aside.*] You can't imagine the urgent Reasons I have to be so particular; nor how much my Peace of mind depends ——

Double: Sir, your most humble Servant: – The next Time I do myself the Honour of waiting on you, it shall be to read you Lectures out of the *Practice of Piety*,[173] or

---

[172] Being tortured, a reference to the stretching torture device of the rack.

[173] *The Practice of Piety: Directing a Christian How to Walk, That He May Please God* (first publication date unknown; second edition 1612), by Anglican Bishop Lewis Bayly. This very long text went through over 50 printings by 1700 and was hugely popular for its inclusion of prayers for many occasions, rules for a pious life and Christian death, and practical tone on issues of faith and piety.

the *Saint's everlasting Rest;*[174] not with a tender Message from a warm, glowing, expecting *Venus.*

Freelove: Stay! You must not, shall not go yet. – Allow me but one Moment's Consideration.

Double: Consideration! 'Slife, the Man that pauses in a Love Affair, wou'd say his Prayers, when he shou'd enjoy his Mistress —— I shall never forgive myself, if I stay any longer.

Freelove: One Moment more, and I resolve. —— It may be *Bellair* she means, I have sometimes flatter'd myself she favour'd me; If it shou'd, and I decline the Invitation, I am undone with her for ever. [*Aside.*] Well, now *Double,* you may take me blindfold, and lead me where you please.

Double: Oh! I thought your Spirit wou'd take Fire at last ——

Freelove: And yet, who knows, in the Humour the dear Wanton[175] seems to be in at present; but this Message, may be only to insnare me farther, and make me the Object of more publick Ridicule: – Hark ye, *Double!* Look me full in the Face! – so!

Double: Well, Sir, and what now?

Freelove: I am looking for Truth in your Eyes, – for there's no Dependance on your Tongue.

Double: What the Duce, more Scruples? Does your Conscience appear to you, like a huge roaring Lyon, with great, saucer Eyes, and frighten you from consenting?

Freelove: No, no, I am more afraid of the Sex, than my own Conscience, or the Devil himself. – I tell thee what, if thou shou'dst be in a Plot to expose me –

Double: A Plot to expose you! Very likely indeed! – a very terrible Plot truly, to lead you in a few Steps to such Delight, as a Man, who was not Ice itself, wou'd ride Post a Thousand Miles for —— A fine Way of exposing you too – to be carried into an Apartment fum'd with richest Odours, and adorn'd with all the

---

[174] *The Saint's Everlasting Rest, or a Treatise of the Blessed State of the Saints in their Enjoyment of God in Glory* (1650), by Richard Baxter, explains how the pious should prepare for 'rest' at the end of life. Ironically, given Double's reference to publicly reading lectures, *Rest* encourages readers to preach sermons privately to themselves.

[175] An ungovernable person, particularly a woman given to romantic entanglements.

wanton Arts, that cou'd delight the loose *Semiramis*[176] – To be lodg'd in an Alcove, that the soft *Persian*,[177] skill'd in Luxury, might envy; to sink in a Bed of Gossamere,[178] bestrew'd with living Roses, fresh in their own native Sweetness. —— A hideous, formidable Plot! And there be folded in the Arms of one so soft, so fair, so joyous, as, by the first delicious Touch, wou'd make old Nestor[179] young; whose Kisses, dew'd with Nectar, wou'd render him immortal; and, like a God, make his Elizium[180] in her Arms for ever. —— Here's a Plot for you! you do well to be afraid on't.

Freelove: No more, dear Temptation! – I'll venture any Thing on such a Prospect – If the Devil wou'd always bait his Snares so well, he cou'd never be without Store of Game.

Double: No, Sir, 'tis your Turn to tempt me now: I am in a Plot against you, you know, and 'tis not fit you shou'd put any Confidence in me, – your Servant, Sir.

Freelove: Come, come, you must forgive me —— and let this Purse be my Advocate —— dispose of me, as you please.

Double: Well, I am too good natur'd, that's certain: —— But you Gentlemen have such prevailing Arguments with you. —— Some little Time after Dinner, take an Opportunity, to slip away from the Company into the Gallery,[181] and, from thence, 'tis but a Step to Paradise.

Freelove: Dear *Double!* only the first Letter of her Name. ——

Double: Such another Word, and you shall never know. ——

Freelove: What a Tyrant the Jade[182] is!

---

[176] Legendary Assyrian queen who asked her second husband, King Ninus of Babylon to make her regent for a day. On that day she had her husband executed and made herself sole leader. During her reign Semiramis was known for having sexual liaisons with soldiers who were then killed so that they could not threaten her power. A play about her life had been mounted at the Haymarket Theatre in the fall of 1733.

[177] A citizen of Persia (now Iran), widely imagined in the eighteenth century to be a place of luxury, beautiful women, and sensual pleasure.

[178] A soft, sheer, gauzelike fabric, from the term for very light cobwebs.

[179] Hero from Greek myth, described in Homer's *Iliad* as having outlived two generations while maintaining much of his mental and physical ability.

[180] A paradise, in reference to the Elysian Fields or Elysian Plains of classical myth.

[181] A covered walking area partially open to the outdoors, with a roof supported by columns.

[182] A derogatory term for an assertive young woman.

Double: There's nothing like using one's Power, while one has it —— away, Sir, away —— I hear my Lady's Voice, and she must not see me in private with you, for the World.

SCENE V.

Lady Lurcher, *and* Double.

Lady Lurcher: Well, my good Girl, what Success? Have you touch'd him in the right Place?

Double: Yes, Madam, and I'll engage he shall do the same by you too.
Lady Lurcher: Cou'd I believe thee, I shou'd run half mad with Joy. – But 'tis impossible; you only flatter me.

Double: Your Ladyship won't say so, when you have him in your Arms. —— He has promis'd to be in the Gallery after Dinner.

Lady Lurcher: Were I an ill Woman[183] now, so dextrous a Creature wou'd be worth a Million! —— But, answer me ingenuously; did you tell him, in so many Words, the Assignation was from me?

Double: Hum! I can't positively say that with a safe Conscience – But I told him it was from a Woman; and, if he cou'd agree to it at a Venture, he can't be displeas'd to find it you.

Lady Lurcher: I don't know that, *Double;* – that insnaring Devil has such a hold of his Heart, I am out of my Wits again for Fear of a Disappointment.

Double: Come, come, Madam, you have no Occasion; do you only put on the Woman, and I'll engage for the Man. — If you won't scruple to advance, he won't have the Face[184] to recede. —— Attack him on the Side of his Constitution![185] waken his Desires! and, whatever Woman has his Heart I'll insure you his Person; for the Time being, however; which is as much as cou'd be done for Lady *Bellair* herself.

---

[183] A woman of low morals.
[184] Impudence, from the control of the face in surprising or distressing circumstance.
[185] Nature of body and character, what one is 'made of'.

Lady Lurcher: That will be some Satisfaction however. – But if I shou'd make this Sacrifice in vain, the Mortification will kill me, unless I can find some Way or other, to make it answer to my Vengeance. —— Let me consider. —— Aye, —— You shall take my Cousin aside presently, pretend to be exceedingly her Friend, and, out of great Tenderness for her, acquaint her with the Assignation.

Double: Lard, Madam! You can't be in Earnest sure?

Lady Lurcher: You shall find I am; nay, I will have you plant her where she may be a Spectator of the Interview. —— Beside all this, you must rail at me very plentifully, and, the severer you are, the sooner she'll believe you. I give you an Indulgence[186] for it.

Double: But, dear Heart, Madam! is not this the ready Road to ruin the whole Design?

Lady Lurcher: No, no; do as I bid you, and leave the rest to me.

Double: Nay, Madam, 'tis your Ladyship's Concern, not mine.

Lady Lurcher: Make no more Words then, but do it. Here she comes; I will go out of the Way, to give you an Opportunity.

SCENE VI.

Double, *and Lady* Bellair.

Double: O dear, Madam! I am glad I have met your Ladyship.

Lady Bellair: What's the matter, *Double!* What has disorder'd you so?

Double: The matter, Madam; I have hardly Patience enough to tell you. – O! 'tis a villainous World, that's certain.

Lady Bellair: Aye! Is the World grown so bad within, this half Hour?

Double: O, Madam! strange things may be done in half that Time.

---

[186] Permission or special privilege, with allusion to the Roman Catholic tradition of the indulgence as remission of the punishment for sin.

Lady Bellair: No doubt on't, if the Parties are agreed.

Double: They are Agreed, Madam. – Why, that's the very thing which provokes me.

Lady Bellair: Who are agreed? Prythee speak out! I have no Talent at Conjecture!

Double: I protest it goes against me, after all. – I am positive your Ladyship has a Regard for him, by the Mention you made of him this Morning; And you can't hear it without some Uneasiness, of Course.

Lady Bellair: Be it what it will, or of whom it will, declare it boldly! —— I have Courage enough to hear it, I warrant you.

Double: Then, again, that your Bosom-Friend should prove such a Viper, and take so much Pains to sting you to Death!

Lady Bellair: Nay, if I am wounded by a Friend, it must be in the dark; and no Caution of my own can put me upon my Guard.

Double: Aye, Madam, but she is my Friend too; and I am afraid I shall never be able to answer it to my Conscience to betray her.

Lady Bellair: You should prefer nothing to your Honesty: If you do, you have no Title to be believ'd at all.

Double: Lard! Madam, Honesty is not the thing: But suppose I should be undone by it?

Lady Bellair: That's few Peoples Case now a-days. – But if you are, I'll make you Amends.

Double: Nay now, Madam, you overcome me with your Generosity, I can hold out no longer. —— In short, Madam, Mr. *Freelove*'s false, and my Lady a Hypocrite.

Lady Bellair: Hah! are you sure of this, *Double?*

Double: Yes indeed, Madam, to my Shame, I may speak it; I was the Go-between,[187] – I carry'd the Message, appointed the Time and Place – and am, as it were, the Confidant on both Sides. —— But, not being able to indure that so good a Lady as you, should be abus'd in so perfidious a manner, —— I resolv'd to

---

[187] A messenger between lovers.

expose them, and, make this honest Confession, as an Atonement for my Share of the Guilt.

Lady Bellair: This is a Story not easily to be credited.

Double: If your Ladyship pleases, —— I'll wait on you to the very Spot, and place you, so that you may be a Witness of all their Doings.

Lady Bellair: I thank you, *Double*; but my own Innocence leaves me no room to be suspicious of any Body else. —— Beside, if it should be true, why should I disturb them? —— And yet, to upbraid[188] them with the Falshood were not much amiss. —— I find I have a Female-Curiosity that will be obey'd; and, in the mean time, I'll try him to the Bottom.

Double: When they are met then, I'll give your Ladyship Notice.

SCENE VII.

Lady Bellair, *and Young* Modern.

Lady Bellair: So, Sir! I see you have taken the Hint I gave you.

Young *Modern:* Yes, Madam! with Joy, with Pride, with Pleasure, and I think am qualify'd for your Cabinet-Council[189] now, or the Devil's in't. —— Will you believe me, Madam? when I look'd first in the Glass, I was frighten'd at my own Figure – and half persuaded myself 'twas some puritanical Devil in my Stead. — — My Valet too, very gravely told me, as I was dressing, that the Masquerade was not till To-morrow. – Nay, the Servants below mistook me at first for Lady *Lurcher's* Physician. —— I don't wonder now that these dull Rogues are so much in the Ladies Secrets. — I'll be sworn *Argus*[190] himself would not dream of a Gallant, under so forbidding a Disguise.

---

[188] Chastise.

[189] Like the modern cabinet, a body of advisors or ministers to a head of state, but also in contemporary use by Swift and others in its older sense as a term derived from counsel given privately or secretly in the cabinet or private apartment.

[190] In Greek myth, Argus may refer to either the hundred-eyed monster slain by Hermes or to Odysseus' dog, who recognized his master upon his return after twenty years.

Lady Bellair: Then the Gallant must not open his Lips I'm sure; for, if he did, his first Speech would betray him. —— What, Sir, do you think this fantastick Outside is all that's requisite to win a Lady's Favour?

Young *Modern:* Why, faith, Madam, I never understood that Hypocrisy was any thing else. —— And, if you'll examine all Bigots, Quacks and Pretenders,[191] you'll find them but mere Out-side all over.

Lady Bellair: Yes, Sir; but there's abundantly more contain'd in their Out-side than Cloaths.

Young *Modern:* Gad, Madam, I'll submit to any thing else in Reason.

Lady Bellair: Aye, and out of Reason too, or you are no Lover for me.

Young *Modern:* Well then, I'll surrender at Discretion to your Ladyship, if that will please you.

Lady Bellair: And 'tis discreet in you to do so. – Henceforward, then, no more swearing, either in Letters, or by Word of Mouth. – Oaths and Tears, in a Lover, are sure Signs of Artifice and Falshood.

Young *Modern:* Not swear how much I love you?

Lady Bellair: No; In the next place, no toying with the Orange-Women[192] at the Play-house, to shrew your Gallantry; no Debaucheries at Taverns, to prove your Generosity; nor drunken Quarrels to extol your Valour; ——

Young *Modern:* For Heaven's Sake, dear Madam —

Lady Bellair: No Riots in the Street at Midnight, for the Credit of beating the Watch,[193] and lying in the Round-house;[194] ——

---

[191] A bigot is a hypocritical person of religion; a quack is a medical charlatan, pretending to information he does not have. In general, a pretender is one who lays claim to something he does not deserve; most of eighteenth-century England termed the son and grandson of deposed King James II "the Pretenders" as they led several military campaigns to claim the British throne.

[192] Women who sold oranges in the theatres were widely assumed to be sexually available.

[193] In smaller centers, the watch comprised generally one unarmed, able-bodied citizen in each parish, who was appointed or elected annually to serve unpaid for a year as parish constable. He worked in cooperation with local justices in maintaining social order. In larger communities like London, members of the watch were paid to patrol the streets at night to prevent disorder and to bring criminals before a justice.

[194] A lockup or holding facility used until an individual could appear in court.

Young *Modern:* How can you be so cruel?

Lady Bellair: And no Visits to the Groom-Porter's,[195] for the Benefit of Gentlemen-Sharpers, and Pick-Pockets of Distinction.

Young *Modern:* 'Zoons, Madam, you must give me leave to swear a little, or I shall expire. –

Lady Bellair: Then I must have your whole Set of Acquaintance chang'd at once; I will not have you seen with profest Rakes of Quality, staunch Topers[196] of a Gallon and a Half at a Sitting; or roaring Gentlemen of the Blade,[197] that value themselves upon having kill'd their Man.

Young *Modern:* 'Sdeath, Madam! You'll banish me from all civil Society.

Lady Bellair: No, no, I'll recommend you to the Conversation of grave and venerable Prelates,[198] who will furnish you with holy, and devout Maxims, sage Homilies, and all the proper Materials to set out a Saint. – 'Twill not be amiss too, that you shou'd be seen at Church every *Sunday*, and, now and then, at Morning and Evening-Prayers[199] ——

Young *Modern:* I hope our Ladyship does not mean to make a Martyr of me.

Lady Bellair: Then, for a proper Face of the true primitive Cast,[200] I wou'd have you step into the City[201] and, in any Assembly of the Elect,[202] you may have what Variety of Choice you please.
Young *Modern:* Is this all, Madam?

---

[195] An officer of the royal household (until George III), the Groom-Porter was responsible for all matters related to gaming within the precincts of the court, including the supplying of cards and dice and the resolution of disputes.

[196] Contemporary slang for an excessive drinker.

[197] Soldiers, but also men who could easily be incited to duel.

[198] High ranking ecclesiastical dignitaries.

[199] During the English Reformation, Divine Office was simplified to Morning and Evening Prayer on weekdays.

[200] A facial expression of purest devotion. The idea of the "Primitive Church" refers to the earliest and thus presumably purest form of Christianity.

[201] Refers to the square mile first developed by the Romans, now known as the City of London, which lies at the heart of the modern conurbation of Greater London. During the eighteenth century, this same square mile held nearly 100 parish churches, many of which were redesigned and rebuilt by Sir Christopher Wren following the Great Fire.

[202] Church congregation.

Lady Bellair: That I can think of at present, I'm afraid. – Oh! no, – I must have you provide yourself with a Library; some Time To-day, I'll furnish you with a proper Catalogue of Authors. —— When this is all punctually comply'd with, I must have you perform Quarentine, like Ships that come from the *Levant*, in the Time of the Plague.[203]

Young *Modern:* I vow to Gad, Madam, 'tis a terrible Task! and a gay Ensign in his first Campain, or a young Poet, on his first Night, or a stammering Senator in his first Speech, cou'd not be more alarm'd than I am. —— But, however, I'll venture upon it boldly; 'tis your Command, and Love the Reward.

Lady Bellair: Bravely resolved! But 'tis no more than I expected from you; and now, while your Spirits are warm, you shall meet your Uncle at once. – I know you have more Grace, than to be asham'd of your Reformation, and more Gallantry than to be hector'd out of it again. —— There! take that Book of holy Meditations! read it devoutly! and dispose yourself to appear Sanctity itself. —— I will send him to you directly; if you stand the first Shock with Courage, you have nothing to fear afterwards; and, when 'tis over, you may expect to see me again to know your Success.

SCENE VIII.

Young Modern *solus.*

Was there ever such a mad-cap Vixen as this? was ever poor Lover made such a Devil of before? But, as long as she loves me in the main, one may bear a little of her Tyranny very well. – Beside, there's Humour in the Frolick, and I wou'd not lose the Diversion with my Uncle for a Million. – Then 'tis tim'd to a Hair's Breadth, just when he had inlarg'd my Stipend, and given me a Commission for Extravagance —— 'Gad, 'twill be excellent Sport, and here he comes. —— Now for a Masque fit for the Devil's own Wearing. —— I have it, I have it! —— That, I think, is worth his while to copy, when he wou'd even cheat an Attorney.

---

[203] During the bubonic plague, which struck Europe between the fourteenth and sixteenth centuries, infected ships carrying trade goods from the Baltic were forced to quarantine at the Levant, a region in the Eastern Mediterranean comprising modern day Lebanon, Israel, and parts of Syria and Turkey.

SCENE IX.[204]

Young Modern, *and* Modern.

Young *Modern:* What sweet Content dwells here? what Pleasure without Alloy? let wild, abandon'd Libertines immerse themselves in their Vices, and call it Life's best Happiness; I make a nobler Choice, and only pity them, for not being sensible of their own Mistake.

Modern: What the Devil, can this whining Fellow want with me? I am sure I never kept such villainous Company in my Life. – Pray, Sir, have you any Business with me?

Young *Modern:* Don't you know me, Sir?

Modern: Oons! it can't be my Nephew, sure.

Young *Modern:* O fie, Sir, give me leave to remonstrate, that, in a Person of your Age, such fearful Expletives, are a double Wickedness.

Modern: Double Damnation! what the Devil ails him?

Young *Modern:* O terrible! he makes my very Hair stand an End!

Modern: Why *Frank*! what Witchcraft, what Enchantment is come over thee?

Young *Modern:* Alas, Sir! you do but disturb my Contemplation! The World and I have done, Sir.

Modern: Mercy forbid. —— Now cou'd I cry for Madness. – *Frank*, – dear *Frank*. – If 'tis a Frolick, I forgive thee with all my Heart. —— But, prithee don't keep me in this Fright any longer?

Young *Modern:* Do you think I wou'd trifle in spiritual Concerns, Sir? my Conscience tells me I have done that too long already.

Modern: Pox of thy Conscience! If 'tis impertinent, don't be troubled with it; away with it at once, as all great Men have done before thee! Conscience quotha! think of the new Equipage I have bespoke thee, of splendid Cloaths, rich Wines, sweet Musick, fine Girls, and all the Pleasures that will make Time laugh, till he forgets to turn his Glass.

---

[204] Corrected from XI in 1735 edition.

Young *Modern:* Good Sir! name these Vanities no more! I have done with them, and, from henceforward, must live as I had never known them.

Modern: O this damn'd old Fellow *Freelove*, he has utterly spoil'd my Boy, and I shall run mad for Vexation. —— Be but wicked for another Year, *Frank*! break but his Heart, and I'll forgive thee, repent as soon as thou wilt!

Young *Modern:* Pray, Sir, don't tempt me to Frailty any more.

Modern: 'Slife, what a Phrase is there! he talks like a Criminal at the Gallows Foot. – Sirrah, Sirrah! are all my Hopes of thee come to this?– have I thrown away so much Money, to make a Monk of thee at last? – I have not Patience to think on't. – If 'twere not for the Law now, I cou'd cut his Throat. – Perhaps, thou art in Love, *Frank*! if thou art, thou shalt have her, if she be to be bought for Money. – I'll fetch thee a Mistress from the Grand Seignior's[205] Seraglio.

Young *Modern:* Oh!

Modern: Do you sigh? Why, if she is not to be had, forget her! – I'll teach thee Secrets shall make thee defy the Sex. – Thou shalt away with me to my Country Seat,[206] and exchange this whorish Air, which is the first Element of Corruption. – There thou shalt rise before the Sun, and make a Breakfast on the Morning Dew, serv'd up by Nature, on some grassy Hill. – 'Tis Nectar, Sirrah! Nectar, and more refreshing, than all the Provocatives to Luxury.

Young *Modern:* Pray excuse me, Sir.

Modern: This done, thou shalt vault into thy Saddle, as if thou wer't all Spirit; heavy as I am, I can still do it without a Stirrup. —— Then, my Hounds uncoupled, my Huntsmen ready, and all the Musick of the Field opening in full Chorus, you shall hear such spiritely Harmony, shall make you quite forget your soft *Italian* Airs,[207] and half persuade you, that you hunted in *Diana's* Train;[208]

---

[205] Generally used in the eighteenth century in reference to the Sultan of Turkey.

[206] Country house or estate.

[207] Not least because of the vogue for the castrato Farenelli on the English stage of the 1730s (mentioned by Cooper in her Preface), things Italian were often linked to softness, effeminacy, and romance.

[208] Followers of Diana, the huntress. Joining Diana's train also traditionally suggests leaving society behind to return to nature.

while Echoe,[209] from the neighbouring Woods and Caves, enamour'd of the Cry, with frequent iterations, doubled every Close.[210]

Young *Modern:* 'Tis all in vain, Sir.

Modern: And, if you grow fatigu'd with Exercise so full of Toil, the Angler's musing Art[211] shall learn you Patience, and every running Brook, or standing Lake, afford you Entertainment.

Young *Modern:* Indeed, Sir, you quite mistake me.

Modern: But, if all this shou'd still prove fruitless, let me again advise thee to another Mistress; and you'll find the Fondness of a second Woman, will efface the Rigour of the first, as the Oil of one Viper heals the Venom of another.[212]

Young *Modern:* Believe me, Sir! I have given over all Thoughts of the Sex, and *Venus* herself wou'd not warm me to Desire again.

Modern:[213] Then thou art an insipid, spiritless Fellow, not worth my Advice, or Affection. – And now, Sir, d'ye see, I'll make use of the Cloaths and Equipage myself; break into the gay World with an Eclat;[214] marry any Woman, under thirty, that will have me, and get Sons and Daugters to disinherit thee, as long as the old Patriarchs.[215]

---

[209] In Greek myth, Echoe pined away for love of Narcissus until nothing remained but her voice

[210] See Introduction page 4 for a source for this passage.

[211] Likely a reference to Izaak Walton's *The Compleat Angler* (1653), a popular book combining amusing and practical information on fishing and English folklore.

[212] Benjamin Gooch's *A Practical Treatise on Wounds and other Chirurgical Subjects* (1767) notes the contemporary belief that 'viper oil or fat, which shou'd be fresh, is a sovereign remedy against the stinging of bees ... and other venomous insects'.

[213] This speech is attributed to Freelove in the 1735 edition. Though Freelove does appear in the next scene, the plan to disinherit Young Modern is obviously spoken by his uncle.

[214] Modern implies the traditional meaning of a great achievement deserving praise, though the term can also refer to an ostentatious or scandalous act, the other way in which Modern's plan to reenter the world of young men might be perceived.

[215] Several of the Biblical patriarchs are reported to have fathered children well beyond their hundredth birthdays (Genesis 5:3–32).

SCENE X.

Young Modern, *and* Freelove.

Young *Modern:* Ha! ha! ha! my dear *Harry*! Thou art come, like a Beau, into the Boxes, in the Middle of the Comedy.[216] —— Ha ! ha ! ha!

Freelove: What's the matter, *Frank?* Why so grave in thy Dress, and so gay in thy Behaviour, prythee?

Young *Modern:* Why you must know, my Dear, this is a Farce of *Bellair*'s! —— She plays the Goddess, I the Saint, and my Uncle the Devil. —— In plain Terms, that dear, pretty, arch Creature, has let me into a Secret ——

Freelove: Not of her own, I hope.

Young *Modern:* Humh! —— not yet. —— She has only put me into the Road —— ——

Freelove: Why, at this rate, *Frank*, you are quite a *Caesar* in Love.

Young *Modern:* Aye, and hope to pass the *Rubicon*[217] in an other Campaign.

Freelove: But the Secret, *Frank*, the Secret!

Young *Modern:* I don't know whether 'tis safe to trust it with a Rival. —— But, however, you are an honest Fellow, and scorn to take Advantages. – D'ye observe this Dress? D'ye see this Book? D'ye understand this Face?

Freelove: Well, what of all this?

Young *Modern:* Why this, Sir, is Love's own Livery, and the only true Secret of being a Gallant in Vogue. —— I had it from her own Mouth, Sir, and, in a Day or

---

[216] The boxes were an expensive seating area generally reserved for the gentry, and were located along the sides of the theatre and across the back of the pit. Fashionable men could have a servant hold their seats until well into the production to allow them to socialize, flirt, and be seen.

[217] To cross triumphantly into forbidden territory. In 49 BCE Julius Caesar led his army out of his own province and across the Rubicon into Italy proper, violating an ancient Roman law and plunging Rome into the civil war that would leave him Emperor.

two, shall be able to give it under my Hand, with *Probatum est*[218] in Capitals at the Bottom.

Freelove: Are you so positive then?

Young *Modern:* In sure and certain Hope, as one may say.

Freelove: Really! – Well, but this could not put your Uncle in such a Passion!

Young *Modern:* Egad! but it has tho' – Why 'twas but this very Day, Man, that he ordered me to launch into all the Expences I could think of, and live away most magnificently, to expose your Father's Avarice to you; and, he's so provok'd at seeing me act so opposite to his Instructions, that he swears bloodily to marry forthwith, and disinherit me.

Freelove: And is this an Affair to laugh at?

Young *Modern:* Yes faith, as I design to manage it.

Freelove: Why, how can you possibly reconcile the Lady's Commands, with your Uncle's Humour.

Young *Modern:* Very easily, my Dear; For, when I have carry'd my Point with her, as I shall infallibly do ——

Freelove: Infallibly?

Young *Modern:* I'll come to an Explanation with my Uncle; and he will be to tickled with the Success, that he'll be Friends with me immediately, and reward my Ingenuity.

Freelove: And so you put on your present Shape, only to serve a Turn ——

Young *Modern:* To be sure: To deceive a Woman, is but fair Play to one's-self.

---

[218] Latin, 'It is proved', a common conclusion to legal documents of the day.

SCENE XI.

Young Modern, Freelove, *and Lady* Bellair.

Lady Bellair: Say you so, Sir? I am very glad then I know your Mind before-hand; and, if I don't prevent you, my Wit will be no better than your Honesty.

Freelove: Poor *Modern!* Ha! ha! ha!

Young *Modern:* 'Slife, Madam! this is such a Surprise! – Beside, Madam, I was talking to my Rival; and you know, Madam, we are never obliged to speak Truth to an Enemy.

Lady Bellair: That Excuse won't serve you, Sir. – For he that is not honourable to his Enemy, will never be true to his Friend.

Young *Modern:* Was there ever such an unfortunate Dog? [*Aside.*] —— I vow to God, Madam, I have so many things to say, that the Devil take me if I can utter one of 'em – One Turn in the Garden, Madam, will compose me instantly, and then –

Lady Bellair: You'll have Time to frame some poor Pretence, or other, to excuse your Falshood; no, no, Sir, I have you at my Mercy now.

Young *Modern:* O dear, Madam, I hope you will not oblige me to be rude. —— I know, by my dear Friend's Looks, he has something of Importance to communicate.

Freelove: Not I indeed, Madam. —— Pray don't spare him!

Young *Modern:* Fie, fie, *Harry*; How can you dissemble so? – I should not forgive myself, to hinder you. –This was a Scrape with a Vengeance! [*Aside.*

SCENE XII.

Freelove, *and Lady* Bellair.

Lady Bellair: Well, Sir, what is this mighty Something of Importance?

Freelove: Only to take my Leave, Madam.

Lady Bellair: 'Tis granted – Sir, your humble Servant.

Freelove: Stay a little longer, Madam, if you please. —— I don't design to trouble you with any Discourse of Love. —— I am as weary of the Subject as you can be.

Lady Bellair: Nay, now if you were the Brazen Head,[219] I would stay to hear you out.

Freelove: How, or which Way I shall hereafter dispose of myself is hardly worth your Curiosity, or my Relation? with what Ambition I have sued for your good Graces, will as little avail me to mention; I therefore wave it, and, if my long and faithful Addresses have any Title to the smallest Regard, you may now discharge the Debt, by granting me a very trifling Favour.

Lady Bellair: A good Preface! Pray proceed, Sir!

Freelove: If you approve my Petition, you must swear to grant it; and, that you may'n't think I have any Reserve in it, to make you uneasy, you may, before-hand, except to every thing you refuse.

Lady Bellair: I must own, nothing seems fairer.

Freelove: Make your Exceptions then! I would not deceive you for an Empire.

Lady Bellair: 'Tis ten to one tho', I shall include the very thing you pray for.

Freelove: I am willing to run that Risque.

Lady Bellair: Very well then! Because you shall not have it to say, I am quite Adamant, I agree to the Premises.

Freelove: Swear then!

Lady Bellair: Hold there! not till we come to except before excepted; and then I fancy there will be nothing left of Value, for you to ask, or I to grant.

Freelove: You have me at your Mercy.

---

[219] A reference to the English folk tale about Medieval philosopher Friar Roger Bacon, who tried to invent a brass head that would speak, in hopes of using it to frighten off England's enemies at strategic landing points. While left under the care of a servant, the head spoke three times ("Time is," "Time was," "Time is Past") and then smashed on the floor.

Lady Bellair: First then, you shan't intreat me to love you.

Freelove: Never! I go on, if you please, Madam.

Lady Bellair: Go on? Do you know what I say?

Freelove: I do, Madam.

Lady Bellair: And are you contented?

Freelove: I must be so.

Lady Bellair: What the deuce wou'd he be at? – You shan't desire to marry me.

Freelove: That's excepted too.

Lady Bellair: You shan't directly, or indirectly solicit to possess me any other Way — I think I shall mortify you by and by ——

Freelove: Granted.

Lady Bellair: Amazing! Is there any Thing a Man would ask of his Mistress, but to love him, marry him, or oblige[220] him without? – You shan't compel me, not to marry, or oblige any other.

Freelove: You are free to all the World.

Lady Bellair: You shan't confine me to a Nunnery or insist on my wearing myself to Skin and Bone with Penance and Mortification.

Freelove: Neither.

Lady Bellair: You shan't desire me to spoil my Face, take Poison, or do any Body a Mischief.

Freelove: Not for the World.

Lady Bellair: I'm half at my Wits End. – I'll neither be limited in Dress and Fashions; or task'd to go naked.

Freelove: My Desires are all modest.

---

[220] Both possess and oblige are euphemisms for sexual intercourse.

Lady Bellair: I won't be debarr'd from Gaming, Plays, Balls, Assemblies, Masquerades ——

Freelove: You are welcome to them all.

Lady Bellair: I never was so puzzel'd in all my Life. —— You shan't ask me how old I am before Company, refuse me Liberty of Speech, confine me from using my Lovers as I please, or listening to their Flatteries, when I am in a Humour to be diverted – None of these? Why then I swear – Stay! I will not be oblig'd to read your hideous Poetry, answer your ridiculous Letters, or be charg'd with Cruelty, for sending them back unopen'd.

Freelove: My Suit is still my own.

Lady Bellair: Well, If I must swear, I do then –

Freelove: By all that's honourable ——

Lady Bellair: Ay, Ay, make Haste! I am out of all Patience to know what it is.

Freelove: Only this, that you would never love me, or desire my Company.

Lady Bellair: Granted! with all my Heart and Soul! – Bless the Man! what a Rout[221] is here indeed? Why I would have done it at a Word speaking.

Freelove: You have oblig'd me, Madam; I am satisfied, and you are safe – Don't be uneasy, for 'tis not likely you shou'd ever break it.[222]

SCENE XIII.

Lady Bellair *sola.*

There is no Danger of it at present! or, if there ever shou'd be, why does he debar me from pursuing my Inclination? If he had only made me swear I did not love him now, it had been reasonable enough; but to injoin me not to do it for the future, is a Hardship I was not aware of – Beside, the Man has Merit too, and, though I never told him so, 'twas no Argument I never shou'd – To be limited! to be prescrib'd! – the very Thought on't makes me uneasy – He knew very well I

---

[221] Fuss.
[222] See Introduction page 4 for a source for this scene.

lov'd Freedom, beyond all Things; and that to forbid me any Thing, was to make me long to enjoy it – Yes, yes, I see his Artifice now, and if I am not even with him, tho' I wound myself at the same Time, say there's neither Wit, or Will in Woman.

The End *of the* Third Act.[223]

ACT IV. SCENE I.

Lady Bellair, *and* Young Modern.

Young *Modern:* LET me but swear, Madam –

Lady Bellair: Should you perjure yourself to Eternity, Sir, 'twill do you no Service.

Young *Modern:* Is there no Way to make my Peace again? – Set me a Task, Madam, that would daunt the Seven Champions,[224] I'll undertake it: Injoin me a Penance that would discipline a whole Convent, I'll endure it – Rot me!

Lady Bellair: Look here, Sir, to save you any farther Expence of Oaths, I must tell you plainly there is but one Thing in the World which can restore your Credit with me, – and that is, to make a Convert of your Uncle too –

Young *Modern:* S'Death, Madam, you might as well bid me persuade the *German* Princes to defend the Empire;[225] the good People of *England* to forswear

---

[223] Corrected from "first act" in the 1735 edition.

[224] The seven major European national saints: Saint George of England, Saint Patrick of Ireland, Saint Andrew of Scotland, Saint David of Wales, Saint Denis of France, Saint James of Spain, and Saint Anthony of Italy, most famously chronicled in an adventure series by Richard Johnson that was widely available in the eighteenth century, *The Seven Champions of Christendom* (1596).

[225] Likely a reference to the Holy Roman Empire, a collection of nearly three hundred territories, duchies, city-states and cantons loosely united under an elected Emperor and covering the lands now known as Germany. In the War of the League of Augsburg (1688–97), the Emperor had formed an alliance with various German princes, as well as Austria, England, the Netherlands, and later Savoy and Spain, against attempted French expansionism. The war came to an inconclusive conclusion with the Treaty of Ryswick, which restored the earlier *status quo*, but by this time the Holy Roman Empire had entered an irreversible decline.

Corruption;[226] or the *French* to fight only for the Peace of *Europe*:[227] —— Why, Madam, he hates the very Mention of any Thing Spiritual as much as Lady *Lurcher* does an Oath –

Lady Bellair: I see you are like the Rest of the Men, all Profession and no Performance; and so, Sir, I shall give myself no more Trouble about you – You may thank my Cousin that I open'd your Letter, or forgave you the Contents – nay, for this very Opportunity of justifying your late Rashness to *Freelove*: —— But, after this trifling, I won't hear the least Plea in your Favour again. ——

Young *Modern:* If 'twas any Thing but this, Madam, the Devil take me if I would make a Word of it; but, if he is once thoroughly provok'd, 'tis as hard to pacify him, as drown the Clamour in *Westminster-Hall*,[228] after a long Vacation.

Lady Bellair: You may thank yourself then for the Difficulty – If you had not been false, I had not been cruel; but as it is, I am inexorable, and, if you undertake it, I myself will be a Witness of the Performance.

Young *Modern:* Gad 'tis a prodigious Risque, Madam, – but, however, I'll venture at all Hazards – Pox on't, if she loves me she's worth winning at any Rate, and, if not, I shall find Means to disintangle myself after all – O the Devil, here he is – and as fine as a Lord too. (*aside.*)

SCENE II.

Lady Bellair, *Young* Modern, Modern.

Modern: Madam, I am your Ladyship's most obedient, humble Servant; Sir I kiss your Hand: Nay, no Ceremony.

Lady Bellair: Now to prove your Gallantry. [*apart to Young* Modern.

---

[226] A reference to the political and financial corruption entrenched in the British government. Prime Minister Robert Walpole not only rose to power as a result of the South Sea Bubble (1720), a stock market crash, but also exemplified the patronage system that enabled him to install his dependents in government offices and control the House of Commons by buying off its members.

[227] The French under Louis XIV had been particularly belligerent in Europe; Britain had been at war with France in both the War of the League of Augsburg (1688–97) and the War of the Spanish Succession (1701–13).

[228] The building that houses London's parliament, which breaks four times per year.

Young *Modern:* Sir, 'tis my Duty –

Modern: Not at all, Sir, you're discharg'd of the Burthen – and so, Sir, I say your Servant again.

Young *Modern:* With Submission, Sir,

Modern: I tell you, Sir, I'll have none of your Submissions – you are now your own Man, Sir, and may treat me upon the Level[229] intirely – The old, troublesome Fellow your Uncle, is now become what his Nephew ought to be, and has thrown off Age and Authority, to shake Hands once more with Freedom and Pleasure.

Young *Modern:* If so, Sir, you can't blame me for taking up the venerable Character you have laid aside – nay, if out of my great Concern for your Credit among wise and good Men here as well as your Happiness hereafter, I take upon me to set before you the dangerous Consequences of this unseasonable Levity — —

Modern: What the Devil, Sir, do you set up for a Ghostly Father?[230] Do you think I am to be preach'd into Patience, and Forbearance?

Young *Modern:* I can't bear to see you run headlong to Perdition,[231] Sir, without the utmost Uneasiness; – Alas, Sir, Life is but a Flower,[232] and it may be cut off before you are aware. –

Modern: One Word more, Sir, of this canting[233] Stuff, and I'll cut yours off before you are aware.

Lady Bellair: But why so passionate, Mr. *Modern*?

Modern: 'Tis enough to make one mad, Madam; he's grown as impertinent, as if he had been bred up to the Trade.[234]

---

[229] As an equal.

[230] Minister or priest.

[231] Hell, or ruin more generally.

[232] Most famously an excerpt from a popular folk song with a *carpe diem* spirit, "A Lover and his Lass" which was also sung on stage in William Shakespeare's *As You Like It* (V iii). The more originary source, and the allusion that suits Young Modern's charade is Job 14: 1–2: 'Man that is born of a woman is of few days, and full of trouble. He cometh forth like a flower, and is cut down'.

[233] A pejorative term for the phraseology of a particular religious sect, also often used to imply disingenuous devotion.

Lady Bellair: In my humble Opinion, Sir, you might be glad he has the Grace to repent so soon.

Modern: Then he should have had the Manners to have stay'd, till I had shew'd him the Way.

Lady Bellair: But you may have nothing to repent of perhaps?

Modern: Yes, my Generosity and Indulgence to him: – I'll tell you what, Madam; when I found my Relish for Pleasure a little pall'd, I gave his Appetites the same Encouragement I had done my own; made him acquainted with Money betimes, that he might never sneak for Want of it; expected him to spend it with a Grace, as I had done before him, and reflect a Pleasure upon me, for having bestowed it so well – But he has thought proper to be a Bigot, it seems, rather than a Gentleman; and, as his Wisdom despises worldly Things, he can never regret the Want of them.

Lady Bellair: You don't mean sure to disappoint him of your Estate?

Modern: Without Mercy – I would as soon leave it to the Church, or an Hospital.

Young *Modern:* Egad I begin to be afraid this will prove a little too serious for a Frolick. (*aside.*

Lady Bellair: What do you turn pale? Sure you are not frighten'd already (*to Young Modern:*) But as you have bred him up in Expectation of it, won't it be cruel to balk him at last?

Modern: Nor in the least, Madam, —— I have order'd 1000 *l.* to set him as a Haberdasher of small Wares;[235] or enable him to turn Pawnbroker, and get an honest Livelyhood, by cheating in Defiance of the Law[236] —— The Gain of either

---

[234] Raised in the church, though Modern's language equates a life in the church to the social status of tradesman or apprentice.

[235] By the eighteenth century, a haberdasher could be either one who sold hats or one who sold small wares pertaining to dress, such as ribbons, buttons, and needles.

[236] Early pawnbroking was unregulated and the very high rates of interest charged by the downmarket 'Dolly Shops' of the eighteenth century made the trade disreputable, although not illegal. At the time of the play, pawnbroking reform—especially the regulation of interest rates—was in the air. Cooper may be alluding to a 1731 petition to Parliament by the City of London to regulate pawnbroking on the grounds that 'by affording an easy method of raising money upon valuables, [a pawnbroker] furnishes the thief and the pickpocket with a better opportunity of selling their stolen goods and enables an intending bankrupt to dispose of the goods he buys on credit for ready money to the defrauding of his creditors'. Regulation of the industry did not occur until 1785.

will be enough to keep him out of an Alms-House,[237] and more may indanger his Soul's Welfare.

Young *Modern:* I am much oblig'd to your Piety, Sir; If the War continues, Money may be scarce, and Interest high, so that the yearly Profits –

Modern: Say you so, Sir? Not a Shilling then! – If you know how to turn the Penny so well, your hypocritical Face will get you Credit in Change-Alley,[238] and you'll fatten like the Cameleon, no Body knows how.[239]

Young *Modern:* What you please, Sir, I shall trust to Providence. My Heart akes confoundedly? [*Aside.*

Lady Bellair: Excellent! There – kiss my Hand, and make yourself easy – you have nothing more to do now. – (*apart to Young Modern:*

Young *Modern:* Abundance to suffer though, I am afraid. (*aside.*

Lady Bellair: But you are rich Sir, and have no other Way of bestowing your Money.

Modern: O a hundred, Madam – though I left Pleasure, Pleasure has not left me – I have, begun to dress again already you see, and I fancy every other Gaiety will become me as well as my Cloaths – However, If I can't spend it fast enough myself, I'll get a young, handsome, frolick Wife to help me; and I fancy, between us, we shall find a Way to make both Ends meet – Will you give me Leave, Madam, to pay my Addresses to your Ladyship? I have a Notion that poor, pitiful Fellow has a hankering the same Way; and I had rather be his Rival, than any Man's in the World – If you like the Proposal, Lady, say so; at Fifty, there is not much Time to be lost in Courtship, and she, that accepts it, shall have for her Jointure my whole Estate.

Lady Bellair: 'Tis really a tempting Offer, Sir.

Modern: Let me tell you, Madam, a healthy Autumn is to be preferr'd to a sickly Spring.

---

[237] Housing for the poor, funded by churches and charitable groups.

[238] A London alley where much of the trading involved in the South Sea Bubble took place from 1710–20.

[239] Because of their limited motion and very intermittent eating, chameleons were long supposed to live on air.

Lady Bellair: You'll indulge me with a little Time to consider of it, I hope, Sir?

Modern: With all my Heart, Madam, and in the Interval, I'll prepare every Thing that's Grand and Magnificent for the Reception of such a Bride – I kiss your Ladyship's Hand —— B'wye Sanctity![240]

SCENE III.

Lady Bellair, *Young* Modern.

Young *Modern:* I hope in Gad your Ladyship is more a Woman of Honour, than to take the Old Fellow at his Word.

Lady Bellair: O 'tis only coming to an Explanation with him, you know, and he'll be Friends with you immediately.

Young *Modern:* But slife, Madam, that's out of my Power now, and both my Fortune and Happiness are intirely at your Mercy.

Lady Bellair: Well, well, do you behave yourself as you should do; go to Church, say your Prayers, and leave the Rest to me – there's the Catalogue of Books I told you of, and, when I give the Word, go and bespeak them immediately.

Young *Modern:* Gad! if she did not love me now, what would become of me? (*aside*) But did not I behave bravely, Madam?

Lady Bellair: Bravely? Heroically! and you shall see how gratefully I'll reward it! First tho' I'd have you go in to *Freelove*; insinuate I wish to see him here, but don't be too express neither; then be within Call, and you shall see Sport[241] that will make you amends I'll warrant you.

Young *Modern:* I am all Obedience.

---

[240] Modern derisively terms his son a personification of holiness as he wishes him goodbye (be on your way).

[241] Entertainment.

SCENE IV.

Lady Bellair, *sola.*

This ridiculous Thing may well be allarm'd; for I believe the Uncle is really in Earnest – the Bribe he offers too, would hardly be refused by some People – and such a Coxcomb ought to be humbled – At present, though nothing but his Trick of *Freelove*'s runs in my Head; and my dear Friend *Lurcher*'s Assignation – I can't lose him that's certain, and yet I must plague him a little longer too – If he withstands her Temptation, I shall have a higher Opinion of his Merit – and if he wavers, I have a Reserve that will bring him about, after all ——

SCENE V.

Lady Bellair, Freelove.

Freelove: I thought, Madam, you had enter'd into some such trifling Obligation as an Oath, or so, never to desire my Company.

Lady Bellair: Well! and you fancied, I suppose, I had not the Heart to keep it.

Freelove: Your Ladyship will allow, I had a shrewd Guess to find out a Woman's Mind –

Lady Bellair: Ay, if you had found it out; but I'm of Opinion you'll discover the Longitude[242] as soon.

Freelove: You wou'd persuade me then, Madam, that you did not send *Frank Modern* for me this Moment ——

Lady Bellair: I? Prodigious! this is such an Abuse of my good Nature – Why he told me you obliged him to seem your Rival, in Order to be in Fact your Advocate – confest you were almost mad for another private Audience, and swore terribly, you wou'd be content with Six Words – But I perceive, what I granted in Compassion to you, you will needs have to be an Indulgence to myself.

---

[242] In 1735, longitude could be easily calculated on land, but was impossible to calculate in open water. 'Finding the longitude' became a catchphrase for something highly desirable, but apparently unattainable.

Freelove: Your Ladyship's very pleasant – But I waited upon you to know your Commands, not to be entertain'd with your Wit.

Lady Bellair: I know you would have it thought so; but, alas! I am not so easily impos'd upon, you had better by half be honest, and confess the Truth – Had not you study'd a moving Speech now, full of Submission and Humility, Sorrow, and Repentance? But being a little out of Countenance when you saw me, forgot every Syllable of it again – Come don't be cast down, if you have a Mind to it; I'll be your Prompter, and furnish you with a new one.

Freelove: Was ever such a Tyrant?

Lady Bellair: Nay, if you grow outragious! I must tell you 'tis a strange Thing that I must be always haunted in this Manner from Place to Place, and that all I can do will not defend me from the Persecution.

Freelove: Come, come, Madam, be sincere for once, and own you sent for me.

Lady Bellair: Lard! Do you think I have no more Grace than to forget my Oath so soon? or that your Charms are so irresistible as to excuse the Perjury?

Freelove: Nay, now, Madam, I have found you out ——

Lady Bellair: Heaven forbid. (*aside.*

Freelove: Your Tongue belies your Heart, and your Eyes your Tongue – Thro' them I can see into your very Soul, and read every Thought that passes there – I know you love me, and this Caprice of yours is all Affectation to hide it – A little I could have allow'd to the Sex, but this over-doing it has spoil'd all.

Lady Bellair: Well, since 'tis in vain to dissemble any longer, I must own I am caught – had you still pursu'd me in the common Path, like *Atalanta*,[243] I had never been overtaken – But Contradictions is the Foible of the Sex, and, if we are driven one Way, we are sure to run the other – I am afraid tho' you can never forgive my former Treatment.

Freelove: Intirely, I love you the better for your Wildness.

---

[243] In Greek myth, a huntress who would not marry unless a man could defeat her in a footrace (and risk being killed for losing). After Aphrodite provides him with golden apples, Hippomenes (in some versions Milanion) wins the race by dropping the apples in Atalanta's path, knowing she will stop to pick them up.

Lady Bellair: But is not this a Breach of my Oath?

Freelove: Pshaw! the Oath was but a Lover's Stratagem – a Trifle not worth your Memory.

Lady Bellair: Pardon me, Sir, though my Thoughts are free as Air, my Humour changeable as *April* Weather, yet all that's sacred in itself, I hold inviolable.

Freelove: Confusion! I am intangled in my own Net (*aside.*) Why, Madam, if you will but hear me – an Oath's – but an Oath – Beside your Lady must needs imagine – I did not expect – 'SDeath, without a little Sophistry,[244] I am undone (*aside.*) Well thought on – I have stumbled upon it at last – You remember, Madam, one of your Stipulations was to have your Humour in all Things; so that, if 'tis your Humour to break your Oath, the Obligation's void.

Lady Bellair: There's something in that, indeed – I am glad you have found a Way to relieve me, for I must own I look upon you now with tender Eyes, and melting Heart – But I must intreat you not to triumph in your Conquest, nor tyranize in Turn, because 'tis in your Power.

Freelove: Don't suspect me of such Arrogance, Madam! I have neither the Pretence, or Inclination for it, cou'd I be certain this Sun-shine humour of yours wou'd always last.

Lady Bellair: If you doubt it, call in Young *Modern*, and I'll confirm it even before your Rival's Face.

Freelove: You are all Goodness! – *Frank Modern! Frank!*

SCENE VI.

Lady Bellair, Freelove, *and Young* Modern.

Lady Bellair: Indeed, Sir, you must pardon me, I can't suffer you to borrow any Money on my Account.

Freelove: Madam?

Lady Bellair: My Necessities are not so urgent as that comes to neither.

---

[244] Deception, especially through deceptive reasoning.

Young *Modern:* Faith, *Harry,* 'tis the wrong Time to borrow Money of me.

Freelove: Sir?

Lady Bellair: Tho' I desire you wou'd continue my Friend, I wou'd not be troublesome to you for the World.

Young *Modern:* What the Devil makes the Man stare so?

Freelove: If you want Money, Madam, I need not borrow it to supply you; I have just received a Trifle from my Father.

Lady Bellair: By no Means, Sir, – When I am Fool enough to love, I may be humble enough to be oblig'd.

Freelove: Pray, Madam, have you taken an Oath to this Gentleman too, never to love me?

Lady Bellair: No, Sir, but I think myself bound in Conscience to keep that I made to you.

Freelove: You are not in Earnest sure?

Lady Bellair: 'Twill be a new Tryal of your Ingenuity to find out whether I am or no; you are a Wit, as well as a Lover – You win Ladies Hearts by Stratagem and Surprize; but how will you secure your, Conquests when they are made? Alas! I had forgot you can see into our Souls, and read every Thought that passes there – Ha, ha, ha, – I am a Barbarian to use him so cruelly. (*aside.*

Young *Modern:* She tickles me to the Soul – This is excellent Sport, indeed! (*aside.*

Lady Bellair: What are you struck dumb, Sir? Or are your Love and Anger together by the Ears,[245] and you can't answer till you know which is Master?

Freelove: I begin to think, Madam, that the whole Sex is not worth either – I am now myself again; and able to bid them all farewel for ever.

Lady Bellair: You will not leave me sure! – You can't be so unkind!

---

[245] Quarreling.

Freelove: When I put myself in your Power again, may you use me, if possible, worse than ever!

Lady Bellair: Nay, then, – Mr. *Modern,* – your Hand – I must always have the Pleasure of parting first, Your Servant, Sir. – Now to the Bookseller's directly, and give Orders for your Library. (*apart to Young Modern:*

SCENE VII.

Freelove *solus.*

So! If this was the Assignation I was to expect, it has made me happy with a Vengeance; if not, I am in the best Humour in the World to wait for another – for, grant she has no Love in her Constitution, she must have Pride: No Woman was ever made without one, or both; and, if I can't win her Affections, I may hurt her Vanity.

SCENE VIII.

Freelove, *Lady* Lurcher.

Lady Lurcher: What, Sir! My fine Cousin has given herself some of her usual Airs, and fretted you for the present; but when the Fit's over, you'll wonder you were angry at all.

Freelove: No, were she Ten Times more bewitching than she is; were every Smile Enchantment, every Accent Musick, every Look a Charm –

Lady Lurcher: Come, come you talk as if you did not know her Power, tho' you have suffer'd so much by it – Why now, at this very Moment, with one tender Glance, one kind Whisper, wou'd she disarm your Rage at once.

Freelove: If I thought it possible, I should despise myself.

Lady Lurcher: Lard! she's a Critick in the very Souls of Men; and knows minutely all their Powers – can tell where Love, or Pride, or Interest most abounds; how these again are mixt; where each is to be assail'd; and how to triumph over all –

Freelove: Is it then her Science[246] to undo Mankind?

Lady Lurcher: Ask your own Heart! Ask every Fellow-Slave that she has led thro' the same Variety of Torture.

Freelove: It shall be my Glory then to break her Chain, and show the Rest a Method to be free – Nay, to prove I'm in Earnest, did I know a Woman that would accept my Hand, tho' she were old, ugly, poor, infamous, and diseased, I wou'd this Minute lead her to the Altar.

Lady Lurcher: This goes admirably! (*aside.*) You need not stoop so low, Sir, – There are Women in the World, every Way equal to my Cousin; in some Things superior, who would make it their Happiness to deliver you out of her Hands – And, I must own, I think you deserve the Compliment.

Freelove: You are very obliging, Madam; but sure if I had the least Pretence to Merit, the inhuman *Bellair* had treated me gentler, nor forc'd me with Regret to hate her.

Lady Lurcher: All Women are not proud, tyrannical, or ungrateful; and I know such as wou'd redeem your good Opinion of the Sex, and give you Cause to bless yourself for the Exchange.

Freelove: This good-natur'd Flattery becomes you, Madam, but it does not reach the Grievance it wou'd cure —— That there are Women who may vie with Angels; only aggravates my Mistake ——

Lady Lurcher: But suppose I myself prevail on a Lady to distinguish you, who has already an Esteem for your Person, Compassion for your Sufferings, and Resentment for your ill Usage; who bas no Pride but to be yours, and can have no Happiness without you, who is your Equal in Rank, above you, at present, in Fortune, and would even court you to accept it?

Freelove: Let her be who she will, I'll make myself her own for ever.

Lady Lurcher: Pardon a Woman's Blushes then – She's now before you.

Freelove: Yourself, Madam! you overwhelm me with your Goodness – I did not think to be taken so suddenly at my Word tho' – But now there's no receding. (*aside.*) Is it possible you shou'd be serious Madam? Or do I only make myself ridiculous in supposing it?

---

[246] An area of studied knowledge.

Lady Lurcher: 'Tis in your Power, Sir, to have what honourable Confirmation you please.

Freelove: Henceforward then, my Hand, and Heart, Madam, are at your Disposal.

Lady Lurcher: Now if *Double* has play'd her right, she is provok'd enough to give him up for ever. (*aside.*) I will now be frank enough to own, Sir, that I have long lov'd you; and to Day was determined to know my Fate – My Woman, I believe, gave me a Hint of it before Dinner and I myself prepared your Father, to engage himself in my Behalf; and the Event will be almost as grateful to his Heart as mine.

SCENE IX.

Lady Lurcher, Freelove, *and Sir* William.

Sir William: Well, Madam, has my Son made your Ladyship any Proposal yet?

Lady Lurcher: No, Sir.

Sir William: Why, surely, Sir, you have taken it into your Head to cheat your Father? What did I give you that prodigious Sum of Money for, Sir? Answer me that! Is this your Gratitude for such a Piece of Generosity? S'Life, Sir, If you don't comply this Minute, I shall find a Way to make you refund, I shall, Sir,

Freelove: 'Tis all over now, Sir.

Sir William: What's over, Sir? Are you married to the great Beauty then? Oons, if you are –

Lady Lurcher: If you'll have but a little Patience, Sir.

Sir William: Never talk on't Madam! 'tis impossible! —— My 800 *l.* I will be demolished on the Wedding-Day, and my whole Estate vanish in Reversions,[247] within a Fortnight[248] after.

Freelove: Believe me, Sir, there's no Danger of either; and your Blessing is all that's wanting to make me happy in this Lady for Life.

---

[247] Loans taken out against an expected inheritance and repaid upon the death of the original estate holder.

[248] Two weeks.

Sir William: Kneel down then you Rogue! Kneel down this Minute! No, hold! This Lady is a greater Blessing than any Father in the Nation can give thee —— Od's my Life, Madam, if he makes you as happy as you deserve, you will find Matrimony a Heaven upon Earth.

Freelove: With your Ladyship's Leave then, the Writings[249] shall be agreed on to Night, and the Licence[250] taken out for To-morrow Morning —— I dare not trust myself till my Resentment cools. *(aside.*

Sir William: Ay ay, Boy! the sooner the better on all Sides —— We'll have the Lawyers directly – and to make all sure, I'll bribe high to get a Parson that shall dispatch his Part of the Business this very Evening, in Spite of the Canon[251] —— Now I have my Thousand sure, and my Friend *Modern* may be as mad as he pleases.

SCENE X.

Lady Lurcher, Freelove, *Sir* William, *Lady* Bellair.

Lady Bellair: But why in such Haste, good People? Are you afraid I should forbid the Banns?[252]

Sir William: O the Devil, has she overheard us? *(aside.*

Lady Lurcher: Confusion! This Turn I was not aware of. *(aside.*

Lady Bellair: What all silent? Lard, Cousin, don't be asham'd! Marriage, like Titles,[253] is honourable, you know, let us come by it how we will —— But, for

---

[249] Legal contracts outlining the distribution of property prior to a marriage, usually including inheritance to future children and provision for a wife in case of widowhood.

[250] Until the 1750s marriage was largely a private matter between two individuals and their kin. Those not wishing to be have their banns announced over three church services could obtain a licence from an appropriate (usually ecclesiastical) authority to marry at a place within its jurisdiction. Marriage by licence was often preferred because it was quicker, more convenient and more discreet, or because it was thought to confer social prestige.

[251] In the eighteenth century, English canon law dictated that marriages take place between 8:00 in the morning and noon.

[252] Banns are the announcement of a forthcoming marriage, so that any necessary objection might be raised. Tradition dictated that the banns be announced publicly three times before a wedding occurs.

[253] Appellations of honour conveying social rank and aristocratic birth.

Goodness Sake, why all this Secrecy, and Cabal about it? Your Ladyship, though a great Fortune, is not under Age; and, allowing you, Sir, to be a Minor, yet, with so wise a Man as your Father for your Guardian, there was no Danger of your being spirited away.

Lady Lurcher: One would think there was, Madam, when you are in such Fear to lose him.

Lady Bellair: But my dear Lady *Lurcher*, I am quite astonish'd, that a Woman of your Importance should condescend to steal a Lover.

Lady Lurcher: I steal him, Madam! He fell into my Hands like a Stray.

Lady Bellair: And so, like the Lady of the Manor, you seiz'd upon him as your Right – But still, methinks, as you knew the Creature had some Time belong'd to me; nay, as he had my Mark[254] upon him still, you might, at least, have enquir'd if I had turn'd him out upon the Common,[255] before you had clapt him into the Pound[256] of Matrimony.

Lady Lurcher: I thought I did you both Service, by taking him into mine. —— In short, Madam Cou'd any Thing be more friendly, than to rid your Hand of a losing Card, and give you a Trump in its stead? – While his Father liv'd, my *Freelove*'s Fortunes were as precarious, as your own; whereas Young *Modern* ——

Lady Bellair: Yes, yes, I know both him and you – and can give a Guess at the odd Confederacy that has pass'd between ye.

Lady Lurcher: I must tell you, Madam, after this Reproach, you ill deserve the tenderness I have shew'd you – I appeal to Sir *William*, whether I did not first solicit his Consent in your Favour.

Lady Bellair: Then I am sure 'twas to set him more against it – But no more Apologies, dear Madam: Your Innocence has no Occasion, nor does the Offence deserve one – Lard! he knows I wou'd have turn'd him over to any Living Creature, and thank'd them for taking him off my Hands.

---

[254] In this extended metaphor of a stray animal, Bellair claims ownership by asserting that Freelove is still marked or branded by their relationship.

[255] Open community space or shared grazing grounds.

[256] As now, a place to keep stray animals until their ownership can be proved.

Freelove: Yes, Madam, I know you have treated me, as if I was form'd to create Aversion – as if I was born your Vassal, made on Purpose to adore you – But I have found the Way to be free at last; and wou'd not be a Slave again –

Lady Bellair: No! and venture to marry! I vow that's very extraordinary – But pray, Sir, how long do you think this Fit of Bravery will last you?

Freelove: As long as I remember the Cruelty that caus'd it. —— In my Opinion, 'tis a Kind of Cowardice in Beauty to insult its Admirers; and Gentleness, in a Woman, is as amiable as Courage in a Man.

Lady Bellair: As I live, this Spirit becomes him. (*aside.*) Very well, Sir! Pray go on!

Lady Lurcher: If he holds this Resolution I am happy. (*aside.*

Freelove: I am very far from thinking, Madam, that my Passion was a Claim for yours – But, if you had soften'd your Disdain with Pity, I had mingled Gratitude with Fondness, nor ever ceas'd to love you for the Hope of any Pleasure, or Fear of any Pain —— But now ——

Lady Bellair: Hold, hold, dear, good *Orlando!*[257] I know you are horridly netled; but I know too you will beg my Pardon, for daring to own it.

Freelove: If ever I do, Madam, –
Lady Bellair: Prithee be quiet! and don't for Shame make any New Vows, till you have performed the Old!

Freelove: The Old!

Lady Bellair: Nay, if you have forgot them – pray read, and refresh your Memory. (*gives him a Letter.*

Sir William: Oons, not a Contract I hope. (*aside.*

Freelove: 'Tis sign'd with my Name, indeed, and looks like my Character.

---

[257] Two intriguing allusions present themselves here. The first is Ludovico Ariosto's 1532 *Orlando Furioso*, in which Orlando responds to the marriage of his beloved to another with a rampage of mad violence. A second possibility is that this is the play's second reference to Shakespeare's *As You Like It*, where Orlando, like Freelove, is a noble man with less wit and cunning than his beloved.

Lady Bellair: Yes, truly, 'tis your Character to the Life.

Freelove: (Reads) *Barbarous, bloody, and inhuman Tygress!* ——

Lady Bellair: That's a Sample of your Breeding, I suppose!

Freelove: Within this half Hour I shall be one of Love's Martyrs ——

Lady Bellair: Did not I tell you how much your Word was to be depended on?

Freelove: And I have already bespoke my Elegy of the Belman[258] ——

Lady Bellair: Horrible! He wou'd murther himself a second Time.

Freelove: I don't value being brought in Lunatick by the Coroner;[259] *I shall only die as I have lived* ——

Lady Bellair: He owns himself distracted you see.

Freelove: My Comfort is, you'll have the Pleasure of being my Executioner, and I the Revenge of haunting you as a Ghost ——

Lady Bellair: Mercy on us! How cou'd you think of going out of the World with so little Charity?

Freelove: Yours to the last Gasp, Freelove. Monstrous! I never saw a Syllable of it before.

Lady Bellair: Why what a Letter was here now, to send a Woman of my tender Disposition —— Heaven knows what Heart-akes it gave me —— I have been ready to swoon at the Mention of a Sword or Pistol; and when I recollected, there were such a World of Apothecaries,[260] I was almost as mad as you are –

Freelove: I must humour her; she has some Design in this. (*aside.*

---

[258] Like a town crier, the bellman was employed to walk London's streets making announcements, including announcing deaths and calling the faithful to pray for the deceased.

[259] The eighteenth-century coroner, as the king's agent and keeper of the peace, was charged with administering the care of lunatics and the protection of their property until they were again competent.

[260] Those who mixed drugs for medicinal purposes, often thought to supply poison if bribed.

Lady Bellair: It makes me weep to think on it still – But I must own, I had rather you had made away with yourself in any Manner, than this.

Freelove: I am much oblig'd to you, Madam.

Lady Bellair: But, if I pity'd you then, I am quite in Pain for you now.

Freelove: Humh! you are?

Lady Bellair: And wou'd preserve you still, if 'tis not your own Fault.

Lady Lurcher: Perdition seize her! With what Art she winds him? (*aside.*

Freelove: If I could believe you were in Earnest, Madam?

Sir William: Don't mind her, Sirrah! I tell you she's a Crocodile, a very Crocodile! and, if she weeps, 'tis Death.[261]

Freelove: But you have fool'd me so often, Madam, that, if I shou'd put it in your Power again, my very Enemies wou'd pity me, my Friends despise me.

Sir William: Brave! Brave again! Ods my Life, the Boy has more Spirit than I thought he had. (*aside.*

Lady Bellair: I protest he half frightens me! (*aside.*) Come, come, a generous Mind can never abuse a Confidence – you shall defer this new Treaty for one Hour, to oblige me, and do what you will afterwards.

Freelove: Such a Trifle as that I may safely, and honourably comply with.

Sir William: If thou dost one Minute, I'll do my best to starve both thee, and all thy Generation.[262]

Freelove: In any Thing but this, Sir, I shall be proud to obey you.

Lady Lurcher: Then, from this Moment, I shall despise thee, more than ever I lov'd thee.

---

[261] Both literary and some ostensibly historical exploration narratives refer to the crocodile's ability to weep like a human being in order to lure its victims.

[262] Children and future generations.

Freelove: What you please, Madam – I am all Gratitude for your intended Favour – But, if possible, I wou'd marry to be happy —— I'll wait your Ladyship's Commands in the Bird-Cage-Walk.[263]

SCENE XI.

Lady Bellair, *Lady* Lurcher, *Sir* William.

Lady Lurcher: Curse on his Gratitude! O, I shall burst with Spleen, for this Disgrace!

Sir William: That ever I shou'd be Father of such a stupid Scoundrel!

Lady Bellair: You see, my pious Cousin! I have not lost all my Power with my Fortune – Now you may bite your Lip[264] at Leisure, or send for your Ladyship's Chaplain, to preach you into Patience and Resignation —— My Dear, your Servant, Ha ha ha.

SCENE XII.

Lady Lurcher, *Sir* William.

Lady Lurcher: Shame, Want, and Ugliness overtake her! May she live to wish, to sue, and be despised as I am! O I am lost, lost to my Pride, my Fame, my Love, and all but my Revenge; and that shall fall with its full Weight upon her, crush her to the Earth, and leave her there to die unpitied.

Sir William: And, if I cou'd bring my disobedient Prodigal to rot on the same Dunghill, they might curse their Destinies together!

Lady Lurcher: Were there no Way to do it, but by my own Destruction, I'd undertake it boldly; nay, think the Time ran slow till 'twas effected.

Sir William: Say you so, Madam? Why then there's a certain Method, which wou'd do it most effectually; and that too, without the least Hazard to ourselves.

---

[263] A fashionable promenade on the west side of St. James's Park, so named because it was originally the site of James I's aviary.

[264] A gesture of frustration.

Lady Lurcher: If it depends on me! conclude it done already!

Sir William: Then 'tis done, Madam, and there's my Hand upon the same.

Lady Lurcher: But when? How? Explain! – I begin to hope he'll meet me half Way. (*aside.*

Sir William: Thus, then, —— Your Ladyship, I think, wou'd have marry'd my Son, – Good! which he has been foolish enough to decline, in Favour of one you hate – very well – and now you wou'd be reveng'd on them both —— Best of all ——

Lady Lurcher: To the Point, dear Sir, I die with Impatience to hear it.

Sir William: Dear Sir! Humh. (*aside.*) I say, therefore, dear Madam! If you'll make a shift[265] with the Father, instead of the Son ——

Lady Lurcher: I understand you now, Sir; but you must allow me to pause on't a Moment —— 'Tis a curs'd Exchange, that's certain – yet it flatters my Revenge too agreeably to be slighted – 'Twas my Desire too, and, by this Means, I shall, at least, have the Fugitive in my Power again, and perhaps, fright him into Compliance, when he sees his Ruin unavoidable – I'll seem to agree to it however; and, if it does not answer that Way, go through with it in Earnest – An Old Husband, I know, is the Devil all over; but some Comfort there's always Help at Hand, to save one. (*aside.*) – Well, Sir *William*, provided you'll disinherit your Son, 'tis a Match as soon as you please.

Sir William: With joy, Madam, with joy! – Next to your Ladyship, 'tis the very Thing I covet most; and, to shew my Generosity, I'll make a noble Addition to your Ladyship's Jointure into the Bargain.

Lady Lurcher: If I am but reveng'd, I desire no more.

Sir William: That you are sure of to your Heart's Content; if Poverty is the wretched Thing I take it to be! One Kiss, Madam, to seal the Contract.

Lady Lurcher: As an Earnest of Revenge, Sir ——

Sir William: And Joys, and Pleasures, and so forth ——

Lady Lurcher: As many for the Time to come, as Love and Duty can afford you.

---

[265] Make do.

Sir William: S'Life! What a lucky Rogue am I to stumble on so much Love and Money together —— Not but I venture hard for't —— A Man of my Years, might very well tremble to engage with a Woman of her Spirit – But, if I find myself over-match'd, I have Friends, enough to lend me a Lift, and she Gold of her own to pay for it. (*aside.*) One Kiss more, dear Madam, and I'll fly for the Spiritual Permit, as one may say, that is the only legal Warrant in the Excise of Love.

SCENE XIII.

Lady Lurcher, Double.

Lady Lurcher: O, *Double*, I am in a most desperate Way! Reduc'd to my very last Stake, and that too, when Love, and Fortune smil'd on me together, and scarce a Danger seem'd to threaten.

Double. Ay, Madam, I told your Ladyship how 'twou'd be —— But I was a Fool forsooth, and not to be believ'd.

Lady Lurcher: Curse on my confidence, fallaceous Cunning! that led me to deceive myself, and plot the very Stratagem that undid me —— Yet who wou'd have imagin'd, that, when she heard herself so solemnly abjur'd, her Pride wou'd let her stoop to lure him back? —— I cou'd have pawn'd my Soul, that, never after, she had thought him worth her Notice.

Double. But, dear Madam, what signifies your Ladyship's teasing yourself about it, now 'tis over? — If there is any after Game[266] to be play'd, I think you shou'd not lose a Moment in complaining, but strike a Master Stroke at once, and, from the Middle of Misfortune, Bring forth Happiness.

Lady Lurcher: Nay, I was not so short-sighted neither, as not to guard against the worst – *Bellair* is now elate with her Success, and full of Gratitude, no doubt, for your Assistance; find her out then this Moment; congratulate her, on her Conquest; advise her to pursue it instantly; tell her there may be Danger in Delay; and offer yourself to be her Instrument —— Within this Hour she has promised *Freelove* Satisfaction for the severe Tryals the has put him too; press her to hasten it; get her to write, if possible, and she'll be glad to make you the Messenger.

Double. But suppose she shou'd, Madam?

---

[266] A scheme to change the results after the original game has ended.

Lady Lurcher: Why then carry it to Young *Modern* immediately, and advise him from me, to insult his Rival with the Favour, as the only Means to get rid of him for ever. —— The Billet will be under Cover,[267] to be sure; and you may do it with all the Safety in the World.

Double. Well, Madam, and what will be the Consequence of this?

Lady Lurcher: How blind thou art grown? Why *Freelove,* full of Expectation of her promis'd Kindness, and vain of having made me her Sacrifice, will be provok'd beyond a Reconciliation, will look Upon her as a trifling capricious Creature, too volatile to be fix'd, and too proud to be grateful.

Double. This has a Face of Success, indeed.

Lady Lurcher: Beside, when this is done, you must find out *Freelove,* and tell him I intreat the Favour of one private Meeting more —— I know he has too much Manners to refuse it; and I'll contrive it shall be after the Explanation with his Rival, when all his Passions are again afloat, when Interest may have Power to melt, and Vengeance move —— I'll even go so far, as to give him a Sight of the Riches he has refus'd ——

Double. Nay, then I'm sure he can hold out no longer.

Lady Lurcher: And, if he still disdains me, convince him he's undone for ever ——
——

Double. How can that be, Madam?

Lady Lurcher: I'll marry his Father the next Moment, and strip him of his Birthright.[268]

Double. This is doing Business, indeed, Madam —— But the finishing Stroke is wanting still —— As I take it, your Ladyship will as little brook your Cousin to vie with you in Splendour, as in Love; and, if you let her secure Old *Modern,* as I know she may, she'll set you at Defiance for Life.

Lady Lurcher: O, if she is not ruin'd every Way I do nothing at all – I apprehend though, the Old Gentleman only addresses her to frighten his Nephew: – But,

---

[267] Enclosed in a plain sheet of paper, and thus formally unaddressed.

[268] Specifically used of the special rights of the first-born son, the title, privileges, and inheritance to which one is entitled by birth. Particularly since Freelove appears to lack siblings, he would be expected to inherit his father's title and the bulk of his estate.

however, for Fear of the worst, it shall be my Business to reconcile them by making it appear that their Conduct is nothing but Artifice on both Sides.

Double. I vow there is some Pleasure in serving a Lady of your Ingenuity —— I love a Woman that's so full of the Sex, as to Prefer Mischief to Love, Love to her Interest, and her Interest to Paradise itself.

Lady Lurcher: Yes, I own myself a very Woman; a Martyr to my Passions, and yet anxious for my Fame —— But, when I am defeated in my Will, blasted in my Pleasure, slighted in my Anger, and scorn'd in my Person; neither Hope of Good, nor Fear of ill, shall frighten or allure me from my Vengeance.

> *In vain shall Pity plead, or Heaven reprove;*
> *Give me Revenge! Let Folly Virtue love!*

The END *of the* Fourth Act.[269]

ACT V. SCENE I.

Young Modern, *and* Double.

Double. LARD, Sir! Where in the World have you been? I have been watching for you, as if you had been the Ten Thousand Pound Prize.[270]

Young *Modern:* You shou'd have ask'd my Queen, my Sultaness; I vow to Gad she's a very *Juno,* and wou'd find Tasks for another *Hercules.*[271]

Double. Ay, and such as he could never accomplish too, perhaps – But 'twas she employ'd me to find you out.

---

[269] Changed from 'Third Act' in the 1735 edition.

[270] A reference to the prize in England's annual state lottery, which was used to raise money for public endeavors such as the Westminster Bridge and the British Museum. The modern equivalent would be approximately £1.14 million.

[271] In Roman myth, Juno is the stepmother of Hercules, the half-god son of Jupiter. After Juno drives him to temporary insanity, he kills his wife and children. The Delphic Oracle instructs him to serve Eurystheus, King of Mycenae (who has stolen his birthright) in penance. When the King cannot think of anything challenging enough for the son of Jupiter, Juno devises the list of tasks that Hercules must complete for redemption, including slaying the Hydra and capturing both the Cretan Bull and Cerberus.

Young *Modern:*   That's strange; when she had sent me to ransack Booksellers Shops; Places I have never shewn my Head in, since I came from the University – I must have a Library now, forsooth, and a Sample of damn'd godly Books, to sanctify my Toilet[272] every Morning, and make my Conversion publick to all my Acquaintance – Then such a Catalogue of holy Jargon she gave me as wou'd set me up for a Non-Con Teacher[273] at once; and serve to edify a whole Congregation of gifted Mechanicks, groaning Beldams, and sleeping Prentices.[274]

Double.   O' my Conscience, she has learn'd this Trick of my Lady; and I'll lay my Life the Catalogue is the same with hers.

Young *Modern:*   There 'tis — you may compare it if you will.

Double.   Ay, exactly! I have all the Titles by Heart, as well as my Lady herself.

Young *Modern:* Egad I don't know how I shall come off though; I have not been able to hit any one Article right — For *War with the Devil*, I have bought *The Devil upon Two Sticks*;[275] for the *Warning to Sinners*, the *History of the* French *Disease*;[276] and Ovid's *Art of Love* instead of *Salve for a wounded Conscience*;[277]

---

[272] The daily processes of grooming and dressing, and the domestic area set aside for them.

[273] A Nonconformist preacher, teaching doctrine outside that sanctified by the Church of England. After the 1662 Act of Uniformity, nonconforming groups were formally expelled from the Church of England and termed Nonconformists.

[274] Mechanik describes a tradesperson or member of the lower classes; beldam refers to an older woman (or derogatorily, a hag); and a prentice is an apprentice. Young Modern assumes that only the unattractive, old and poor would be likely to subscribe to Nonconformism.

[275] *War with the Devil: or the Young Man's Conflict with the Powers of Darkness: In a Dialogue* (1673), an allegorical narrative of moral instruction by Benjamin Keats, is replaced by *The Devil Upon Two Sticks* (originally, *Le Diable Boiteaux*, 1673), a satire available in England in translation beginning in 1708.

[276] The ESTC reveals two similarly titled works: the anonymous *A Warning to Sinners, being a True Relation of a Poor Woman who is Daily to be Seen in Rosemary-Lane* (1660) and *A Warning to Sinners by the Just Hand of God* (1677), on drunkenness and adultery in William Dennis's murder of Thomas Gately. Both are pamphlets of a similar nature, and the title here may be simply shorthand for didactic dissenting warning narratives. *Warning to Sinners* is replaced by what is likely Nahum Tate's translation of *Syphilis, or, A Poetical History of the French Disease* (1696). Originally published in Latin by Girolamo Fracastoro in 1530, the *History* is an attempt at a medical explanation of the origins of syphilis in Europe, and eventually concludes that the Gauls were responsible.

[277] Ovid's famed treatise on love is a fairly frank discussion of the gamesmanship involved in the pursuit of sex for pleasure; it was widely available in translation in the

Then *Judgments on profane Swearers*, I have supply'd with *The Duty of taking the Oaths*;[278] Dr. Dismal's *Spiritual Groans*, with *The Musical Miscellany*;[279] The *Reasons for the Unreasonableness of Reason in Matters of Faith*, with the *Essay on the Profund*;[280] The *Mysteriousness of Mysteries, no Mystery at all*, with *The Tale of a Tub*;[281] and so Egad of the Rest.

Double. Well, I vow and protest you have done it purely —— But, dear Heart, Sir, you are in no Danger of disobliging now —— You are safe arriv'd in the Port, and have nothing to do but cast Anchor, as soon as you please.

Young *Modern:* O ho! Has she thought proper to come to at last? I knew 'twas impossible she shou'd escape me – Well, but hark ye my dear precious Devil! What Token has she sent? Ha!

Double. A tender Billet, Sir, delivered with a soft Whisper, to my dear *Modern* —— *(gives the Letter.)* What the Duce no Reward? Tho' I made the Messenger myself too —— S'Life I'll be even with him. *(aside.*

---

eighteenth century. It replaces *The Cause and Cure of a Wounded Conscience* (1647), by Church of England clergyman Thomas Fuller.

[278] The ESTC shows no similar title, but Young Modern may refer to *The Swearer Silenced, or the Evil and Danger of Prophane Swearing and Perjury Demonstrated by Many Arguments and Examples of God's Judgment upon Sinful Swearers* (1689) by Nonconforming Presbyterian minister Thomas Doolittle. *The Duty of Taking the* Oaths may refer to Samuel Pufendorf's *De officio hominis et civis* (1673), chapter XI of which is titled 'On the Duty of Those Who Take Oaths'. The text first appeared in English translation in London, as *The Whole Duty of Man, According to the Law of Nature* in 1691. Unlike many Christian political theologians, Pufendorf refused to ground his natural law ethics in the ideal of human holiness; rather, he grounded them in the need for sociability, which he regarded as simply a means to an end.

[279] Again the ESTC shows no identical title, but one possibility is *The Groans of Believers under their Burdens* (1722) by Ebenezer Erskine. What is clearly intended as a didactic text, however, is replaced by Young Modern with the six volume series *A Musical Miscellany, being a collection of choice songs and lyrics* (1729–31), printed in London by John Watts.

[280] The title on reason appears to be a parody of various titles in the ongoing philosophical debates on the possibility or impossibility of substantiating faith with reason, including John Locke's 1695 *The Reasonableness of Christianity*. The text that replaces it is unclear, but may be Matthew Concanen's 1728 'A Supplement to the Profund' (an attack on Alexander Pope's *Peri Bathos*).

[281] Possibly a reference to John Toland's 1696 *Christianity Not Mysterious* and Peter Browne's 1697 response, *A Letter in Answer to a Book Entitled Christianity Not Mysterious*. Both authors are supposed to have inspired Jonathan Swift's allegorical *A Tale of a Tub*, which satirizes epistemological issues of reason and mysticism in Roman Catholicism, Calvinism, and Anglicanism.

Young *Modern:* (Reads) Hum Hum.

Convinc'd of your Affection, sensible of my Severity, —— my Heart has long been yours. Come back instantly to my Cousin's —— Have something of Importance to communicate ——
Yours, Bellair.

Now, the Devil take me if I have not a great Mind to coy it in my Turn —— Pretend to be in Jest all this while, and make her think it a Blessing that I will stoop to pity her.

Double. O fie, Sir, you can't be so hard Hearted sure!

Young *Modern:* I can't say I am absolutely resolv'd on't – yet, to humble a proud Beauty, has something almost irresistible in it.

Double. 'Tis my Lady's Advice, Sir, the first Thing you do, should be to communicate this Advantage to your Rival.

Young *Modern:* That I am bound to do by Treaty, – and Egad, I had rather forget my Conquest, than my Triumph —— *apropos* —— Here he comes! and if I may guess by his Looks, in a special Mood to feel my Raillery, and rot me if I spare him!

Double. A very pretty Fellow, truly! that had rather insult his Rival, than enjoy his Mistress. (*aside.*

SCENE II.

Young Modern, Freelove.

Freelove: I have waited till I am quite out of Patience – But, no doubt, she is so pleas'd with herself, that she has never once thrown away a Thought on me. (*apart.*

Young *Modern:* Now is he as sullen, as if he had the Gift of second Sight,[282] and cou'd foresee his Misfortune: But I'll rouze him from his Visions with a Vengeance – My dear *Harry!* thou art the most welcome Man alive – wish me Joy, you Rogue! wish me Joy.

---

[282] The ability to see the future.

Freelove: If you are dispos'd to be merry, Sir, I am not in a Humour to interrupt you.

Young *Modern:* Prithee don't be so peevish, my Dear! you are my Friend, and have a Right to share with me.

Freelove: Was there ever such an Impertinent?

Young *Modern:* In short, Sir, I can throw off the Masque when I please, and swear, and drink, and wench, and game *cum Privelegeo.*[283]

Freelove: S'Death, Sir, what's all this to me? You may go to the Devil by what Road you please, for any Thing I care.

Young *Modern:* But don't you, remember, *Harry*, a certain Agreement between you and I, with Respect to a certain Lady? —— Wherein 'twas stipulated, that which of us two carried her first should declare his Right, and the other make his Leg, and march off the Premises?

Freelove: Well, Sir, and what's all this to the Purpose?

Young *Modern:* Nay, no Passion, my Dear. —— 'Tis contrary to Articles.[284] —— The Devil take me, now, if I am not infinitely concern'd for you. Ha!

Freelove: Death and Vengeance, Sir, if you have any Thing to say, out with it! and truce with your ridiculous Apologies!

Young *Modern:* In two Words then! *Harry! Bellair* has declared herself mine, Sir, mine; and, if *Jove*[285] himself, were to become my Rival, and harlequin it thro' all his amorous Disguises, to gain her Heart would be in vain.

Freelove: Amazing! Can this be possible?

Young *Modern:* Possible! 'tis Gospel, Sir, Gospel, and you are a Heretick, and will be damn'd, d'ye see, if you don't believe it.

---

[283] Latin: literally 'with privilege', a phrase traditionally found at the bottom of the title page of the King James version of the New Testament, signifying copyright.

[284] The clauses or provisions of a contract, here, the agreement made earlier on courting Bellair.

[285] In Roman myth, an alternate form of Jupiter, the most powerful of the gods, also known for a series of seductions (or rapes) while in disguise, including impregnating Leda while disguised as a swan, Danae as a shower of gold, and Europa as a bull.

Freelove: Confusion! if 'twere a Falshood, he wou'd not dare to assert it so confidently. —— O Woman! Woman! But the Reproach rather belongs to Nature than them; they were made to cousin us, tho' nothing but the Devil can cousin them; and if they were to be honest, they would defeat the End of their Creation.

Young *Modern:* Upon my Soul, I am sorry to see thee take it to Heart so.

Freelove: Damn your Sorrow, Sir!

Young *Modern:* Bless us! how he swears? Why, have but a little Patience, Man, and, in a Month or two, I'll resign her to thee; nay, pawn my Honour, in the mean while, that she shan't be the worse for wearing, —— that's fair now.

Freelove: One such slighting Word more of her, Sir, and I am your Enemy.

Young *Modern:* Was there ever such an odd Fellow? He's angry that I have her, and as angry that I wou'd part with her again. [*Aside*] Perhaps, then, you don't believe me after all: but do you know her Hand, my Dear.

Freelove: I have seen it.

Young *Modern:* There then, —— read, Sir, and don't give your self, or me, any further Trouble. [*Gives a Letter.*]

Freelove: [*Reads.*] 'Tis even so; and now I have no Remedy but Despair. Strange Capriciousness of Destiny to compel us to covet our own Misery!

Young *Modern:* Well! now you are convinc'd, my Dear, I hope we are good Friends again.

Freelove: O as ever, Sir, as ever. [*Folding up the Letter.*]

Young *Modern:* You'll return my Billet, tho'?

Freelove: Not till I have made what Use of it, I think proper.

Young *Modern:* Positively!

Freelove: Positively!

Young *Modern:* Then, by, all that's great and noble.

Freelove: What?

Young *Modern:* You may keep it. —— As long as I sit down to the Feast, I don't care who has the Invitation.

Freelove: If your Mistress shou'd not bid you welcome without it, you know upon what Terms to recover it when you please.

Young *Modern:* I can give a shrewd Guess. —— But egad! I have more Sense than to accept them.

SCENE III.

Young Modern, *Lady* Bellair.

Young *Modern:* My Life! my Angel! my Goddess!

Lady Bellair: Heyday! What has inspired you with this sudden Transport, Mr. *Modern*?

Young *Modern:* You, you, my Charmer! I am in Heaven, and can utter nothing but Raptures of Love and Joy.

Lady Bellair: Surprising! I have heard Devotion – has turn'd some People's Brains,[286] but could never suspect it would be your Case. – Sure you have not busied your self with any of the abstruse Controversies, that wou'd puzzle a whole Convocation, to settle the Truth on either Side.

Young *Modern:* Lard, Madam! I have not had Time yet to furnish myself with a Creed,[287] —— and when you and I are *Tete a Tete*,[288] I have something else to think of; Fraud and Dissimulation, have nothing to do with Love. —— Besides, I know your Ladyship despises both in your Heart, and that your real Principles are adapted to serve your Pleasures.

Lady Bellair: But then, Mr. *Modern*, my Pleasures always justify my Principles.

---

[286] Likely a reference to the evangelical revival known as Methodism, which became popular in the 1730s and relied on a new form of emotional preaching, which shocked the Anglican Church and the upper classes, and was sometimes linked to madness.

[287] A specific articulation of beliefs.

[288] Together privately, head to head.

Young *Modern:* Come, come, Madam, as I have put on this Disguise to screen your Reputation without Doors, I think I have a Title to the Benefit of it within; and now you have honoured me with your Confidence, 'tis but losing Time to dissemble longer.

Lady Bellair: Where? When? How, for Goodness Sake?

Young *Modern:* Your Ladyship has utterly forgot then the Billet you sent me by *Double?*

Lady Bellair: By *Double?* I begin to be confounded. [*Aside.*

Young *Modern:* Yes, Madam, that I receiv'd a few Minutes ago.

Lady Bellair: That treacherous Gipsy has betray'd me; and poor *Freelove*, by this Time, is half mad at my Ingratitude. [*Aside.*

Young *Modern:* Nay, never be asham'd on't, Madam; you are not the first Lady that has done me a Favour.

Lady Bellair: Insolent Coxcomb! But I'll find a Way to humble him, yet: [*Aside.*] Well, Sir, I am sure you are too much a Man of Honour, to abuse my Weakness.

Young *Modern:* No doubt on't, Madam; —— Lard! you are as safe as if I was, indeed, a Son of the Church, and my Preferment[289] depended on my Hypocrisy.

Lady Bellair: If you would have me believe you, restore my Billet this Moment.

Young *Modern:* I beg your Pardon, Madam, —— 'tis the only Proof you have given me of your Passion.

Lady Bellair: And shall be the only one, if you make the least Scruple to obey me.

Young *Modern:* What the Plague shall I do now? [*Aside.*] As I hope to be sav'd, Madam, ——the Devil take me! [*Feeling for the Letter.*] there is Legerdemain[290] sure. ——

Lady Bellair: Legerdemain! No, no; your Vanity, I suppose, has betray'd it to some of your swearing Companions; or, perhaps, to *Freelove*, your Rival; and he had too much Honour, to trust it in your Hands again.

---

[289] An appointment to a remunerative position in the church.
[290] Sleight of hand, or stealing of the letter.

Young *Modern:* She deals with the Devil sure! What Lie shall I invent to come off? Swearing signifies nothing. [*Aside.*

Lady Bellair: I know, by your Silence, I have found you out. —— But it is what I expected, and I did it on purpose to expose you. —— Nay, the Letter was designed at first for him, and I took this Method of conveying it thro' your Hands, that he might have his Intelligence, and you disgrace your self, at that same Instant.

Young *Modern:* What the Devil, don't you love me, then, at last?

Lady Bellair: Yes, for my Diversion, as Children do a Rattle. – You will serve well enough to look Babies in one's Eyes, say foolish Things, and play over a thousand Monkey Tricks, to fill up an idle Hour, and give one a quicker Relish for better Company.

Young *Modern:* Egad, Madam, I would not advise you to carry the Jest too far. —— I can be angry upon Occasion.

Lady Bellair: Cou'd it so? And leave one I warrant in a Huff, like Pistol[291] in the Play.

Young *Modern:* There are more fine Ladies in the World, Madam.

Lady Bellair: And the same Taylors, Barbers, and Dancing-Masters, that made you, to dress up more pretty Fellows; Nay, I'll engage to write a Receipt myself, for the Making.

Young *Modern:* A Receipt, Madam! a Receipt!

Lady Bellair: Aye, and they shall walk, and talk, and dress, and sing, and dance with any Plaister-crown'd Puppets of you all.

Young *Modern:* I vow to Gad, Madam, you dissemble to a Miracle.

Lady Bellair: Indeed, you flatter me. —— I have no Talent that way. —— I can't help owning, now, for my Life, that I have seen thro' the little Cabal of my Cousin and you to betray me; and that I despise, alike, the pious Hypocrite, and the avow'd Debauchee.

---

[291] A bombastic but basically honest soldier in Shakespeare's *Henry* plays and in *The Merry Wives of Windsor* (1602).

Young *Modern:* Your Ladyship, then, may as well confess, your own Designs upon my Uncle too, and that 'tis the Estate you are fond of, not the Man; I can see through your Cabals now, and if I don't defeat them, rot me!

SCENE IV.

Lady Bellair, Freelove.

Lady Bellair: Now for *Freelove,* and his new Resentment. —— The Mischief was most maliciously tim'd, that's certain. —— However, 'tis but to see him, and all's well of Course.

Freelove: I cou'd not leave the House, Madam, till I had thanked you for your late Goodness, and Generosity, —— It implies such thorough good Nature, Sincerity and Honour.

Lady Bellair: Well said! —— A Favour I see, is not thrown away upon you. —— As I live, you are improved upon it already. —— Why, is not this better than raving about Flames, and Wounds, and Darts; or threatning to hang or drown your self in a Pet,[292] because I was not to be mov'd by such awkward Wooing.

Freelove: Oh! your Ladyship has made a very effectual Cure. —— The Medicine, indeed, was a little bitter; but I have made a Shift to get it down. – In short, Madam, I can bear your ill Usage no longer, I have lov'd you generously, serv'd you faithfully, endur'd your Contempt patiently, and thought to have parted with you bravely. —— But that last Relief your Artifice deny'd me.

Lady Bellair: Have a Care! the Fit's returning again.

Freelove: I heard you, believ'd you, and made my self accessary to my own Undoing.

Lady Bellair: Bless me, how it grows upon him? Shall I call for a little Hartshorn?[293]

Freelove: For which, may I be made a Slave to all the Vanities of all your Sex; may I be vex'd with all their Passions, liable to all their Frailties.

Lady Bellair: Nay, now you are stark staring mad again.

---

[292] In a petulant sulk.
[293] Smelling salts made from the ammonia in deer antlers.

Freelove: If ever I put any Confidence in your Promises, believe your Tears, or regard your Protestations more! —— From hence forward, I'll grow a Rebel to Beauty, an Enemy to Love, and never think of the Sex, but to despise and loath it. To be a fine Lady, is to have Graces to enchant, and Insolence to abuse; and, to be a Lover, is to live in Purgatory, and worship the Devil.

Lady Bellair: So, so, give it Vent! 'twill be the sooner over.

Freelove: As long as I have Sense to know my Injuries, I never will forgive them.

Lady Bellair: I protest, 'tis more stubborn than I expected!

Freelove: No sham Letters will do now, no counterfeit Pity, nor affected Innocence. —— I have undeniable Proofs of your Falshood, and 'tis not in your Power to evade them.

Lady Bellair: You'll repent this on your Knees, presently!

Freelove: Never, while this guilty Letter justifies my Resentment.

Lady Bellair: Ha! ha! ha!

Freelove: Confusion! am I still to be your Jest? But 'tis my Comfort, this is the last Time.

Lady Bellair: Not by a thousand. —— I shan't let you escape so. —— Here you huff about with the very Letter in your Hand, that I sent on purpose to make you easy.

Freelove: S'death, Madam, what is there in my Face, that makes you think I am to easy to be imposed upon?

Lady Bellair: Nay, I like your Face well enough.

Freelove: You think this Trifling becomes you, I suppose. —— But let me tell you, Madam, to be past Conviction, is to be almost past Blushing too.

Lady Bellair: Why, are not you convinc'd then, dear Wisdom! to shew your Modesty? As I take it 'tis I that am imposed upon: For if I had sent this Letter to any Body else, how should it fall into your Power?

Freelove: By the Folly and Vanity of him you trusted, Madam?

Lady Bellair: And, is this all your Demonstration?

Freelove: All! is it possible to have more?

Lady Bellair: You shall see that immediately. —— Who's there? Send *Double* hither.

SCENE V.

Lady Bellair, Freelove, Double.

Double: Mr. *Freelove* here! nay, then, Impudence assist me! or as my Lady says, my dear Reputation's lost for ever. [*Aside.*

Lady Bellair: Pray *Double,* did not I send you with a Billet to this Gentleman?

Double: Yes, Madam, to be sure; I should be a base one to deny it.

Lady Bellair: Look you there, Sir! What's become of your Demonstration now?

Freelove: And pray did you deliver it as you were directed?

Double: No, Sir, but I gave it to young Mr. *Modern*, for you, and that was all one, you know, Sir.

Freelove: Hum! not altogether, because he put the Favour upon me for his own.

Double: Lard bless me! I am ready to sink into the Earth. ——How could he be such a base Wretch? By my Virginity, Madam, I thought no more Harm, than it was my dying Day. ——

Freelove: Virginity, hum! – a good Word to save an Oath.[294] You see, Madam, I was not entirely out in my Demonstration, neither.

Lady Bellair: But I am not quite easy yet. —— You know, *Double,* I am not very suspicious, by my having put myself once already in your Power. But when I have Reason to be alarmed; nothing but the clearest Integrity can restore my Confidence. – If therefore, you wou'd have me believe you innocent, tell me sincerely, whether this Mistake of yours was not an Artifice of my Cousin's? —— I know you can have no Intent to hurt me yourself.

---

[294] By swearing on her (probably non-existent) virginity, Double leaves room for dissimulation in her oath.

Freelove: And, if she has made it your Interest; it shall be doubly so to be honest, and disappoint her.

Double: Nay, if there's any Thing to be got by it, it may be worth one's while. [*Aside.*] Why, really, Sir, you're so very obliging, and your Ladyship's so good, that I han't the Heart to deny you any thing. – First and foremost, then, 'twas by my Lady's Instigations and the Devil's together, that I was seduced, to send for your Creditors to dun[295] you this Morning; then to vouch with her, to Mr. *Modern,* how your Ladyship lov'd him, that he might offer you Terms; after this, to carry an Assignation to you, Sir; then discover that again to you, Madam, that you might either defeat him upon it, or put such a Confidence in me, as might be made the means of your Ruin, – and, accordingly, your Ladyship trusted me with this same Letter, which, I must own, I gave to Mr. *Modern,* for himself.

Freelove: Well! but the Use of this Treachery?

Double: My Lady, supposed, that, on his communicating it to you, as he was instructed, you wou'd be so incensed at Lady *Bellair,* as never to see her again.

Lady Bellair: Grant he had. ——

Double: I had Orders to invite him to one private Interview more with her.

Freelove: And, if I should comply? ——

Double: She wou'd tempt you with a Sight of the Riches, you had before refused.

Freelove: But, if I had still continued obstinate? –

Double: She has it in her Power to marry your Father, and disinherit you.

Lady Bellair: Was there ever such a Fury! —— Hark you, *Double!* —— Have you a Mind to have all this forgot, and earn a hundred Pound in Hand, and as much more hereafter?

Double: To be sure, Madam, in an honest Way; or any other, rather than fail. [*Aside.*

Lady Bellair: Do what I bid you then. [*Whispers* Double.] As they are exactly alike, you understand me. —— 'Tis a very natural Mistake, and may be easily forgiven.

---

[295] To demand money.

Double: Lard! I'll venture any thing to serve you, Madam. – You'll see my Lady, then, Sir.

Freelove: Never, I would converse with the Plague as soon.

Lady Bellair: Yes, this once to oblige me. —— I have a Design to serve in it of some Moment. —— Tell her, he will, *Double.* —— But not a Word that you have seen me, for your Life.

Double: If I do, Madam, may I —— lose the two hundred Pounds.

Freelove: No, one is your own already. [*Gives her a Note.*

SCENE VI.

Lady Bellair, *and* Freelove.

Lady Bellair: Well, Sir! How do you find yourself now?

Freelove: Happier a thousand times than I deserve. ——

Lady Bellair: You wise, lordly Creatures, then, may sometimes be in the wrong; nay, reason yourselves into Difficulties, and take Pains to be miserable.

Freelove: I confess, Madam, I have found it so, to my Confusion.

Lady Bellair: I told you I shou'd bring you on your Knees again!

Freelove: I ought to continue so for ever, Madam. –

Lady Bellair: No, no, I am not so unreasonable neither.

Freelove: Words can't describe the Excess of my Gratitude, the Fulness of my Joy!

Lady Bellair: Indeed I am much of your Mind.

Freelove: It shall be the Business of my Life, to –

Lady Bellair: Aye, aye, and Business enough too. – But, if you wou'd set out right, away with Jealousy for ever! 'Tis a Canker[296] that preys on the Heart of Love. —— Tho' I am free in Principles, I am not fickle in Temper; and as I can't love without Reason, neither can I change without Provocation. ——

Freelove: And do you confess, at last, you love me?

Lady Bellair: Yes, yes; I do. —— Lard! What wou'd the Man have more?

Freelove: Your Heart, Madam, your Heart in Exchange for my own.

Lady Bellair: There then! —— Take it! ——

Freelove: O Extacy!

Lady Bellair: Pshaw! I hate Raptures! You see I don't blush to own my Sentiments; and, if I have the Softness of my own Sex, I have at the same time, the Courage of yours. ——

Freelove: You are the Delight of our Sex, Madam, and the Glory of your Own.

Lady Bellair: No Flattery, dear *Freelove*, I despise it, tho' a Woman: My Actions are meant to follow Nature, not Applause, —— I can by no means think Love a Crime in itself, or more so in us than you: Neither can I be persuaded, that 'tis any Immodesty to confess its Power; or Virtues to be, or seem insensible of it.

Freelove: No, 'tis rather an Addition to every Charm; and if ever I abuse your Confidence in me ——

Lady Bellair: Idle! Protestations are useless, where there's Sincerity in the Heart. As long as you love me, I know you'll be constant; and when you cease to do so, Vows and Promises will never hold you: Neither shou'd they, against your Inclination.

Freelove: Let us then fear nothing more than Loss of each other; and wish for nothing so much as to prevent it. —— This will make a Desire to please mutual, and keep up the Spirit of Passion on both sides.

Lady Bellair: I hate the insolent Tranquillity that subsists where Duty steps into the Place of Love, as much as the noisy Wrangling of Hatred and Contempt. ——

---

[296] A spreading sore or ulcer.

Freelove: If we have the Sense to avoid these Extremes, every Day will compliment us with a new Choice of each other, and make us happier than the last.

Lady Bellair: But, if we are both fatally mistaken in our Hopes, and Harmony can never be the Result of our Union —— Let us separate the Moment we find our Error. —— If 'tis my Fault, I'll never upbraid you with Inconstancy; if yours, I'll never think you worth the keeping.

Freelove: Nothing can be nobler —— I am ev'ry way your Captive.

Lady Bellair: Well, no more Speeches at present, but away, and look for your Father, —— you'll find it necessary he shou'd be near at your next Interview with my honourable Rival; and whatever she puts into your Hands, be sure to examine thoroughly. —— Go! —— You'll need no further Instructions.

Freelove: 'Tis my Pleasure to obey you.

SCENE VII.

Lady Bellair *and* Modern.

Modern: A Whoreson Hypocrite! A sanctified Knave! 'Slife, a thorough-pac'd Statesman cou'd do no more than lie and cousin on both Sides. —— Will you have his Ears, Madam?[297] I have not chastis'd a Scoundrel Time out of Mind; and 'twill do me good —— I shall live Twenty Years the longer for it.

Lady Bellair: Bless me, Sir! Who is this horrible Traitor?

Modern: My Nephew, Madam, my Nephew: Who, but he, cou'd think of injuring so fine a Creature?

Lady Bellair: It does not appear to me, Sir, that he had any such Design.

Modern: You are too good to own it, Madam: But your Cousin has told me all —— For fear I shou'd cut him off from my Estate, forsooth, – as if I could sooner pardon him for a Wrong to another, than Disobedience to myself. —— No, no, since he is so good at Tricks, let him live by them. —— I am ready to make good my late Offer, Madam, and shall be happy if you think it worth your Acceptance.

---

[297] The removal of one ear or both to shame and identify criminals, usually on the pillory, dates back to Tudor times. Modern, horrified by his son's duplicity, offers to brand Young Modern publicly to compensate Bellair for his treatment of her.

Lady Bellair: You are too obliging, Sir. —— But I have a Thousand Reasons to decline it.

Modern: If you had Ten Thousand, Madam, they are not half the Value of my Estate.

Lady Bellair: Pardon me, Sir, 'twas I put your Nephew on the Frolick; and tho' 'twas done to mortify his Vanity, 'twould be monstrous in me to take the Forfeit.[298]

Modern: But, 'Slife, Madam, he never intended to run the Hazard. —— You only meant to expose him; but he resolv'd to ruin you. —— This is but Self-Defence then. —— A Revenge that is your Due.

Lady Bellair: Aye; but, Mr. *Modern*, Revenge does not agree with my Temper; and if it redresses one Injury, seldom fails to inflict a greater.

Modern: Come, Madam, think of it once more. —— Three Thousand Pounds a Year[299] is no Trifle; and Faith, Lady, I shall be no very grievous Incumbrance.

Lady Bellair: O! None all, Sir, —— But, the greater the Offer, the more I think myself oblig'd to refuse it. —— Every new Instance of Splendor, wou'd be a new Reproach to me: And, what makes other People's Happiness, wou'd be my Misery.
——

Modern: Is it possible, Madam? Are you a Woman? Answer me to that. Are you a Woman, I say?

Lady Bellair: Why! What do you think I am, Mr. *Modern*?

Modern: By this Light, an Angel. Hitherto, Madam, I have only address'd you in Resentment to my Nephew; but now, in Justice to your Merit, and in Pursuit of my own Happiness. —— 'Tis a Shame such Beauty and Virtue shou'd be liable to any future Insult for the want of Fortune.

Lady Bellair: Nay, Sir, I wou'd no more be outdone in Generosity, than I wou'd be guilty of Injustice, and still to refuse the Compliment, is the best way to shew my Gratitude for it.

Modern: I don't know how it is, Madam, but I begin to feel something of a Pain here, that a Man of my Years shou'd be entirely free from. —— But I think, if

---

[298] To take the money that her prank may cause Young Modern to lose.

[299] A substantial income equal to over £341,000 per year in modern terms.

such a Weakness is ever excusable, 'tis when Reason itself borrows the Darts of Love, and we are wounded by Desire and Esteem together.

Lady Bellair: You are very gallant, Sir. – But tho' I have many Reasons to be vain of such a Conquest, I shou'd be asham'd to indulge my Pride at the Expence of my Sincerity. —— Less than my whole Heart, is not fit for me to give, or you to receive; and that is not in my Power to bestow. Pardon the Freedom I take in telling you so. —— I dare not trifle a Moment, with a Man, who has treated me so nobly. ——

Modern: Generous Creature!

Lady Bellair: All my Tenderness and Affection is already disposed of, to one who deserves it all. —— One who, in his very Childhood, while all Innocence and Sweetness, woo'd me with all his pretty Toys, and lisp'd out the softest, dearest Things, —— hung on my Lips like Love himself, and, in a Thousand rosy Dimples, smil'd me into Fondness; till riper Years, and differing Educations, damp'd our mutual Ardour. —— Yet had you been his equal in Years, (for Love allows of no Disparity)[300] and began your Addresses at the same time, I don't know but your frank, honest Manner, had carried the Day.

Modern: I am lost in Admiration. ——

Lady Bellair: As it is, my Love only takes Place of my Ambition, that's all; and I chuse to be happy rather than great. —— Henceforward, then, think of me no more! both for your own sake and mine. At present the Wound is but slight; to proceed may make it deeper: And it wou'd hurt me to hear it, even in my Lover's Arms.

Modern: Well, Madam, If I can't instantly obey you, I'll do something to convince you, I endeavour'd to copy your Example. ——

Lady Bellair: If you wou'd do any thing more to oblige me, dissuade Sir *William Freelove* from marrying my Cousin.

Modern: With all the Pleasure in the World, Madam.

---

[300] A significant age difference was thought to be an impediment to a good love match, though property marriages still widely ignored the objection.

SCENE VIII.

Lady Bellair, Modern, *Sir* William, *and* Freelove.

Freelove: Hear me but two Syllables, Sir!

Sir William: Not one, Sir. 'Tis my Turn to be deaf now.

Freelove: It concerns your Honour, Sir ——

Sir William: As I take it, Sir, my Honour is no Concern of yours.

Freelove: 'Twill be none of your Lady's, I am afraid.

Sir William: You hope, you mean, Sirrah! But I shall balk your Malice; I shall, Sir.

Modern: Aye, marry! And be undone! Do!

Sir William: Undone!

Modern: Certainly! Infallibly!

Sir William: Why, my Wife that is to be, is rich, rich, rich.

Modern: And young too, or worse, in the full Strength and Vigour of her Age. You may have the Affair in your Head indeed – But I fancy you are not Head all over.[301]

Sir William: 'Slife, Sir, I'd have you know, She hates young Fellows mortally.

Lady Bellair: She has not been long of that Mind, Sir *William.*

Sir William: No Matter, Madam, no Matter! – She's none of your Libertines, but a good Soul, that makes Piety and Devotion her Pleasure.

Modern: Piety and Devotion! Prudery and Hypocrisy! I'll pawn my Soul she's a damn'd incroaching Tyrant, that wou'd not part with one Inch of her Right,

---

[301] Refers to the head as the center of the intellect and reason, as opposed to the body and heart as the source of emotion and desire. Thus Modern asserts that Sir William may think that he is able to keep up with his young wife's desires, but his body may not support him.

without more than an Equivalent some other way. —— And, as much a Phoenix[302] as she is, she will hardly burn in her Nest, rather than fly abroad to save herself.

Lady Bellair: But then, Sir, you'll have the Pleasure of being courted almost as much as your Lady, and not a Man will have the Face to pay his Addresses to her, before he has made a Friend of you.

Modern: Right, Madam: Nothing gives such a Spirit to Cuckoldom, as to make the Husband help to put on his own Horns.[303]

Sir William: Alack-a-day, Sir, I am not so easily impos'd upon.

Modern: Perhaps then, you design to make yourself your own Spy, and, by your very Suspicions, let the World know, that she wants nothing but Opportunity, to do you the Favour. –

Lady Bellair: Or, suppose her all Virtue, besure she'll find her Account in it; make it a Plea for all Power, all Liberty, all Expence.

Modern: Aye, with such Haughtiness and Clamour, as if she was a Child of Thunder —— Insomuch that you'll be glad to compound with her, at last, to give it up, that her Pleasure may be your Peace. – Then again, tho' she has no Generosity, she has a World of Ostentation; and no Pride, no Fashion, no Pleasure, no Extravagance, will escape her, cost what it will.

Lady Bellair: And all this you must not dare to oppose, tho' she should add Gaming to the List, and hazard your whole Estate at a Cast.[304]

Sir William: Must not dare?

Modern: No, for fear she shou'd recollect there's one Amusement wanting still, that no Consideration cou'd atone for.

Sir William: Well, well, her own Fortune will do all this, without any Damage to mine.

---

[302] The mythical bird that would burn itself to ashes and then rise again to life. Lurcher has emerged from each failed plan with another ready to begin.

[303] A man whose wife had been unfaithful was termed a cuckold, and was often marked in the popular imagination with the horns of a stag.

[304] A throw of the dice or risky act.

Lady Bellair: Suppose, tho' like many other sharping Widows, she has put it out of her own Power already.[305]

Sir William: Bless us, that wou'd be terrible indeed!

Lady Bellair: Or, grant she has not, there's much Reason to believe, that all her Wealth is not very honestly come by.

Sir William: That's no great matter. —— I know few Estates that are.

Lady Bellair: But what if she shou'd be compell'd to make Restitution?

Sir William: How! Restitution? If this was not Malice now ——

Lady Bellair: You shall be convinc'd to the contrary, if 'tis not your own Fault.

Freelove: Nay more, Sir, that this Marriage is her last Shift, and in my Power still, to break it off when I please.

Sir William: If this cou'd be made appear ——

Freelove: If you'll withdraw but a few Minutes with this Lady and Mr. *Modern*, it shall to Demonstration. ——

Sir William: No foul Play in the mean time then. ——

Freelove: None, as I wou'd deserve your Blessing, or enjoy my Birth-Right.

SCENE IX.

Freelove *and Lady* Lurcher.

Lady Lurcher: I once believ'd, Sir, that my Pride wou'd never let me stoop to sollicit any Man – But Love has got the Ascendant now, and I have no Pretence to save my Blushes, but the Merit of the Object. ——

---

[305] Widows who scheme to trick men into marriage for their money. In Congreve's *The Way of the World* (1700), for example, the remarried widow Arabella Fainall has made a secret legal contract before her marriage to put all of her fortune in trust to another man so that it cannot be claimed by her second husband, despite marital property laws that would typically grant a husband full control over his wife's assets.

Freelove: Love, Madam? I thought your Favours to me had only been Friendship to your Cousin. –

Lady Lurcher: Cruel! To upbraid me with an Artifice I cou'd not avoid. – Had not I uncommon Softness in my Disposition, the most sensible Concern for your Welfare, the most inviolable Esteem for your Person, I shou'd rather pursue my Revenge than Love, rather insult than pity your Misfortune. —— But such Conduct wou'd better suit other Characters: The artful, designing, mercenary Coquet, who trafficks with her Charms, makes an Auction of her Beauty, and sets it up to the highest Bidder —— Your giddy, variable *Bellair.*

Freelove: This is a Home Charge, Madam; and, however capricious she has been to me, I can't tell how to think she deserves it.

Lady Lurcher: Fie, fie, Mr. *Freelove!* Has not she play'd the whole Game upon you? Has not she flatter'd your Hopes, then sent you into Despair? And, to crown all, has not she deserted you at last, and made the very Concession to your Rival she had promis'd to you? Don't offer to palliate, or excuse it! I know you are convinc'd of her Falshood, and, if ever you think of her more, deserve to be chronicled as one that no Injury cou'd provoke, nor Favour oblige.

Freelove: That wou'd be very severe indeed!

Lady Lurcher: Break off her Hold from your Heart then! And dare to be free! —— You see I can lay aside my Resentment, mortify my Pride, and forget all the Woman in me, to wooe you to it —— Stoop even to accept you on any Terms, your Heart yet glowing with my Rival's Image, averse to mine; and if ever to be won, complying more out of Anger to her, than Love to me. ——

Freelove: But suppose, Madam, I shou'd begin to be sensible of my Error, have not you already engaged yourself to my Father?[306]

Lady Lurcher: But verbally, when only Scorn and Rage were uppermost. —— From this Moment the very Remembrance of it is cancell'd. ——

Freelove: Then his Resentment falls on me, and all my Hopes of Fortune are undone; or I must live as an Incumbrance upon yours, and thank your Ladyship annually for my Pension. ——

Lady Lurcher: I'll rid you of that Fear immediately, —— [*goes to the Door*] *Double*, the Casket! There, Sir, I put you in Possession of my all, nor ever will

---

[306] Corrected from 'alrea dyngag'd' in the 1735 edition.

recall the Grant. —— Nay, don't be modest, but examine the Contents; they'll pay your Trouble richly, and prove how tenderly I love you.

Freelove: Now, if *Double* is for once but faithful, —— She is, she is, I can hardly contain my Joy. [*Aside.*

Lady Lurcher: Well, Sir! Does it answer ——

Freelove: Oh, abundantly, Madam! —— Hum, hum. —— A choice Collection of excellent new Receipts for the Complexion, Hair, Lips, Teeth, &c.[307] As I live, Madam, a complete Magazine of Beauty! ——

Lady Lurcher: I tremble every Joint of me. —— How in the World came those Papers there? [*Aside.*

Freelove: Hum! —— Some Select Passages of *Rochester*'s Poems;[308] hah! and, inclos'd in a Leaf of the Common Prayer, certain amorous Miniatures from *Italy.*
——

Lady Lurcher: Oh that She-Devil! I can hold no longer, [*Aside*] This is some strange Mistake, Sir, my Woman has given me the wrong Casket; I must beg you to return it again.

Freelove: I thought you said, Madam, you never wou'd recall the Grant.

Lady Bellair: Undone! undone!

Freelove: [*Reads.*] Counterpart, —— Settlement for Life.[309] —— Dear Doctor *Lenitive.*[310] —— I protest, Madam, I admire your Gratitude. ——

Lady Lurcher: Dear Sir! let me conjure you to proceed no farther!

Freelove: Only examine the Contents, Madam, according to your Ladyship's Commands, [*Reads.*] Letters from Mr. *Ironside.*

[307] Such recipes are evidence that Lurcher's appearance is false, and that she is neither as young nor as pretty as she seems. In addition, 'etcetera' and '&c' could also be used at this time as euphemisms for the female genitalia, and so more alteration may also be implied.

[308] John Wilmot, Earl of Rochester, the most famous and most extreme libertine of the Restoration era, well known for his abundant sexual and obscene poetry.

[309] Apparently in exchange for her secrecy in sexual matters, Lady Lurcher has bestowed a lifetime income on her doctor lover.

[310] A lenitive is a term used for medical devices or medications intended to be soothing.

Lady Lurcher: If all I'm worth can move you, Sir, ——

Freelove: You must pardon a Lover's Curiosity, Madam. —— I had been a Pensioner in very good Company it seems.

Lady Lurcher: On my Knees, Sir, ——

Freelove: Oh dear Madam! Why shou'd you be asham'd of your Liberalities? [*Reads.*] Assignment of Ten Thousand Pounds from Sir *Jeremy Bellair*, to Sir *Lawrence Lurcher*, in Trust for Lady *Lucy Bellair*.

Lady Lurcher: Nay, then there's no Remedy, —— I am snar'd in my own Cunning, and baited with my own Follies.

Freelove: Why aye, Madam, this will pay my Trouble richly indeed!

Lady Lurcher: Perhaps not, Sir. —— The Acknowledgment of the Trust I took care to possess myself of, and destroy'd long ago, to invalidate the Claim.

Freelove: Prodigious! and do you glory in it too?

Lady Lurcher: I do; and, if you had the least Spark of my Spirit, you wou'd do the same, and not be so scandalously concern'd for one ——

Freelove: Come, come, no more of that, Madam, for own Sake. —— *Double*, your Creature, has discover'd all, and there is not a Treachery you have been guilty of, that is not apparent enough to make Impudence itself asham'd

Lady Lurcher: This is a Plot to betray me then! But I'll keep the Ten Thousand Pound, and blush once for all.

Freelove: Then you shall have Reason to fix constant Fever in your Cheeks. —— I'll forget you're a Woman, to mark you out as a Fiend. This secret Hoard of Vices, like *Pandora*'s Plagues, shall be expos'd to make you hated thro' the World.[311] —— —— Your Patch-work, borrow'd Charms, and real Imperfections; your studied Piety[312] by Day; your loose Intrigues by Night; your Bargains and Rewards for Infamy; Names, Times, and Circumstances shall be all describ'd at

---

[311] In Greek myth, Pandora was the first woman on earth, created as a vengeance upon man. She arrived with a box that she was forbidden to open; when opened the box released all of the evils put into the box by the gods, providing the origins of sorrow, mischief, toil and disease.

[312] Practiced and thus artificial piety.

large, —— Hypocrisy itself shall be unmask'd in you, and guilty Truth start blushing from beneath it.

Lady Lurcher: O, I cou'd curse myself to the Centre, for trusting that perfidious Creature. —— My Reputation, my dear Reputation!

Freelove: Bid adieu to it for ever!

Lady Lurcher: 'Tis impossible I shou'd survive it. – O! I can't bear to be pointed at as a Monster. – Dear, dear Mr. *Freelove,* pity me!

Freelove: Restore the Ten Thousand Pound then, and you shall be as white as Snow.

Lady Lurcher: Then will my Rival be happy, and I shall die to see it.

Freelove: There's no Alterative.

Lady Lurcher: Hard, hard Conditions! an Estate for a Name!

Freelove: Now, or never!

Lady Lurcher: Well, if it must be so! [*Writes.*] There then! [*Gives a Note.*] and now, Sir, the Casket!

Freelove: No, Madam, that must be Security for the Payment. —— Beside, your Ladyship must give me Leave to trust the Secret with my Father first, in my own Defence.

Lady Lurcher: Confusion! Disappointed again!

Freelove: When that is done, it shall be restor'd intire, and this Adventure be no more remember'd by either of us. —— At present, I would advise you to retire to your Closet, till your Cousin leaves the House. – You look much disorder'd, —— I am sorry for you, and wou'd spare you the Pain of seeing her any more.

Lady Lurcher: O Shame! how dearly do we purchase thee?

SCENE X.

Freelove, *Lady* Bellair, *Sir* William, Modern.

Sir William: My dear Boy! thou hast sav'd me just in the nick, i'faith. —— We have overheard all, and, o'my Conscience, I tremble still at the Danger I have escap'd. —— Sirrah! thou shall't marry who thou will't, — this Lady, or any other Lady, with my Blessing into the Bargain.

Freelove: I will make it my Study to deserve this Indulgence, Sir. —— These Papers, Madam, are yours, —— and I restore them with more Joy, than she cou'd keep them. —— But give me Leave to inquire how so large a Sum cou'd be left in such Hands unknown to you? Or by what Stratagem she cou'd get her Husband's Acknowledgment of the Receipt into her Power?

Lady Bellair: The Intricacy, I'm of Opinion, is now easy to be explain'd. — You are to understand that when I consented to sell my Jointure, to make my Husband's Affairs easy, he told me with a Smile, that nothing but Distress would teach me the Value of Money; and in such a Case, an unexpected Supply would do me double Service, – added, I should not repent my Generosity, and said no more. —— The next Summer after this, Sir, Sir *Lawrence Lurcher* invited us to spend the Season at his Seat in the Country, and there having been a long Intimacy in the Family, we readily accepted it. —— There my Husband was seiz'd with his last Sickness; and tho' I seldom stirr'd from his Bed-side, I had one Day left him but a few Moments asleep, Lady *Lurcher* sitting by him in my stead, when of a sudden he rung the Bell with the utmost Precipitation; I ran immediately back, met her coming out of the Chamber very abruptly, and found him in the Agonies of Death, with great Surprise and Uneasiness in his Face. – He had still Sense enough to point to a Beaureau that was open in the Room, —— mention'd my Cousin, Receipts, Ten Thousand Pounds; and then expir'd in my Arms. —— This was all a Mystery to me, and his Friend Sir *Lawrence* had not the Honesty to unriddle it, but dying soon after, left her sole Executrix:[313] Now, what Light these Particulars may let into the Affair, I may be too much prejudic'd to determine. —— But I can't help wishing, that my Cousin had been less anxious for her Reputation, and more for her Virtue.

Modern: 'Twou'd not have cost her half the Trouble, and done her infinitely greater Service — But come, Sir *William*, this young Gentleman is unprovided for still, and if you would have the Credit of being thought his Father, behave like one to him; for shame, give him a Fortune suitable to his Spirit, and don't provoke him to pray for your Death, because 'tis not in his Power to live while you do.

Sir William: Humph!

---

[313] A female executor or administrator of the conditions of a will.

Freelove: When I deserve it, I presume you have so much Generosity to deny me.

Modern: 'Slife, he must do it this Moment then, or he has neither Generosity or Gratitude.

Sir William: Will not this busy Gentleman then, take the Merit of it to himself?

Modern: Not I, indeed, Sir. —— But the Pleasure I will I have a Share in, in spite of your Teeth.

Sir William: Well then, I will settle five hundred a Year upon him directly, and now I hope you'll allow me Gratitude and Generosity too.

Modern: Aye, but make it a thousand; and I'll cut any Man's Throat, that mutters to the contrary.

SCENE the Last.

Lady Bellair, *Sir* William, Modern, *Young* Modern.

Young *Modern:* Your Servant, Madam. —— Gentlemen yours. —— Once more, Sir, [*To Modern:*] you men see me in *statu quo:*[314] That is to say, as mad, frolick, profuse, and wicked as your Heart can wish. —— You must know, I was but a white-wash'd Saint, mere Out-side —— But a little bad Weather has spoiled my Complexion, and now I am a down right Sinner again. —— To Night, I'll to the Tavern, where the best Burgundy, the richest Banquets, the gayest Friends, and loveliest Women, shall mingle Luxuries, and not a Bugbear Thought intrude, to dash the wild Extravagance of Joy.

Modern: You will?

Young *Modern:* To oblige you, Sir. ——

Modern: To oblige me? Thou Fool! do'st think, because I hate Hypocrisy, I love a Profligate, an abandon'd Debauchee? —— 'Tis true, I bid thee follow Pleasure, incouraged thee to make the most of Life, before Age came on, and Appetite decay'd. —— But then I bid thee too be honest, brave and generous; bid thee mingle Virtue with Enjoyment, and feast thy Understanding, still beyond the Sense. —— For this, I threw my Purse before thee, and suffered thee to supply thy

---

[314] Latin, "as things were before."

self to thy own Wishes: But now I see thou hast mistaken my Goodness, and that thy Soul has nothing great or noble in it, I'll suit my Bounty to thy Merits, and make thee, from thy Wants, acquire thy Virtue.

Young *Modern:* Egad! if no Body was to get no more by Religion, there wou'd be no —— [*Aside.*

Modern: And to prove that this Conduct of mine is not Avarice, but Equity, —— This Lady, shall now receive what thou hast lost, and be my Heiress in Reversion.[315]

Lady Bellair: Once more, Sir, I must have Leave to refuse your Bounty —— I have now, no Occasion for it; and this Gentleman may live to deserve it better.

Modern: You are still above me, Madam. —— But this you must indulge me in: —— The Plate,[316] Equipage and Furniture, I bespoke to Day for my own Use; you must accept for your's. —— Your sudden Departure from this House, will make them convenient for you. —— And I shall still think you are too proud to be obliged, if you will not let me redeem the jewels you so nobly parted with, and make them your own again.

Lady Bellair: You have not left it in my Power, either to refuse your Liberality, or acknowledge it as I ought. —— These are the only Actions I can envy, and such as I only wou'd be rich and great to imitate —— Pleasure, I have ever thought the chiefest Good; but that Pleasure is to be found no where, but in obeying Reason and Virtue.

Falshood a while, may gild a worthless Name,
But Truth untainted, is the Soul of Fame.

---

[315] Upon Modern's death, Bellair would receive his entire estate.
[316] Silver or gold utensils.

EPILOGUE.
By a FRIEND.

WELL, Gentlemen, the Comedy is ended,
And, if it takes, it need not be defended;
If not, the finest Speaker in the Nation,
Can hardly talk it into Reputation.

Some Faults are left, for those that love to rail;
As Seamen throw out Barrels to the Whale;[317]
And some, for want of Judgment to write better:
And those may serve to exercise good Nature:
We grant, to be severe on Plays is common,
But who wou'd set their Wit against a Woman?
If you prevail, the Triumph is but small;
Alas! thro' Weakness, we are apt to fall!
But then these Criticks have such savage Hearts,
They stick at nothing, so they shew their Parts:
If then, our Author trip in Quest of Honour,
Without Remorse, they're sure to fall upon her.

Yet some, methinks, shou'd look with gentler Eyes,
And lend her, gallantly, their Hands to rise;
'Twas to oblige, she run this mighty Venture,
And, when a Woman sues, you shou'd content her;

If Bellair's but a Libertine in Name,
And makes her Freedom, but refine her Flame;
If, baulk'd of what your wanton Hopes expected,
You see her constant, and a Beau rejected:
Our Author's Muse, you'll find, not half so coy,
'Tis her avow'd Desire, to give you Joy;
And if you kindly meet her first Endeavour,
She hopes, in Time, to please you altogether.

---

[317] A version of a maritime colloquialism meaning to create diversion in order to avoid real danger. In whaling, when a ship was threatened by whales, a tub or barrel might be thrown into the sea to divert their attention.

Appendix A

Elizabeth Cooper's Announcement of her Benefit Performance

The Grub Street Journal 226 (25 April 1734)

To Mr. Bavius,

Sir,

A woman-correspondent, is what I believe you are seldom troubled with, and therefore, for the novelty's sake, as well as the complaisance which is allowed to the sex, I take it for granted, you will indulge me with a place in your paper.

By the persuasion of my friends I have, this last winter, ventured to make my appearance on the *stage*, tho' a way of life entirely foreign to what I have hitherto been used to; and have been taught to believe, that, in time, I need not despair of some success.

The character of LADY EASY, in the *Careless husband*, which is to be presented on friday next for my benefit, at the Theatre-royal in Lincoln's-inn fields, may, however, be thought too great an attempt, for, almost, a first tryal: I therefore, thought myself obliged to make some apology for it; that I might not be condemned for that which may seem a choice, but is, in fact, necessity.

I know, that when the abilities of a player are little known, there is the same need of novelty to excite curiosity and attention: and, as I have little interest to depend upon, but what I gain'd in a different station of life, 'tis my duty to do my utmost for their entertainment.

If therefore, the character should not be supported as well as I ought, I hope the diffidence natural to such severe trials as these, will be my excuse; and that every candid and impartial spectator will conclude, that habit, and longer use to the stage, will, at length, enable me to get the better of that disadvantage. I am, Sir,

your very humble servant,

E. Cooper

Appendix B

Review of *The Rival Widows*

The Prompter 34 (7 March 1735)

FELICITER AUDET.
Hor.

With HAPPY BOLDNESS *She attempts the* Part,
While Nature *paves her Way, in Spite of Art.*

FRIDAY, MARCH 7. 1735

IT is a wise World we live in: Every Day affords Examples of some new Improvement. Formerly, *Poets* were content to instruct the *Actors*, and let their Wit be convey'd to the Audience by those whose proper Business it was, who studied for that Purpose, and were paid for that End. But this Method is now grown stale, and Authors must turn Actors too. Poets no longer must depend on the Merit of their Pieces, however good; nor the Skill of the Actors, however great; but must study to act the *principal Parts* themselves. A NEW Play will want NOVELTY, if the Actors, *only*, represent it, should this Custom take Root, and spread over the *Theatrick-Soil*, as *Weeds* are *apt* enough to *grow there*.

As I am acquainted with almost all the Dramatick Writers of the Stage, and cannot find the executive Genius of the Actor in many of them, I am the more concern'd, lest this should grow into a Fashion on *their* Account, well knowing, that very often the *Success* of a Piece depends on the *skilful Performance* of the Actor.

I shall therefore take the Liberty, in this Day's Paper, without Offence to the Fair Sex, to *prompt* that aspiring Genius, who has lately introduced this Custom on the Stage, and crush it in it's Infancy.

THE Person I mean, is the ingenious Mrs *E. Cooper*, Author of The *Fair Libertine*, who play'd that Part for her own Benefit, on *Thursday* last Week; and, as I am informed, intends to appear again in the same Character.

THREE Motives may have induced this Fair Lady, to this dangerous Enterprize. – The first, To recommend herself to the Town as an Actress. The second, To eclipse, by her superior Merit, one of the most graceful Actresses we have on the Stage. And the third, To appear in a Character more *natural* to *her* than to Mrs. *Horton*, who performed it the first and second Nights; by which lucky Circumstance in her Favour, she might possibly hope to succeed in the other Two.

IT is an Observation, proper enough to be made in this Place, that when Jealousy (not that which arises from Love, but that which results from a Rivalship of Perfections) takes Possession of a Female Breast, nothing seems *beyond* a Lady's Power, that she imagines may *take from* the *Merit* of her *fancied Competitor*.

SELF-OPINION, without any other Spur, is apt enough to carry us too far; but when increased by such a Passion as this I am speaking of, our Wonder ceases, when any too adventurous Enterprize is the Consequence of it.

A Lady moderately covetous of Reputation, would have been satisfied with having distinguish'd herself out of the common Road of her Sex; and received thankfully, IF SHE HAD ANY RIGHT TO IT, the Share of Praise due to her Wit, without attempting any thing farther: But Women, thro' an *Oversprightliness* of *Constitution*, generally are in Extremes; if GOOD, BETTER than *Men*, if BAD, WORSE,; more *tenderly*, and *constantly* LOVING, when they do LOVE; more *firmly*, and *desperately* HATING, when they do HATE.

THE Desire of recommending herself to the Town as a Actress, was in itself *laudable*, and *right*, however BOLD the Method of doing it may be thought; But where will not *Love of Fame* and *Emulation* carry the FAIR ASPIRER?

WITHOUT saying too much in Favour of Mrs. *Horton*, she is, undoubtedly, the finest Figure on any Stage, at present; – consider'd as an Actress, I don't see who goes beyond her, in personating the fine Lady in genteel Comedy.

THE *Fair Libertine*, from the Picture drawn of her requires an Actress that should unite Beauty of Person with Grace of Action: See her Description. "*Freel.–* A Rose at fairest, neither a Bud, nor Fullblown, is but a faint Emblem of her Beauty. – The Painters need no other Model for a living *Venus*; and Nature form'd her as a Mould for smiling *Cupids*, to propagate a Race of Beauties to insnare another Age. Then she has Wit enough to supply the present Dearth of it on the Stage, and good Nature, to make that Wit agreeable even at Court. In short, she's *gay*, without *Levity*; *Libertine*, without *Scandal*; *Generous*, without *Design*, and *well-bred*, without AFFECTATION."

For as to the Character of her Mind, from which she derives the Title of *Libertine*, that neither requires *Beauty* of *Person*, nor *Grace* of *Action*, PRIMARILY; for a very disagreeable Woman may have the Sentiments of Lady *Bellair*. –

HOW far Mrs. *Cooper*'s Person may justly oppose itself to Mrs. *Horton*'s, in Point of *Beauty*, I leave to the Admirers of each to decide. – Perhaps (contrary to most of my Sex) I am partial to a Face I am acquainted with, and the Novelty of Mrs. *Cooper*'s failed, for that Reason, of one Admirer in me, in Prejudice of Mrs. *Horton*'s. I am so much in this way of thinking, that cou'd I recall the *Dead*, whom once I saw tread the Stage, I should, I believe, give them the Preference, in Opposition to those to whom I now owe the Pleasure I taste in such Representations; and this, without Ingratitude to my *present Benefactors*.

NEITHER will I venture to determine, how far the Method Mrs. *Cooper* chose to recommend herself to the Town, as an Actress, may pass without the Imputation of *Vanity*, or an *over-rating* of her *Perfections*. – That is a Point I shall chuse to leave, to be decided by a Letter printed in the *Daily Advertiser*, as a grateful Acknowledgement to the Town, for the kind Reception they gave her. I think nothing can better decide it than that Letter, since it is hardly possible to suppose a Lady of her CONSCIOUS MERIT, would stoop to return Thanks for a Reception she did not meet with.

As well pleased as I am, at the Town's Acquisition of an Actress, that, with BUT ONE REHEARSAL, cou'd deserve the good Opinion of an Audience, in a Character where Mrs. *Horton* appeared *originally*, and could not but be *fresh* in ev'ry Body's *Eye* at that very Time, I can't help, out of *personal Regard* for this latter, giving one Sigh, at her being so *unexpectedly*, and so *suprizingly eclipsed*. – But there is nothing so advantageous, as to *look* a Character; that alone oft turns the Scale. – 'Tis this that makes Mr. *Cibber* so admired in the different Characters he represents. – Tho' *his* Genius is *infinitely* COMPREHENSIVE; and in *Iago*, *Syphax*, and *Richard the Third*, he looks as much the Villain, as in *Foppington* the *Coxcomb*; Sir *J. Brute*, the *Drunken Debaucher*; and *Fondle-wife*, the *Old puritanick Cuckold*, – not forgetting Sir *Francis Wronghead*, to which he has a *natural Right*.

THE *Fair Libertine* then being a Character Mrs. *Cooper* was very fond of, no Wonder she enter'd into it, more than Mrs. *Horton*, who cou'd not be supposed to have the same natural Affection for it; and of Course, just gave it as much Spirit as might be necessary to make her appear, what she was designed, the *principal Character*. Mrs. *Cooper*, on the contrary, who drew the Character from the Life, and had a *double* Interest in procuring its *Admiration*, neglected *nothing* that might add to its *natural Force*; and having SAT herself, as People imagine, for the Picture she, or somebody else, *drew* for her, knew where to make the Lights strong, and the Shadows *bold*, and *contrasted*. – And thus Mrs. *Horton*, tho' a *finer Woman*, and more *graceful Actress*, had the Mortification to be herself eclipsed, by the HAPPY BOLDNESS of her *Fair Competitor*.

I should now say something as to the Merit of the Performance itself, but that this Lady, who is every where alike SURPRISING and SINGULAR, has left me nothing to add to the Character she gives of it in her Preface.

"I have chosen a Tale, says she, that is not very barren of Incidents, neither are those Incidents FORC'D, or *unnatural, ill-tim'd*, or *superfluous*."

NOT to mention any other, I suppose the Incident of *Young Modern*'s Transformation into a *Puritanick Saint*, by which he disobliges a generous Uncle, who had just considerably increased his Fortune, is sufficiently justified, by ITS BEING HINTED to him by a *Fantastick Mistress*, who laughs at him for it, and is neither FORC'D, UNNATURAL, ILL-TIM'd, or SUPERFLUOUS!

"SOME of the Characters are meant to be *new*, and the rest not mere Copies, or void of Entertainment. – I have endeavoured to *contrast* them too, and shew them by each other's Light."

SIR *William Freelove* and Mr. *Modern* are not mere Copies from the *'Squire of Alsatia*; there is indeed a Variation in them, but, unfortunately for the worse, which makes them fall as much short of the Merit of one, and Humour of the other old Gentleman in that Play, as *Young Freelove* and *Young Modern* do in their respective Characters, of the Son and Nephew in *Shadwell*'s.

LADY *Bellair*, and *Lady Lurcher*, have a strong Resemblance, in several Places, with Mrs. *Millamant* and Mrs. *Marwood*, in the *Way of the World;* but still with the same Variation; and *Double* is but a second Edition of Mrs. *Foible*'s *Double Treachery*.

"ONE I have labour'd to make Principal, to be the SOUL of the Piece, and to be seen and referred to almost tho' the whole Action. – It happens indeed to be a WOMAN, and I flatter myself, I shall have no Apology to make to the Ladies, for having drawn her capable of thinking for herself, and acting on the Principles of NATURE and TRUTH.

I question if the Ladies will thank Mrs. *Cooper* for the Picture she has drawn. – However it was

An Offering to the Sex design'd. –

They may perhaps think *her way of stripping Nature stark-naked, a little too libertine*, and *bold*, for their Imitation, and that *she* cannot quite JUSTIFY herself, as she wou'd do.

"IT has been my Endeavour to preserve what the Criticks call *Unities*.

I believe Mrs. *Cooper* has forgot one essential *Unity, viz.* That of *Character*: – For there is not one *Person* in the Play, but who, in one Part of other, UNCHARACTERIZES him, or her self, and CHANGES oftner than the Scenes.

WHAT follows in the Preface, is only applicable to the most correct Play; and I shall, therefore, CHARITABLY suppose, with her, that The *Rival Widows* yields to none yet wrote, if it deserves the Application she so generously makes in her modest Preface.

I did intent, in this Day's Paper, only to *prompt* her in Relation to the *bold Flight* she attempted; but when one engages with a Lady, one does not know where to stop.

I must therefore, for the present, content myself with ent'ring a Caveat against any Poet's following her Example, except the facetious *Jemmy Worsdale*, who is born an Actor naturally, and may attempt almost any Character, with Success, and without Fear of Reprisals; for none can imitate his.

Appendix C

Argument in Support of the Proposed Licensing Act

The Daily Gazetteer (6 and 8 June 1737)

To the Printer of the DAILY GAZETTEER.

S I R,

IT has been the immutable Practice of the Gentlemen in the Opposition, to represent every *Law*, supported by the *Friends of the Administration*, as a *Violation* of the *British Liberty*. It would certainly be a melancholy Consideration, had we any Reason to believe the Truth of this Suggestion; the Sense of which I take to be, that the *Friends* of the *Administration* are no *Friends* to *Liberty*. I say, the Sense of it; for tho' the Writers in the Service of these Gentlemen are ever carping at other People's *Style*, and giving themselves Airs of *Superiority* in *Science*, yet it is certain, that they themselves are not *infallible*, but make *Slips* as well as other Authors, of which I take the *Phrase*, before-mentioned to be one. The *Author* of the *Craftsman* of the 28th of *May* tells us, that he is very sensible that the *Patrons* of the *Stage* may start several *plausible Objections* against the *Bill* now depending, for its *Regulation*, and may represent it as an *Infringement* on *British Liberty*. I should be glad if this Gentleman, who is so well acquainted with *plausible Objections*, and *modest Representations*, would be so good as to explain to us, how any *Act* of *Parliament* can be an *Infringement* on *British Liberty*; for as I take it, the Excellence of the *British Constitution* is, that the *Representations* of the *People* have a Power of *framing* and *passing Laws* for restraining the *Prejudice* of such Things by *Individuals*, as would be prejudicial to the *Society*; and I conceive, that when this *Power* is exerted to prevent the *Depravation* of People's *Morals*, it can be no more said to be an *Infringement* on the *British Liberty*, than when it is used to *secure* their *Property*: And on these Principles I conclude that a *Bill* for ordaining an *Act* made in the 12th Year of the late *Queen*, is in its Nature as just and reasonable, as the *Laws* against *Gipsies, Fortune-tellers,* or *Deer-stealers*; all of whom sought to make themselves *rich* and *merry*, at the *Cost* of *unwary People*.

THE same Gentlemen, I mean those at the Head of the Opposition, have, on this Occasion, been pleased to Trumpet aloud, that whatever the *Fate* of the *Bill* may be, they have *triumphed* in Point of *Argument*; and that whatever *Power* the *Friends* of the *Administration* may have in *Voting*, the *Power* of *Reasoning* is not *with them*; in respect of which I will venture to affirm, that they are much *mistaken,* and that the *Reason* of the *Thing* is very clearly with the *Friends* of the *Bill*; and this I will not only *say* but *prove,* to the Satisfaction of every *disinterested Man,* tho' I despair of doing it to the *Satisfaction* of the *Malcontents,* who are resolved to be *satisfied* with *nothing* while they are *out,* and who, I am afraid, would give us small Cause to be *satisfied* with *any thing* if they were *in.* But not to follow the Fashion of those great *Writers* with whom I contend, which is first to start *Points* of *Importance,* and then to run off to personal *Altercations,* and a *gibing* kind of *Satire,* quite beside the *Point*: I will keep close to my Subject, and in order to treat it as methodically as I can, I will *first* answer the principal *Objections* which these Gentlemen have *raised*; I will next give a *short History* of the *Regulations* which have from time to time been made, in regard to the *Stage*; and, lastly, I will *propose* the *Reasons* which support the intended *Regulation,* and shew, that they are so far from being *slight* or *superficial,* that they are very *cogent* and *substantial,* perfectly agreeable to the Nature of our *Constitution,* and not at all injurious to any *Body* of *Men* whatsoever.

WITH regard to *Objections,* the Principal are *these*; that as the great End of *Dramatick Entertainments* is to expose *Vice* and *Folly,* and especially the *Vices* and *Follies* of People in *high Life,* the proposed Restriction would entirely destroy that *End,* and in consequence thereof, would be an *Encouragement* to *publick Vice,* and discountenance *publick Virtue*: That it is directly contrary to the Practice of *Greece* and *Rome,* and also the *Customs* of our *Ancestors*; that the *Licentiousness* of *two* or *three* Poets, ought not to induct any Restraint of the Stage in *general,* because that would be punishing the *Innocent* instead of the *Guilty*; that it is contrary to *Law,* to abolish *Patents* which have been declared *Legal,* or to convert them into *Temporary Licences,* during Pleasure, and that any new *Restriction* is *needless,* because the Lord Chamberlain had a very *large Power* heretofore, which hath been *exerted* more than *once.*

As to the *First Objection,* which is infinitely the *strongest,* I conceive it may be very easily answered, because the Force of it consists in begging the *Question.* It is to be *supposed,* that a *Lord Chamberlain* will License no *Plays,* but such as encourage *publick Vice,* and discourage *publick Virtue,* otherwise the *Objection* has nothing to do with the Bill, and that the present or any future Lord Chamberlain will Licence *any* such *Plays,* much more *Licence none* but *such,* is, what, I think, cannot be *supposed,* without doing Violence to *common Sense* and *Reason,* as it evidently does Violence to the *present Bill,* which is so far from being favourable to such Plays, that the very *Intent* of *vesting* such *Power* in the *Lord Chamberlain* by *Act* of *Parliament,* is to prevent the exhibiting of such *Plays* to the People, and thereby corrupting their *Morals* as well as turning their *Heads*; and I appeal to every sober *Housekeeper* in *London* and *Westminster,* for the *Truth* of this Proposition, *That the present* Spirit of Tumult, Contempt *of* Laws, Sacred *and* Civil, *and that* Proneness *to* sensual Pleasures, which deform the Manners *of the* present Age, *could ever have taken Place, but from the* Licentiousness *of the* Stage *for many Years past.*

As to the *Second Objection,* That the Restriction proposed is contrary to the *Practice* of *Greece* and *Rome,* I say that it is false, and will undertake to prove it, when I come to the *History* of the *Stage*. A Writer in the Paper called *Common Sense*, mentions *Aristophanes*, and plumes himself mightily on the *Liberties* taken by that *Writer*; and, in general, by the Old *Comedy* amongst the *Athenians*. I cannot help thinking, that if this *Gentleman* had considered what he was saying attentively, and had reflected that possibly some of his *Readers* might be acquainted with the *Greek History* as well as himself, he would not have insisted so much on this *Head*. There are *two* Instances in the *Athenian History*, of the Liberties taken by *Comick* Writers, of representing great *Characters* upon the *Stage*, and attacking such *Men* personally as were eminent in the *State*; the *first without* and the *latter with Success*. When *Pericles* was at the Head of the *Athenian Councils*, which, by the Way, was when the *People* of *Athens* were the most considerable in *Greece*, as the *Greeks* were the most *considerable People* in the *known World*, the *Comick Writers* treated him not only with the utmost *Freedom*, but with the utmost Rudeness. They upbraided him with the *Shape* of his *Head*; They reviled him for his *great Eloquence*, and they called that *Authority* which he had acquired by his vast *Capacity*, and which he managed, as *Thucydides* tells us, with great *Integrity*, as a *Tyranny* equal to that of *Pisistratus*. Nor did their *Rage* stop there; they *libelled* the whole *Family* of *Pericles;* they attacked his *Wife,* his *Son*, his *Servants*, and, in short, every Body that had any Thing to do with him. And why? Because they were themselves the *Creatures* of an *Opposition,* always *maligning*, always *defeated* by him; tho' they attained Strength enough to *ruin* the *State* after he was *dead*. Such was the Behaviour of the *Comick Poets* towards *Pericles*. Let us now consider the second Instance. *Aristophanes* and his *Companions* attacked *Socrates*, the *best Man* in the Age he lived I and perhaps the best Man of any *Age*, unbless'd with *Divine Revelation*. They attacked him as an *Enemy* to *Religion*: But what *Religion*? The *Religion* of the *Common People* of *Athens,* a *Composition* of the *vilest* and *grossest* Superstitions that ever were *invented* or *believed*. *Aristophanes* particularly represented him as a *Worshipper* of the *Clouds*, which was the *Title* he gave his *Comedy*; and by the Opinions he therein attributes to Socrates, he makes him a mere *Atheist*, a most *immoral Man*, a mere *Dealer* in *Words*, a *Deceiver* of the *People*, a *Corrupter* of *Youth*, and an *Enemy* to *Mankind*: Every *Circumstance* of which was diametrically opposite to his true *Character*: And, with all due Deference to *Antiquity*, this *Play* is as virulent and as outrageous a *Libel* as ever was written; tho' it must be allowed that there is a great deal of *Humour* and *Wit* in it. But what were its Consequences? Why the unthinking *Man*, the easy wrought on *Herd*, swallowed all the *Poet* said, and cherished this *Rancour* in their Hearts, till by a *Conspiracy* of *Sophists* and *Poetasters*, the *best Man* and the *noblest Patriot* in *Athens*, was talk'd to *Death*; to the everlasting *Infamy* of that *People*, and to the *eternal Scandal* of those *base Men*, whose Envy and Malice made them *Instruments* in so *foul* a *Deed*; which they lived to see justly *punished* in *themselves*, the *Athenians*, when they came to their *Senses*, refusing to give them the *Necessaries* of *Life*, to fetch *Fire*, or *light* a *Candle* in their *Houses*. These are the *glorious Precedents* for *Licentious Comedy*.

THE *Third Objection* arises from a supposed *Want* of *Equity*, in restraining the *Stage* for the Offences of *two* or *three Poets*. Well then, it is admitted that *two* or *three Poets* have *Offended*, which is a Point I beg these *Gentlemen* will not *retract*. But is it not better to point out the *Danger* of *Offending* to these *Poets* and their *Brethren*, or to put it out of their *Power* to *Offend*, than to *punish* them for *Offences* which, I warrant you, they will say were unwarily committed? Besides, there are no *Penalties* laid on the *Wits*, it is the *Actors* only who are *Restrained*; and while *Libels* may be *Written, Sung*, and *Said*, nay, *Printed* and *Published* too, with tolerable *Impunity*; surely the taking Care that the King's *Own Servants*, for such only, as the *Law* stands, ought to be permitted as *Players*, should not be permitted as *Players* to revile his *Administration*, or excite his *People* to *Disobedience*, might pass for a necessary *Precaution*. If the other Method had been *taken*, if the *Authors* of these *Seditious Plays* and the *Actors* of them, had been *prosecuted* and *punished*, then the *Cruelty* of the *Ministry*, and the *Expediency* of this *Method* now taken, would have been most pathetically display'd in the *Craftsman*. *Laws* for the *Punishment of Crimes* never committed, have ever been esteemed *harsh* and *injurious*; Laws for Repressing *Licentiousness*, when its ill Effects have been *felt*, have been hitherto looked on as highly *just*, and as strong Instances of *Gentleness* and *Moderation*. How the present Case comes to operate so strongly, as to change the ordinary *Notions* of *Right* and *Wrong*, is what I would be glad to learn from any of our *Playhouse Patriots*, or the *Wits* in their *Service*. And, I hope, they will excuse me, if, till I am better *informed*, I think the *Objection* before stated, very *trifling*, or rather nothing at all to the *Purpose*.

THE *Fourth Objection* is of such a *Nature* that One can scare mention it without a *Smile*. These *Gentlemen*, who every Day make free with the *Royal Character*, are all of a sudden in a *Pannick*, lest any Injustice should be done to those who act under the *Royal Patents*. But is it not strange, that those who are concerned in *Point* of *Interest*, should not have found this out as well as they? Or would it not exercise the *Talents* of one of these *Patrons* of the *Stage*, to draw up a Petition in favour of all the *Patentees*, setting forth the Hardships they shall lye under, if they may not *skreen* themselves by the *Royal Authority*, for representing Plays which *reflect* thereon?

THE *last Objection* is, That the Lord *Chamberlain* exercised this *Authority before*, and therefore it is preposterous to *grant* it him now. But if he executed it *legally* before, what *Sort* of *People* were those who clamour'd so loudly against it? And if he has not a *legal Power* of hindering the *Representations* of *Seditious* and *Immoral Plays*, what Sort of People are *those* who oppose its being given him? Surely no other than the Enemies to the *Present Government*, under which we enjoy *Liberty* and *Property*, in safer and more ample Proportion, than ever it was *enjoyed* by our *Ancestors*.

Yours, &c.

R. F.

Wednesday, June 8. 1737

IT is surprising, the Clamour that is raised against the *Bill for restraining the Licentiousness of the Stage*; when there is not one sober, impartial Man, but must see and acknowledge, that the *Personal* Abuse of *Majesty* itself, as well as the encouraging and promoting all manner of Vice and Immorality, is carried to such a Length, that if some speedy and effectual Stop be not put to such daring Licentiousness, we can expect nothing less, than to fall a Sacrifice to *Those*, who lie in wait to destroy us.

IT would be in vain to go about to conceal the almost irreparable Mischief this Licentiousness in *Writing* alone, has been the Occasion of; and should the same Licentiousness be suffered to be brought into common Practice upon the *Stage*, it is not only true, that the most upright and able Administration can never support itself; but it is equally certain and true, that the best Government, and the honestest and wisest Prince, that ever filled a Throne, must be reduced to the most imminent Danger; and it is well, if the most fatal Consequences do not follow from it.

IT is therefore become absolutely necessary for the *Legislature* to interpose, and no to suffer the same Licentiousness to be practised on the *Stage*, as is in the weekly and almost daily *Libels*.

THE most sacred Persons and Things may be represented, even by *writing*, in so ridiculous a Dress, as to create a very great Contempt and Prejudice in the Minds of the People; but when the same Persons and Things are ridiculed and reviled on the *Stage*, and ridiculous Representation of them is so much the more *lively* and *strong*, that it cannot fail, in a short course of Time, utterly to deface and root out of the Minds of Men all manner of Regard and Respect for those Persons and Things.

THIS is so self-evident, that it must be the greatest Stupidity or Impudence in any Man, to put the Licentiousness of the *Press* and the *Stage* upon the same foot; as if there were the same Reason to restrain the one, as the other; or, as if the Licentiousness of the *Press* could possibly be attended with the same fatal Consequences, as the Licentiousness of the *Stage*.

HAVING premised this in the general, let us examine a little more particularly what is advanced by the Writer of the last *Craftsman* on this Subject.

'THE chief Reason (says he) given for a Law for restraining the Liberty of the *Stage*, is the present Licentiousness of the *Stage*, and the Immorality of the People, which is imputed to it.'

He goes on. 'Now supposing the Fact to be true, I can see no Reason for any particular Interposition of the *Legislature* upon this account; all dramatick Writers and Players being already under the Cognizance of the Law, when they transgress their Bounds, and subject to Prosecution like other *Libellers*, or immoral Persons.'

IT is very true; 'all dramatick Writers and Players are subject to the same Prosecution as other *Libellers*.' But how fallaciously is this urged? He would insinuate to his Readers, what he cannot but know to be utterly false and impossible in Fact; that *Players* and *Libellers*, because they are under the

Cognizance of the Law, and subject to Prosecution, may, for that Reason, be restrained from transgressing their Bounds; or in other Words, That *Libelling*, whether by writing or acting on the *Stage*, may be prevented by Prosecution at Law.

HAVE we not seen Prosecutions at Law brought against Libellers in *writing*, and is not Libelling in that Way practised, at this Time, if it be possible, in ten Times a greater Degree than ever? And is not this a demonstrative Proof, that it is impossible to put a Stop to this Evil by any Prosecutions at Law? And I defy this Writer to shew, that all Prosecutions at Law against Libelling on the *Stage*, will not be *evaded* by the very same Arts. And can he see no Reason then for any particular Interposition of the Legislature upon this Account?

'BUT the Case (says he, speaking of the Reasons given for restraining the Licentiousness of the *Stage*) is directly the Reverse; for the Immorality of the People is so far from being owing to the Licentiousness of the *Stage*, that the Licentiousness of the *Stage* is immediately owing to the Immorality of the People.'

THIS, I confess, is a pretty jingle of Words; but does not in the least overthrow the Reason given for restraining the Licentiousness of the *Stage*; that it is *one* Cause of the Immorality of the People; or, that the Licentiousness of the *Stage* has a very powerful influence to encrease the Immorality of the People.

WHO was ever so absurd, as he would insinuate, as to assert, that the Immorality of the People, was *wholly* or immediately owing to the Licentiousness of the *Stage*? NO, all that is contended for is, that the People are made much more immoral, and that Immorality spreads itself much wider. By reason of the Licentiousness of the *Stage*.

'THE Licentiousness of the *Stage* is undoubtedly owing to the Immorality of the people.' But to argue from thence, 'That the Immorality of the People is not in a *great* Degree owing to the Licentiousness of the *Stage*;' is egregiously stupid or trifling. The People might, and most certainly would be immoral, were the *Stage* utterly abolished; but by the Licentiousness of the *Stage*, they are made much more immoral, than they would be if no *Players* were allowed.

THIS Writer considers, in the next Place, the Effect which a law for laying a Restraint on the Licentiousness of the *Stage*, must have upon Liberty in general.

'THE Bounds, *says he*, of Liberty and Licentiousness are so extremely nice, that it is very difficult to distinguish exactly between them; But it is certain, that there can be *no* Liberty, where there is *no* Room for extending it too far.'

IF this were apply'd to the Liberty of the *Press* only, I acknowledge it to be very true. You must allow an *absolute* uncontroulable Liberty of *Writing*, or *all* Liberty of *Writing* must be annull'd and taken away. There is no possible *Medium*.

IF a Liberty of *Writing* against a *bad* Prince, or a *bad* Administration be allow'd of, the *same* Liberty must, of Necessity, be allow'd against the *best* Administration, and the *best* of Princes. And the Reason is very plain; because, if a *good* Prince, and a *good* Administration, will make themselves the *absolute* Judges of what is fit and proper to be publish'd in *Writing*, the *worst* of Princes, or Administrations, have the *same* Right of exercising the *same* Privilege or Power; and, consequently, the Liberty of *Writing* must be wholly taken away.

BUT, for Goodness sake, what has this to do with the Licentiousness of the *Stage*? Or does it follow, That, 'Because there can be *no* Liberty, where there is *no* Room left for extending it too far;' therefore there can be *no* Liberty, where there is not *Room* left of *extending* it to the Overthrow of all *good* Government, as well as *bad*.

IS it not excellent Reasoning, That because *some* Room ought to be left of extending Liberty too far, in *one* Instance; therefore *all* the Room ought to be left, and in *all* Instances, that the most inveterate and determin'd Enemies to the Government can contrive and invent?

IS it impossible, that Licentiousness should be carry'd to such a Heighth, and in so *many* Instances, as to make it absolutely necessary to restrain, and put a Stop to it in *some* Instances? Or, because Licentiousness ought to be suffered, or connived at, in *some* Instances, ought it therefore to be tolerated in *every* Instance, that any Man can devise? Surely, no Man in his Senses can assert this.

AND yet, as absurd and monstrous as this is, this is the Scheme this Writer builds upon. In his Way of Reasoning, if the Liberty of the *Press* ought to be allowed, so likewise ought the Liberty of the *Stage*. Or, if you put the Liberty of the *Stage* under any Restraint, therefore it is equally justifiable to subject the Liberty of the *Press to the* same *Restraint*; tho' there is not the *Connexion* between, or any just *Consequence* that can be drawn, from allowing the Liberty of the *Press*, to allowing the Liberty of the *Stage*.

THE Truth is, in whatever *Instances* Liberty be allowed, *no* Restraint ought or can be laid on that Liberty without destroying it.

IF the Liberty of the *Press* has, in the *worst* and most dangerous Times, been found *sufficient* to make the People, in general, sensible of the Evils that threaten'd them, and to excite them to unite as one Man to defend and protect their Liberties: What possible Reason can be assign'd, or imagin'd, that the *same* Liberty should not be *sufficient* at *all* Times, to protect them from the like Dangers?

IF, because Licentiousness in *Writing* ought to be suffered, therefore Licentiousness in *all* other Instances has an equal Right to be tolerated, no Government can support itself. There must be a Power in the Legislature to determine in *what* Instances Licentiousness shall be suffered; or the certain Consequence will be Anarchy and Confusion.

HAD those who oppose the Men in Power, turned their Ridicule against *Things* alone, and not against *Persons*; Had they only ridiculed or exposed *Male-Administration*, I need not tell this Writer, that there had been no Occasion for the Legislature to interpose in restraining the Licentiousness of the *Stage*.

HOWEVER, I cannot blame him for being under a *Panick*, lest *Modern Patriotism* should be turn'd into Ridicule on the *Stage*. But as to this too he may make himself perfectly easy: For to speak the Truth, the *Patriotism* of *these* Days is so exceedingly ridiculous in itself, that it is *below* all Ridicule.

FOR can any Thing be more *ridiculous*, than to hear Men *declaiming* against the Power of the *Crown*, for not other Reason but because they are not *employ'd* by the *Crown*?

THIS is the *Whole* of *Modern Patriotism*. And could any Thing make it *more* ridiculous, it must be to hear a celebrated *Writer* and *Patriot* bemoaning himself and his Country; 'That by the present Bill for restraining the Licentiousness of the *Stage*, all the Indulgence will be shewn to *One* Side, and none to the *Other*: That *Players* will be licens'd to flatter the *Men* in Power, and to *laugh* at those who *oppose* them: And, That Patriotism, – *Poor expiring Patriotism!* – will be turn'd into *Ridicule*.'

Appendix D

Lord Chesterfield's Address to Parliament Against the Proposed Licensing Act

My Lords,

THE Bill now before you I apprehend to be of a very extraordinary, a very dangerous Nature. It seems designed not only as a Restraint on the Licentiousness of the Stage, but it will prove a most arbitrary Restraint on the Liberty of the Stage; and, I fear, it looks yet farther, I fear, it tends towards a Restraint on the Liberty of the Press, which will be along Stride towards the Destruction of Liberty itself. It is not only a Bill, my Lords, of a very extraordinary Nature, but it has been brought in at a very extraordinary Season, and pushed with most extraordinary Dispatch. When I consider how near it was to the End of the Session, and how long this Session had been protracted beyond the usual Time of the Year; when I considered that this Bill passed through the other House with so much Precipitancy, as even to get the Start of a Bill which deserved all the Respect, and all the Dispatch, the Forms of either House of Parliament could of, it set me upon inquiring, what could be the reason for introducing this Bill at so unseasonable a time, and pressing it forward in a manner so very singular and uncommon. I have made all possible Inquiry, and as yet, I must confess, I am at a loss to find out the great Occasion. I have, it is true, learned from common Report without Doors, that a most seditious, a most heinous Farce had been offered to one of the Theatres, a Farce for which the Authors ought to be punished in the most exemplary Manner: But what was the Consequence? The Master of that Theatre behaved as he was in Duty bound, and as common Prudence directed: He not only refused to bring it upon the Stage, but carried it to a certain honourable Gentleman in the Administration, as the surest Method of having it absolutely suppressed. Could this be the Occasion of introducing such an extraordinary Bill, at such an extraordinary Season, and pushing it in so extraordinary a Manner? Surely no; – The dutiful Behaviour of the Players, the prudent Caution they shewed upon that Occasion, can never be a Reason for subjecting them to such an arbitrary Restraint: It is an Argument in their Favour, and a material one, in my Opinion, against the Bill. Nay farther, if we consider all Circumstances, it is to me a full Proof that the Laws not in being are sufficient for punishing those Players who shall venture to bring any seditious Libel upon the Stage, and consequently sufficient for deterring all Players from acting any thing that may have the least Tendency toward giving a reasonable Offence.

I do not, my Lords, pretend to be a Lawyer, I do not pretend to know perfectly the Power and Extent of our Laws, but I have conversed with those that do, and by them I have been told, that our Laws are sufficient for punishing any Person that shall dare to represent upon the Stage what may appear, either by the Words or the Representation, to be blasphemous, seditious, or immoral. I must own, indeed, I have observed of late a remarkable Licentiousness in the Stage. There have but very lately been two Plays acted, which, one would have thought, should have given the greatest Offence, and yet both were suffered to be often represented without Disturbance, without Censure. In one, the Author thought fit to represent the three great Professions, Religion, Physick, and the Law, as inconsistent with Common Sense: In the other, a most tragical Story was brought upon the Stage, a Catastrophe too recent, too melancholy, and of too solemn a Nature, to be heard of any where but from the Pulpit. How these Pieces came to pass unpunished, I do not know: If I am rightly informed, it was not for want of Law, but for want of Prosecution, without which no Law can be made effectual: But if there was any neglect in this Case, I am convinced it was not with a Design to prepare the Minds of the People, and to make them think a new Law necessary.

Our Stage ought certainly, my Lords, to be kept within Bounds; but for this, our Laws as they stand at present are sufficient: If our Stage-players at any Time exceed those Bounds, they ought to be prosecuted, they may be punished: We have Precedents, we have Examples of Persons having been punished for Things less criminal than either of the two Pieces I have mentioned. A new Law must therefore be unnecessary, and in the present Case it cannot be unnecessary without being dangerous: Every unnecessary Restraint on Licentiousness is a Fetter upon the Legs, is a Shackle upon the Hands of Liberty. One of the greatest Blessings we enjoy, one of the greatest Blessings a People, my Lords, can enjoy, is Liberty; – but every Good in this Life has its Allay of Evil: – Licentiousness is the Allay of Liberty; it is an Ebullition, an Excrescence; – it is a Speck upon the Eye of the Political Body, which I can never touch but with a gentle, – with a trembling Hand, lest I destroy the Body, lest I injure the Eye upon which it is apt to appear. If the Stage becomes at any Time licentious; if a Play appears to be a Libel upon the Government, or upon any particular Man, the King's Courts are open, the Laws are sufficient for punishing the Offender; and in this Case the Person injured has a singular Advantage; he can be under no Difficulty to prove who is the Publisher; the Players themselves are the Publishers, and there can be no want of Evidence to convict them.

But, my Lords, suppose it true, that the Laws now in being are not sufficient for putting a Check to or preventing the licentiousness of the Stage; suppose it absolutely necessary some new Law should be made for that purpose; yet it must be granted that such a Law ought to be maturely considered, and every Clause, every Sentence, nay every Word of it well weighed and examined, lest under some of those Methods, presumed or pretended to be necessary for restraining licentiousness, a Power should lie concealed, which might be afterwards made Use of for giving a dangerous Wound to Liberty. Such a Law ought not to be introduced at the Close of a Session, nor ought we, in the passing of such a Law, to depart from any of the Forms prescribed by our Ancestors for preventing Deceit and Surprize. There is such a Connection between licentiousness and Liberty, that it is not easy to correct the one, without dangerously wounding the other: It is extremely hard to distinguish the true limit between them: like a changeable Silk, we can easily see there are two different Colours, but we cannot easily discover where the one ends, or where the other begins. – There can be no great or immediate Danger from the licentiousness of the Stage: I hope it will not be pretended that our Government may, before next Winter, be overturned by such licentiousness, even though our Stage were at present under no sort of legal Controul. Why then may we not delay till next Session passing any Law against the licentiousness of the Stage? Neither our Government can be altered, nor our Constitution overturned by such a Delay; but by passing a Law rashly and unadvisedly, our Constitution may at once be destroyed, and our Government rendered arbitrary. Can we then put a small, a short-lived inconvenience in the Ballance with perpetual Slavery? Can it be supposed that a Parliament of *Great Britain* will so much as risque the latter, for the sake of avoiding the former?

Surely, my Lords, this is not to be expected, were the licentiousness of the Stage much greater than it is, were the insufficiency of our Laws more obvious than can be pretended; but when we complain of the licentiousness of the Stage, and of the insufficiency of our Laws, I fear we have more Reason to complain of bad measures in our Polity, and a general Decay of Virtue and Morality among the People. In publick as well as private Life, the only way to prevent being ridiculed or censured, is to avoid all ridiculous or wicked Measures, and to pursue such only as are virtuous and worthy. The People never endeavour to ridicule those they love and esteem, nor will they suffer them to be ridiculed: If any one attempts it, the Ridicule returns upon the Author he makes himself only the Object of publick Hatred and Contempt. The Actions or Behaviour of a private Man may pass unobserved, and consequently unapplauded, uncensured; but the Actions of those in high Stations, can neither pass without Notice, nor without censure or Applause; and therefore an Administration without Esteem, without Authority among the People, let their Power be never so great, let their Power be never so arbitrary, they will be ridiculed: The severest Edicts, the most terrible Punishments, cannot entirely prevent it. If any man therefore thinks he has been censured; if any Man thinks he has been ridiculed upon any of our publick Theatres, let him examine his Actions he will find the Cause, let him alter his Conduct he will find a Remedy. As no Man is perfect, as no Man is infallible, the greatest may err, the most circumspect may be guilty of some piece of ridiculous Behaviour. It is not Licentiousness, it is an useful Liberty always indulged the Stage in a free Country, that some great Men may there meet with a just Reproof, which none of their Friends will be free enough or rather faithful enough to give them. Of this we have a famous instance in the *Roman* History. The great *Pompey*, after the many Victories he had obtained, and the great Conquests he had made, had certainly a good Title to the Esteem of the People of *Rome*; yet that great Man, by some Error in his Conduct, became an Object of general Dislike; and therefore, in the Representation of an old Play, when *Diphilus*, the Actor, came to repeat these

Words, *Nostra Miseria tu es Magnus*, the Audience immediately applied them to *Pompey*, who at that time was as well known by the Name *Magnus*, as by the name *Pompey*; and were so highly pleased with the Satyr, that, as *Cicero* says, they made the Actor repeat the Words an hundred times over: An Account of this was immediately sent to *Pompey*, who, instead of resenting it as an Injury, was so wise as to take it for a just Reproof: he examined his Conduct, he altered his Measures, he regained by degrees the Esteem of the People, and then he neither feared the Wit, nor felt the Satyr of the Stage. This is an Example which ought to be followed by great Men in all Countries. Such Accidents will often happen in every free Country, and many such would probably have afterwards happened at *Rome*, if they had continued to enjoy their Liberty in the Stage, came soon after, I suppose, to be called Licentiousness; for we are told that *Augustus*, after having established his Empire, restored Order in *Rome* by restraining Licentiousness. God forbid! We should in this Country have Order restored, or Licentiousness restrained, at so dear a Rate as the People of *Rome* paid for it to *Augustus*.

In the Case I have mentioned, my Lords, it was not the Poet that wrote, for it was an old Play, nor the Players that acted, for they only repeated the Words of the Play; it was the People who pointed the Satyr; and the Case will always be the same: When a Man has the Misfortune to incur the Hatred or Contempt of the People, when public Measures are despised, the Audience will apply what never was, what could not be designed as a Satyr on the present Times. Nay, even tho' the People should not apply, those who are conscious of Guilt, those who are conscious of the Wickedness, or the Weakness of their own Conduct, will take to themselves what the Author never designed. A public Thief is as apt to take the Satyr as he is apt to take the Money, which was never designed for him. We have an Instance of this in the Case of a famous Comedian of the last Age; a Comedian who was not only a good Poet, but an honest Man, and a quiet and good Subject. The famous *Moliere*, when he wrote his *Tartuffe*, which is certainly an excellent and a good moral Comedy, did not design to satirize any great Man of that Age; yet a great Man in *France* at that Time took it to himself, and fancied the Author had taken him as a Model for one of the principal and one of the worst Characters in that Comedy: by good Luck he was not the Licenser, otherwise the Kingdom of *France* had never had the Pleasure, the Happiness, I may say, of seeing that Play acted; but when the Players first proposed to act it at *Paris*, he had Interest enough to get it forbid. *Moliere*, who knew himself Innocent of what was laid to his Charge, complained to his Patron the Prince of *Conti*, that as his Play was designed only to expose Hypocrisy, and a false Pretence to Religion, it was very hard it should be forbid being acted, when at the same Time they were suffered to expose Religion itself every Night publicly upon the *Italian* Stage: To which the Prince wittily answered, *'Tis true,* Moliere, *Harlequin ridicules Heaven, and exposes Religion; but you have done much worse – you have ridiculed the first Minister of Religion.*

I am as much for restraining the Licentiousness of the Stage, and every other fort of Licentiousness, as any of Lordships can be; but, my Lords, I am, I shall always be extremely cautious and fearful of making the least Encroachment upon

Liberty; and therefore, when a new Law is proposed against Licentiousness, I shall always be for considering it deliberately and maturely, before I venture to give my Consent to its being passed. This is a sufficient Reason for my being against passing this Bill at so unseasonable a Time, and in so extraordinary a Manner; but I have my Reasons for being against the Bill itself, some of which I shall beg leave to explain to your Lordships. The Bill, my Lords, at first view, may seem to be designed only against the Stage, but to me it plainly appears to point somewhere else. It is an Arrow that does but glance upon the Stage, the mortal Wound seems designed against the Liberty of the Press. By this Bill you prevent a Play's being acted, but you do not prevent its being printed; therefore, if a License should be refused for its being acted, we may depend on it the Play will be printed. It will be printed and published, my Lords, with the refusal in capital Letters on the Title Page. People are always fond of what is forbidden. *Libri prohibiti* are in all Countries diligently and generally sought after. It will be much easier to procure a Refusal, than it ever was to procure a good House, or a good Sale: Therefore we may expect, that Plays will be wrote on purpose to have a Refusal: This will certainly procure a good Sale: Thus will Satyrs be spread and dispersed through the whole Nation, and thus every Man in the Kingdom may and probably will, read for Sixpence, what a few only could have seen acted, and that not under the expence of half a Crown. We shall then be told, What! Will you allow an infamous Libel to be printed and dispersed, which you would not allow to be acted? You have agreed to a Law for preventing its being acted, can you refuse your Assent to a Law for preventing its being printed and published? I should really, my Lords, be glad to hear what Excuse, what Reason one could give for being against the latter, after having agreed to the former; for, I protest I cannot suggest to myself the least Shadow of an excuse. If we agree to the Bill now before us, we must perhaps next Session, agree to a Bill for preventing any Play's being printed without a Licence. Then Satyrs will be wrote by way of Novels, secret Histories, Dialogues, or under some such Title; and thereupon we shall be told, What! Will you allow an infamous Libel to be printed and dispersed, only because it does not bear the Title of a Play? Thus, my Lords, from the Precedent now before us, we shall be induced, nay we can find no Reason for refusing to lay the Press under a general Licence, and then we may bid adieu to the Liberties of *Great Britain.*

But suppose, my Lords, it were necessary to make a new Law for restraining the Licentiousness of the Stage, which I am very far from granting, yet I shall never be for establishing such Power as is proposed by this Bill. If Poets and Players are to be restrained, let them be restrained as other Subjects are, by the known Laws of their Country; if they offend, let them be tried as every *Englishman* ought to be, by God and their Country. Do not let us subject them to the arbitrary Will and Pleasure of any one Man. A Power lodged in the Hands of one single Man, to judge and determine, without any Limination, without any Controul or Appeal, is a sort of Power unknown to our Laws, inconsistent with our Constitution. It is a higher, a more absolute Power than we trust even to the King himself; and therefore I must think, we ought not to vest any such Power in his Majesty's Lord Chamberlain. When I say this, I am sure I do not mean to give the least, the most distant Offence to the noble Duke who now fills the Post of Lord Chamberlain: His natural Candour and love of Justice, would not, I know, permit him to exercise any Power but with the strictest regard to the Rules of Justice and Humanity. Were we sure his Successors in that high Office would always be Persons of such distinguished Merit, even the Power to be establish'd by this Bill could give me no farther Alarm, than lest it should be made a Precedent for introducing other new Powers of the same Nature. This, indeed, is an Alarm which cannot be avoided, which cannot be prevented by any Hope, by any Consideration; it is an Alarm which, I think, every Man must take, who has a due Regard to the Constitution and Liberties of his Country.

I shall admit, my Lords, that the Stage ought not upon any Occasion to meddle with Politics, and for this very Reason, among the rest, I am against the Bill now before us: This Bill will be so far from preventing the Stage's meddling with Politics, that I fear it will be the Occasion of its meddling with nothing else; but then it will be a political Stage *ex parte*. It will be made subservient to the Politics and Schemes of the Court only. The Licentiousness of the Stage will be encouraged instead of being restrained; but, like Court-journalists, it will be licentious only against the Patrons of Liberty, and the Protectors of the People. Whatever Man, whatever Party opposes the Court in any of their most destructive Schemes, will, upon the Stage be represented in the most ridiculous Light the Hirelings of a Court can contrive. True Patriotism and Love of Public Good will be represented as Madness, or as a Cloak for Envy, Disappointment and Malice; while the most flagitious Crimes, the most extravagant Vices and Follies, if they are fashionable at Court, will be disguised and dressed up in the Habit of the most amiable Virtues. This has formerly been the Case: – In King *Charles* IId's Days the Play-house was under a Licence. What was the Consequence? – The Play-house retaled nothing but the Politics, the Vices, and the Follies of the Court: Not to expose them; no – but to recommend them; tho' it must be granted their Politics were often as bad as their Vices, and much more pernicious than their other Follies. 'Tis true, the Court had, at that Time, a great deal of Wit; it was then indeed full of Men of true Wit and great Humour; but it was the more dangerous; for the Courtiers did then, as thorough-paced Courtiers always will do, they sacrificed their Honour, by making their Wit and their Humour subservient to the Court only; and what made it still more dangerous, no Man could appear upon the Stage against them. We know that *Dryden*, the Poet Laureat of that Reign, always represents the Cavaliers as honest, brave, merry Fellows, and fine Gentlemen: Indeed his fine Gentleman, as he generally draws him, is an atheistical, lewd, abandoned Fellow, which was at that Time, it seems, the fashionable Character at Court. On the other Hand, he always represents the Dissenters as hypocritical, dissembling Rogues, or stupid senseless Boobies. – When the Court had a mind to fall out with the *Dutch*, he wrote his *Amboyna*, in which he represents the *Dutch* as a Pack of avaritious, cruel, ungrateful Rascals. – And when the Exclusion Bill was moved in Parliament, he wrote his *Duke of Guise*, in which those who were for preserving the Religion of their Country, were exposed under the Character of the Duke of *Guise* and his Party, who leagued together, for excluding *Henry* IV. Of

France from the Throne, on account of his Religion. – The City of *London* too, was made to feel the partial and mercenary Licentiousness of the Stage at that Time; for the Citizens having at that Time, as well as now, a great deal of Property, they had a mind to preserve that Property, and therefore they opposed some of the arbitrary Measures which were then begun, but pursued more openly in the following Reign; for which Reason they were then always represented upon the Stage, as a Parcel of designing Knaves, dissembling Hypocrites, griping Usurers, and – Cuckolds into the Bargain.

My Lords, the proper Business of the Stage, and that for which only it is useful, is to expose those Vices and Follies, which the Laws cannot lay hold of, and to recommend those Beauties and Virtues, which Ministers and Courtiers seldom either imitate or reward; but by laying it under a Licence, and under an arbitrary Court-licence too, you will, in my Opinion, intirely pervert its Use; for tho' I have the greatest Esteem for that noble Duke, in whose Hands this Power is at present designed to fall, tho' I have an intire Confidence in his Judgment and Impartiality; yet I may suppose that a leaning towards the Fashions of a Court is sometimes hard to be avoided. – It may be very difficult to make one who is every Day at Court believe that to be a Vice or Folly, which he sees daily practised by those he loves and esteems. – By Custom even Deformity itself becomes familiar, and at last agreeable. – To such a Person, let his natural Impartiality be never so great, that may appear a Libel against the Court, which is only a most just and a most necessary Satyr upon the fashionable Vices and Follies of the Court. Courtiers, my Lords, are too polite to reprove one another; the only Place where they can meet with any just Reproof, is a free, tho' not a licentious Stage; and as every Sort of Vice and Folly, generally in all Countries, begins at Court, and from thence spreads thro' the Country, by laying the Stage under an arbitrary Court-licence, instead of leaving it what it is, and always ought to be, a gentle Scourge for the Vices of Great Men and Courtiers, you will make it a Canal for propagating and conveying their Vices and Follies thro' the whole Kingdom.

From hence, my Lords, I think it must appear, that the Bill now before us cannot so properly be called a Bill for restraining the Licentiousness, as it may be called a Bill for restraining the Liberty of the Stage, and for restraining it too in that Branch which in all Countries has been the most useful; therefore I must look upon the Bill as a most dangerous Encroachment upon Liberty in general. Nay farther, my Lords, it is not only an Encroachment on Property. With, my Lords, is a Sort of Property: It is the Property of those that have it, and too often the only Property they have to depend on. It is, indeed, but a precarious Dependance. Thank God! We – my Lords, have a Dependance of another Kind; we have a much less precarious Support, and therefore cannot feel the Inconveniencies of the Bill now before us; but it is our Duty to encourage and protect Wit, whosoever's Property it may be. Those gentlemen who have any such Property, are all, I hope, our Friends: Do not let us subject them to any unnecessary or arbitrary Restraint. I must own, I cannot easily agree to the laying of any tax upon Wit; but by this Bill it is to be heavily taxed, – it is to be excised; – for if this Bill passes, it cannot be retaled in a proper Way without a Permit; and the Lord Chamberlain is to have the

Honour of being chief Gauger, Supervisor, Commissioner, Judge and Jury: But what is still more hard, tho' the poor Author, the Proprietor I should say, cannot perhaps dine till he has found out and agreed with a Purchaser; yet before he can propose to seek for a Purchaser, he must patiently submit to have his Goods rummaged at this new Excise-office, where they may be detained for fourteen Days, and even then he may find them returned as prohibited Goods, by which his chief and best Market will be for ever shut against him; and that without any Cause, without the least Shadow of Reason, either from the Laws of his Country, or the Laws of the Stage.

These Hardships, this Hazard, which every Gentleman will be exposed to who writes any thing for the Stage, must certainly prevent every Man of a generous and free Spirit from attempting any thing in that way; and as the Stage has always been the proper Chanel for Wit and Humour, therefore, my Lords, when I speak against this Bill, I must think I plead the Cause of Wit, I plead the Cause of Humour, I plead the Cause of the *British* Stage, and of every Gentleman of Taste in the Kingdom: But it is not, my Lords, for the Sake of Wit only; even for the Sake of his Majesty's Lord Chamberlain, I must be against this Bill. The noble Duke who has now the Honour to execute that Office, has, I am sure, as little Inclination to disoblige as any Man; but if this Bill passes, he must disoblige, he may disoblige some of his most intimate Friends. It is impossible to write a Play, but some of the Characters, or some of the Satyr, may be interpreted so as to point at some Person or other, perhaps at some Person in an eminent Station: When it comes to be acted, the People will make the Application, and the Person against whom the Application is made, will think himself injured, and will, at least privately, resent it: At present this Resentment can be directed only against the Author; but when an Author's Play appears with my Lord Chamberlain's Passport, every such Resentment will be turned from the Author, and pointed directly against the Lord Chamberlain, who by his Stamp made the Piece current. What an unthankful Office are we therefore by this Bill to put upon his Majesty's Lord Chamberlain! an Office which can no way contribute to his Honour or Profit, and yet such a one as must necessarily gain him a great deal of ill will, and create him a number of Enemies.

The last Reason I shall trouble your Lordships with for my being against the Bill, is, that in my Opinion, it will no way answer the End proposed: I mean the End openly proposes, and, I am sure, the only End which your Lordships propose. To prevent the acting of a Play which has any Tendency to Blasphemy, Immorality, Sedition, or private Scandal, can signify nothing, unless you can likewise prevent its being printed and published. On the contrary, if you prevent its being acted, and admit of its being printed and published, you will propagate the Mischief: Your Prohibition will prove a Bellows which will blow up the Fire you intend to extinguish. This Bill can therefore be of no Use for preventing either the publick or the private Injury intended by such a Play; and consequently can be of no manner of Use, unless it can be designed as a Precedent, as a leading Step towards another, for subjecting the Press likewise to a Licenser. For such a wicked

Purpose it may, indeed, be of great Use; and in that Light, it may most properly be called a Step towards arbitrary Power.

Let us consider, my Lords, that arbitrary power has seldom or never been introduced into any country at once. It must be introduced by slow degrees, and as it were step by step, left the people should perceive its approach. The barriers and fences of the people's liberty must be plucked up one by one, and some plausible pretences must be found for removing or hood-winking, one after another, those sentries who are posted by the constitution of every free country, for warning the people of their danger. When these preparatory Steps are once made, the People may then, indeed, with Regret see Slavery and arbitrary Power making long Strides over their Land, but it will then be too late to think of preventing or avoiding the impending Ruin. The Stage, my Lords, and the Press, are two of our Out-sentries; if we remove then, – if we hood-wink them, – if we throw them in Fetters, – the Enemy may surprise us. Therefore I must look upon the Bill now before us as a Step, and a most necessary Step too, for introducing arbitrary Power into this Kingdom: It is a step so necessary, that, if ever any future ambitious King, or guilty Minister, should form to himself so wicked a Design, he will have Reason to thank us for having done so much of the Work to his Hand; but such Thanks, or Thanks from such a Man, I am convinced every one of your Lordships would blush to receive, – and scorn to deserve.

6 First Scroll of *The Licensing Act of 1737*, Parliamentary Archives, HL/PO/PU/1/1736/10G2n31

Appendix E

The Licensing Act of 1737

An Act to explain and amend so much of an Act made in the Twelfth Year of the Reign of Queen *Anne*, intituled, *An Act for reducing the Laws relating to Rogues, Vagabonds, sturdy Beggars, and Vagrants, into one Act of Parliament; and for the more effectual punishing such Rogues, Vagabonds, Sturdy Beggars, and Vagrants, and sending them whither they ought to be sent,* as relates to common Players of Interludes.

WHEREAS by an Act of Parliament made in the Twelfth Year of the Reign of Her late Majesty Queen *Anne*, intituled, *An Act for reducing the Laws relating to Rogues, Vagabonds, sturdy Beggars, and Vagrants, into one Act of Parliament; and for the more effectual punishing such Rogues, Vagabonds, Sturdy Beggars, and Vagrants, and sending them whither they ought to be sent*, it was enacted, That all Persons pretending themselves to be Patent Gatherers or Collectors for Prisons, Gaols, or Hospitals, and wandering abroad for that Purpose, all Fencers, Bearwards, common Players of Interludes, and other Persons therein named and expressed, shall be deemed Rogues and Vagabonds: And whereas some Doubts have arisen concerning so much of the said Act as relates to common Players of Interludes: Now for explaining and amending the same, be it declared and enacted by the King's most Excellent Majesty, by and with the Advice and Consent of the Lords Spiritual and Temporal, and Commons, in this present Parliament assembled, and by the Authority of the same, That from and after the Twenty fourth Day of June, One thousand seven hundred and thirty seven, every Person who shall, for Hire, Gain, or Reward, act, represent, or perform, or cause to be acted, represented, or performed, any Interlude, Tragedy, Comedy, Opera, Play, Farce, or other Entertainment of the Stage, or any Part or Parts therein, in case such Person shall not have any legal Settlement in the Place where the same shall be acted, represented, or performed, without Authority by virtue of Letters Patent from His Majesty, His Heirs, Successors, or Predecessors, or without Licence from the Lord Chamberlain of His Majesty's Houshold for the time being, shall be deemed to be a Rogue and a Vagabond within the Intent and Meaning of the said recited Act, and shall be liable and subject to all such Penalties and Punishments, and by such Methods of Conviction, as are inflicted on or appointed by the said Act for the Punishment of Rogues and Vagabonds who shall be found wandering, begging, and misordering themselves, within the Intent and Meaning of the said recited Act.

II. And be it further enacted by the Authority aforesaid, That if any person having or not having a legal Settlement as aforesaid shall, without such Authority or Licence as aforesaid, act, represent, or perform, or cause to be acted, represented, or performed, for Hire, Gain, or Reward, any Interlude, Tragedy, Comedy, Opera, Play, Farce, or other Entertainment of the Stage, or any Part or Parts therein, every such Person shall for every such Offence forfeit the Sum of Fifty Pounds; and in case the said Sum of Fifty Pounds shall be paid, levied, or recovered, such Offender shall not for the same Offence suffer any of the Pains or Penalties inflicted by the said recited Act.

III. And be it further enacted by the Authority aforesaid, That from and after the said Twenty fourth Day of June, One thousand seven hundred and thirty seven, no Person shall for Hire, Gain, or Reward, act, perform, represent, or cause to be acted, performed, or represented, any new Interlude, Tragedy, Comedy, Opera, Play, Farce, or other Entertainment of the Stage, or any Part or Parts therein; or any new Act, Scene, or other Part added to any old Interlude, Tragedy, Comedy, Opera, Play, Farce, or other Entertainment of the Stage, or any new Prologue, or Epilogue, unless a true Copy thereof be sent to the Lord Chamberlain of the King's Houshold for the time being fourteen Days at least before the acting, representing, or performing thereof, together with an Account of the Playhouse or other Place where the same shall be and the Time when the same is intended to be first acted, represented, or performed, signed by the Master or Manager, or one of the Masters or Managers of such Playhouse, or Place, or Company of Actors therein.

IV. And be it further enacted by the Authority aforesaid, That from and after the said Twenty fourth Day of June, One thousand seven hundred and thirty seven, it shall and may be lawful to and for the said Lord Chamberlain for the time being, from time to time, and when, and as often as he shall think fit, to prohibit the acting, performing, or representing, any Interlude, Tragedy, Comedy, Opera, Play, Farce, or other Entertainment of the Stage, or any Act, Scene, or Part thereof, or any Prologue or Epilogue; and in case any Person or Persons shall for Hire, Gain, or Reward, act, perform , or represent, or cause to be acted, performed, or represented, any new Interlude, Tragedy, Comedy, Opera, Play, Farce, or other Entertainment of the Stage, or any Act, Scene, or Part thereof, or any Prologue or Epilogue, before a Copy thereof shall be sent as aforesaid with such Account as aforesaid, or shall for Hire, Gain, or Reward, act, perform , or represent, or cause to be acted, performed, or represented, any Interlude, Tragedy, Comedy, Opera, Play, Farce, or other Entertainment of the Stage, or any Act, Scene, or Part thereof, or any Prologue or Epilogue, contrary to such Prohibition as aforesaid; every Person so offending shall for every such Offence forfeit the Sum of Fifty Pounds, and every Grant, Licence, and Authority (in case there be any such) by or under which the said Master or Masters or Manager or Managers set up, formed, or continued such Playhouse, or such Company of Actors, shall cease, determine, and become absolutely void to all Intents and Purposes whatsoever.

V. Provided always, That no Person or Persons shall be authorized by virtue of any Letters Patent from his Majesty, His Heirs, Successors or Predecessors, or by the Licence of the Lord Chamberlain of His Majesty's Houshold for the time being, to act, represent, or perform, for Hire, Gain, or Reward, any Interlude, Tragedy, Comedy, Opera, Play, Farce, or other Entertainment of the Stage, or any Part or Parts therein, in any Part of Great Britain, except in the City of

Westminster, and within the Liberties thereof, and in such Places where His Majesty, His Heirs, or Successors, shall in their Royal Persons reside, and during such Residence only; any thing in this Act contained to the contrary in any wise notwithstanding.

VI. And be it further enacted by the Authority aforesaid, That all the pecuniary Penalties inflicted by this Act for Offences committed within that Part of Great Britain called England, Wales, and the Town of Berwick upon Tweed, shall be recovered by Bill, Plaint, on Information, in any of His Majesty's Courts of Record at Westminster, in which no Essoign Protection or Wager of Law shall be allowed; and for Offences committed in that Part of Great Britain called Scotland, by Action or Summary Complaint before the Court of Session or Justiciary there; or for Offences committed in any Part of Great Britain, in a summary Way before Two Justices of the Peace for any County, Stewartry, Riding, Division, or Liberty, where any such Offence shall be committed, by the Oath or Oaths of One or more credible Witness or Witnesses, or by the Confession of the Offender, the same to be levied by Distress and Sale of the Offenders Goods and Chattels, tendering the Overplus to such Offender, if any there be above the Penalty and Charge of Distress; and for want of sufficient Distress the Offender shall be committed to any House of Correction in any such County, Stewartry, Riding, Division, or Liberty, for any Time not exceeding Six Months, there to be kept to hard Labour, or to the Common Gaol of any such County, Stewartry, Riding, Division, or Liberty, for any time not exceeding Six Months, there to remain without Bail or Mainprize; and if any Person or Persons shall think him, her, or themselves aggrieved by the Order or Orders of such Justices of the Peace, it shall and may be lawful for such Person or Persons to appeal therefrom to the next general Quarter Sessions to be held for the said County, Stewartry, Riding, Division, or Liberty, whose Order therein shall be final and conclusive; and the said Penalties for any Offence against this Act shall belong, one Moiety thereof to the Informer or Person suing or prosecuting for the same, the other Moiety to the Poor of the Parish where such offence shall be committed.

VII. And be it further enacted by the Authority aforesaid, That if any Interlude, Tragedy, Comedy, Opera, Play, Farce, or other Entertainment of the Stage, or any Act, Scene, or Part thereof, shall be acted, represented, or performed in any House or Place where Wine, Ale, Beer, or other Liquors shall be sold or retaled, the same shall be deemed to be acted, represented, and performed for Gain, Hire, or Reward.

VIII. And be it further enacted by the Authority aforesaid, That no Person shall be liable to be prosecuted for any Offence against this Act, unless such Prosecution shall be commenced within the Space of Six Kalendar Months after the Offence committed; and if any Action, or Suit, shall be commenced or brought against any Justice of the Peace or any other Person for doing, or causing to be done, any thing in pursuance of this Act, such Action or Suit shall be commenced within Six Kalendar Months next after the Fact done; and the Defendant or Defendants in such Action or Suit shall and may plead the General Issue, and give the special Matter in Evidence; and if upon such Action, or Suit, a Verdict shall be given for the Defendant or Defendants, or the Plaintiff or Plaintiffs or Prosecutor shall become nonsuit, or shall not prosecute his, or their said action, or Suit, then the Defendant or Defendants shall have treble Costs, and shall have the like Remedy for the same, as any Defendant or Defendants have in other Cases by Law.

THE
Hiftorical and Poetical Medley:
OR
MUSES LIBRARY;
BEING

A Choice and Faithful Collection of the beft
Antient Englifh Poetry, from the Times of
EDWARD the Confeffor, to the Reign of
King JAMES the Firft.

WITH

The Lives and Characters of the known Writers
taken from the moft Authentick Memoirs.

BEING

The moft valuable Collection of the Kind now
extant, affording Entertainment upon all Subjects
whatfoever.

Nec veniam Antiquis fed honorem & præmia pofci. Hor.

LONDON:
Printed for T. DAVIES, in *Duke's Court* over-againft St. *Martin's* Church, in St. *Martin's Lane.* 1738.

7   Title Page, *The Muses Library*, 1737, William R. Ready Division of
Archives and Research Collections, McMaster University

Appendix F

Elizabeth Cooper's Preface to
The Muses Library (1737)

THE Muses Library; Or a Series of *English* POETRY, FROM THE *SAXONS*, to the Reign of King *CHARLES* II.

CONTAINING,
The Lives and Characters of all the known Writers in that Interval, the Names of their Patrons; Complete Episodes, by way of Specimen of the larger Pieces, very near the intire Works of some, and large Quotations from others.
BEING
A General Collection of almost all the old valuable Poetry extant, now so industriously enquir'd after, tho' rarely to be found, but in the Studies of the Curious, and affording Entertainment on all Subjects, Philosophical, Historical, Moral, Satyrical, Allegorical, Critical, Heroick, Pastoral, Gallant, Amorous, Courtly, and Sublime,
BY
Langland, Chaucer, Lidgate, Occleve, Harding, Barclay, Fabian, *Skelton*, Howard, Early of Surrey, Sir T. Wyat, Dr. Bourd, Sackville, Earl of Dorset, Churchyard, *Higgens*, Warner, Gascoign, Turberville, Nash, Sir Philip Sidney, Grevill L. Brook, Spencer, Sir *John Harrington, Chalkhill, Fairfax, Sir John Davis, W. Raleigh, Sir Edw. Dyer, Daniel, &c.*

To the truly Honourable Society for the Encouragement of Learning.

My Lords and Gentlemen,

AS the illustrious Families of the *Howards, Sidneys, Sackvilles, Grevilles,* &c. have all an Interest in, and consequently should have a Respect for the Merit, and Fame of their most eminent Predecessors; 'tis morally impossible that a Work of this Nature shou'd want a Patron; yet I chuse rather to wave all private Applications, and address it to you: You have prov'd your selves ally'd to the Genius of those great Persons; their Descendants may be only Heirs to their Titles; and as you only have condescended to attempt the making a Provision for the *living* Learned, I may the more reasonably hope for your Assistance to preserve the Memories of the *Dead.*

Perhaps, there are but few single Names important enough to appear at the Head of so Elegant a List; and if, for want of Judgment, I should make a wrong Choice, the Absurdity would be too flagrant to be forgiven. But by inscribing it to you, I run no such Danger: The severest Critick in Manners must allow 'tis address'd with the greatest Propriety imaginable. –

To patronise a Series of *English Poetry*, is, I presume, a Part of your Scheme; for the Establishment of an Author's Fame, may be said to be the most effectual Provision for his Fortune, and, as I have more at large, observ'd in the Preface, what is attempted here in Favour of former Ages, may, by your Patronage, be made a Benefit to the Present, and reach to all Posterity.

But, beside the Obligations of Decorum, I feel my self bound in Gratitude, as an Author, tho' of the humblest Class, thus publickly to express my Sensibility of the Concern you have shewn for the Interest of Learning: Tho' I my self may have no Title to any Share of the Advantage. 'Tis a great, seasonable, and humane Design, and all who have Generosity, Benevolence, or Politeness, must applaud it. – It has a far more illustrious Origin than the Grand *Academy-Royal* at *Paris,* and, I hope, the Effects will be answerable; to the Increase of our own Honour, the Improvement of Science, and Service to the Nation in General.

I am, with the greatest Zeal, and Devotion,

My Lords and Gentlemen,
　　　　　　Your most Obedient,
　　　　　　　　Humble Servant,

E. COOPER.

THE PREFACE.

We are all apt to make our own Opinions, the Standard of Excellency, and I must plead guilty to my Share of this general Weakness: What has given my Pleasure in my Closet, I have undertaken to recommend to the Publick; not presuming to inform the Judgment, but only awaken the Attention; and rather endeavouring to preserve what is valuable of others, than advance any thing of my own. – The mere Hint of a good-natur'd, and not unuseful Design, is all the Merit I can pretend to. – 'Tis true I attempt to clear the Ground, and lay in the Materials, but leave the Building to be rais'd, and finish'd by more masterly Hands.

What is said of the Nightengale's singing with her Breast against a Thorn, may be justly apply'd to the Poets. – Their Harmony gives Pleasure to Others, but is compos'd with Pain to Themselves: And what is not to gratify a real Want, or fashionable Luxury, Few care to purchase: Thus Poetry has been, almost universally, a Drug, and its Authors have sacrific'd the Substance *of present Life to the* Shadow *of future Fame. Fame, Fame alone they have fondly fancy'd an Equivalent for all they wanted beside, and the World has often been so malicious, or careless, as even to defeat them of that imaginary Good. – I am told, Time and Ignorance have devour'd many important Names which even the universal Languages flatter'd with a sure Immortality: 'Tis no Wonder, therefore, that Ours, rude, and barbarous, as it formerly was, should be so little able to defend its Authors from such incroaching Enemies. – Those, who read the ensuing Volume with Attention, will be convinc'd that Sense, and Genius have been of long standing in this Island; and 'tis not so much the Fault of our Writers, as the Language it self, that they are not read with Pleasure at this Day. – This, naturally, provokes an Enquiry, whether 'tis in the same Vagrant Condition still; or whether the Fame of our most admir'd Moderns, is not almost as precarious, as that of their now obsolete Predecessors has prov'd to be; agreeable to that Line in the celebrated* Essay on Criticism.

And what now *Chaucer* is, shall *Dryden* be.

If this is the Case, as, according to my little knowledge, I think there is some Reason to fear, is it now high Time to think of some Expedient to cure this Evil; and secure the Poet in his Idol-Reputation however? I don't take upon me to say that Learning is of as much Importance here, as in France; *or that we shou'd be at the Trouble, and Expence of a Publick Academy for the Improvement of our Language; But, if any slight Essay can be made towards it, which, at a small Expence, may make a shift to supply that Defect, till a better Scheme shall be found, 'tis humbly hop'd that a moderate Encouragement will not be wanting.*

Such, to the best of my poor Ability, is now presented to the Publick, a Sort of Poetical Chronicle: *which begins with the first Dawnings of polite Literature in* England, *and is propos'd to be continu'd to the highest Perfection, it has hitherto attain'd; That, in Spite of Difficulties, and Discouragements, it may be hardly possible for us to recede into our first Barbarism; or again lose sight of the true*

Point of Excellence, which Poetry, beyond all other Sciences, makes its peculiar Glory to aim at.

Of what real Value polite Literature is to a Nation, is too sublime a Task for me to meddle with; I therefore chuse to refer my Readers to their own Experience, and the admirable Writings of Sir Philip Sidney*; Lord* Bacon*, Lord* Shaftsbury, *and innumerable other elegant Authors; the joint Sentiment of all the refin'd Spirits that ever had a Being, and the following excellent Rapture, in particular, of the ingenious Mr.* Daniel, *in his Poem call'd* Musophilus.

Perhaps the Words, thou scornest now,
May live, the speaking Picture of the Mind,
The Extract of the Soul, that labour'd, how
To leave the Image of herself behind;
Wherein Posterity, that love to know,
The just Proportion of our Spirits may find.

For these Lines are the Veins, the Arteries,
And undecaying Life-Strings of those Hearts
That still shall pant, and still shall exercise
The Motion, Spirit and Nature both imparts,
And shall, with those alive so sympathise,
As, nourisht with their Powers, injoy their parts.

O blessed Letters, that combine in One
All Ages past, and make One live with All:
By you, we doe confer with who are gone,
And the Dead-Living unto Council call:
By you, th'Unborne shall have Communion
Of what we feel, and what doth us befall.

Soul of the World! Knowledge! without thee,
What hath the Earth, that truly glorious is?
Why should our Pride make such a Stir to be,
To be forgot? What good is like to this,
To doe worthy the Writing, and to write
Worthy the Reading, and the World's Delight?

And afterwards, alluding to Stone-Henge *on* Salisbury *Plain.*

And whereto serves that wondrous *Trophy* now,
That on the goodly Plaine, near *Wilton* stands?
That huge, dump Heap, that cannot tell us how,
Nor what, nor whence it is, nor with whose Hands,
Nor for whose Glory, it was set to shew
How much our Pride mocks that of other Lands?

Whereon, when as the gazing Passenger
Hath greedy look't with Admiration,
And fain would know his Birth, and what he were,

How there erected, and how long agone:
Enquires, and asks his Fellow-Traveller,
What he hath heard, and his Opinion:
    And he knows nothing. Then he turns again,
And looks, and sighs, and then admires afresh,
And in himselfe, with Sorrow, doth complain
The Misery of dark Forgetfulness:
Angry with *Time* that nothing should remain,
Our greatest Wonder's Wonder to express!

But, to wave any farther Authorities, we need only look back to the Days of Langland, *the first* English *Poet we can meet with, who employ'd his Muse for the Refinement of Manners, and, in the Rudeness of his Lines, we plainly discover the Rudeness of the Age he wrote in. –* Chaucer, *not the next Writer, tho' the next extraordinary Genius, encountered the Follies of Mankind, as well as their Vices, and blended the acutest Raillery, with the most insinuating Humour. – By his Writings, it plainly appears that Poetry, and Politeness grew up together; and had like to have been bury'd in his Grave; For War, and Faction, immediately after restor'd Ignorance, and Dulness almost to their antient Authority. Writers there were; but Tast, Judgment, and Manner were lost: Their Works were cloudy as the Times they liv'd in, and, till* Barclay, *and* Skelton, *there was scarce a Hope that Knowledge would ever favour us with a second Dawn .– But soon after these, Lord* Surrey, *having tasted of the* Italian *Delicacy, naturaliz'd it here, gave us an Idea of refin'd Gallantry, and taught Love to polish us into Virtue.*
– Before this Impression was worn off, Lord Buckhurst *arose, and introduc'd the Charms of Allegory, and Fable, to allure Greatness, into a Love of Humanity, and make Power the Servant of Justice:* Spencer *made a Noble Use of so fine a Model, overflowing with Tenderness, Courtesy, and Benevolence, reconciling Magnificence and Decorum, Love and Fidelity; and, together with* Fairfax, *opening to us a new World of Ornament, Elegance, and Taste: After these Lord* Brook, *and Sir* John Davis *corrected the Luxuriancy of Fable, inrich'd our Understandings with the deepest Knowledge, and distinguish'd Use from Ostentation, Learning from Pedantry –* Donne, *and* Corbet *added Wit to Satire, and restor'd the almost forgotten Way of making Reproof it self entertaining;* Carew, *and* Waller *taught Panegyrick to be delicate, Passion to be courtly, and rode the* Pegasus *of Wit, with the Curb of good Manners;* D'Avenant *blended Address and Politeness with the severest Lessons of Temperance, and Morality; and the divine* Milton *reconcil'd the Graces of them all, and added a Strength, Solidity, and Majesty of his own, that None can equal, Few can imitate, and All admire.*
So many and variously-accomplish'd Minds were necessary to remove the Gothique *Rudeness that was handed down to us by our unpolish'd Fore-Fathers; and, I think, 'tis manifest all the Ornaments of Humanity, are owing to our Poetical Writers, if not our most shining Virtues. 'Tis not reasonable, therefore, that while the Work remains, the Artist should be forgot; and yet, 'tis certain, very*

Few of these great Men are generally known to the present Age: And tho' Chaucer *and* Spencer *are ever nam'd with much Respect, not many are intimately acquainted with their Beauties. – The Monumental Statues of the Dead have, in all Ages, and Nations, been esteem'd sacred; but the Writings of the Learned, of all others, deserve the highest Veneration; The Last bear the Resemblance of the Soul, the First only of the Body. The First are dumb, inanimate, and require the Historian to explain them; while the Last live, converse, reason, instruct, and afford to the Contemplative, one of their sincerest Pleasures. They are likewise to Authors, what Actions are to Heroes; In His Annals you must admire the one, in his Studies the other; and an elegant Poem should be as lasting a Memorial of the Scholar's Wit, as a pompous Trophy of the General's Conduct, or the Soldier's Valour. And yet, for want of certain periodical reviews of the Learning of former Ages, not only many inestimable Pieces have been lost, but Science it self has been in the most imminent Danger.*

I have often thought there is a Kind of Contagion in minds, as well as Bodies; what we admire, we fondly wish to imitate; and, thus, while a Few excellent Authors throw a Glory on the Studies they pursue, Disciples will not be wanting to imitate them: But, when those Studies fall into Disesteem, and Neglect, instead of being profess'd, and encourag'd, 'tis more than probable they will not be understood. I have read 'twas thus in Greece, *and* Rome, *and all the considerable Nations of* Europe *beside: In* England *'tis notorious; and I wish our share of Reproach on this Head, may be confin'd to the Ignorance, and Inhumanity of former Times.*

'Tis true, not only every Age, but every Year produces Numbers of new Pieces, and 'twould be impossible to preserve them all; neither indeed, would all deserve it: But should we govern our Choice with Judgment, and Impartiality, the Task would be easy, and every good Author would receive the Benefit of it. – 'Twill be in vain to object that Merit is its own Preservative: For, beside Numberless other Instances, most of the Poems in this Volume are a Proof to the contrary, and still many more than I have reserv'd for the next. Yet, let them be enquir'd for among the Booksellers, and the Difficulty of procuring them will be a sufficient Proof how little they are know, and how near they are to be lost in Oblivion. – This I am a Witness of my self, and 'tis with great Trouble and Charge, I have been able to collect a sufficient Number for my present Purpose: nor, without the generous Assistance of the Candid Mr. Oldys, *would even this, have been in my Power: And, after all, there are still some omitted; which, if I can procure, shall be annex'd by way of Supplement, together with a Glossary, at the End of the Work.*

Let me then, at least, be pardon'd for attempting to set up a Bulwark between Time, and Merit? I have heard that a certain modern Virtuoso, had a Project to discover the Age of the World, by the Saltness of the Sea, the Effect of which could not be known for Hundreds of Years after. – I flatter my self, that the Success of mine need not be quite so remov'd; nor is it more Romantick, or less Useful. The Alterations of a Language are of some Consequence to be known, tho' inferior to those of Nature; and this some Satisfaction to be acquainted with the Lives of Authors, as well as their Works: This Undertaking includes all, nor is merely calculated for those which are already Obsolete; but, if it can be suppos'd that any of the Moderns would ever be in the same Danger, or any future Writer should do me to Honour to continue the Series, may prove some little Support even to Them. In a Word, it may serve as a perpetual Index to our Poetry, a Test of all foreign Innovations in our Language, a general Register of all the little, occasional Pieces, of our Holy-Day Writers (as Mr. Dryden *prettily calls them) which might otherwise be lost; and a grateful Record of all the Patrons that, in* England, *have done Honour to the* Muses.

Before I conclude, 'tis my Duty to acknowledge that no less than Three[*] *Writers have undertaken, simply, the Lives of the Poets, beside Mr.* Wood, *who confines himself to those educated at* Oxford; *That Sir* Thomas Pope Blunt, *has wrote Remarks on a Few of them, and Two or Three have had their Works republish'd in our own Times; what use I have made of all, or any of these Circumstances, will be obvious; as well as what is peculiarly my own. – This, however, I may, with Modesty, hint, that many mistakes in Facts are rectify'd, several Lives are added, the Characters of the Authors are not taken on Content, or from Authority, but a serious Examination of their Works; and some of the most beautiful Passages, or entire Poems, I could chuse, are added to constitute a* Series of Poetry *(which has never been aim'd at any where else) and compleat one of the most valuable Collections, that ever was made publick.*

How far I have succeeded, is submitted to the Understanding of every impartial, and sensible Reader: To which I the more cheerfully resign my self, as introducing more Beauties of others, to be my Advocates, than I can have Faults of my own to be forgiven.

To what has been said, on the Design of this Work in general, I, at first, intended to add some Account of the Progress of Criticism in England; *from Sir* Philip Sidney, *the Art of* English *Poesy (written by Mr.* Puttenham, *a Gentleman Pensioner to Queen* Elizabeth:) *Sir* John Harrington, Ben Johnson, &c. *But this part of my Task I am oblig'd to postpone, for want of Room, to my next Volume; and shall conclude with rectifying a Mistake of my own in the Life of Mr.* Fairfax: *Where 'tis said; that Author is crouded by Mr.* Philips *into his Supplement, which should have been said of Mr.* Sacville: *And begging Pardon for the* Errata *which have escap'd me, not thro' neglect, but want of sufficient Experience in Affairs of this Nature.*

---

[*] *Mr.* Phillips, *Mr.* Winstanly *and Mr.* Jacob.

Bibliography

Anderson, Misty. *Female Playwrights and Eighteenth-century Comedy: Negotiating Marriage on the London Stage*. New York: Palgrave, 2002.

Baker, David Erskine. *Biographia Dramatica, or Companion* to the *Play-house*. 4 vols. London, 1764.

Barker-Benfield, G.J. *The Culture of Sensibility: Sex and Society in Eighteenth-century Britain*. Chicago: U of Chicago P, 1992.

Battestin, Martin C., with Ruthe R. Battestin. *Henry Fielding: A Life*. London: Routledge, 1989.

Bevis, Richard W. *English Drama: Restoration and Eighteenth Century, 1660–1789*. London and New York: Longman, 1988.

Burnim, Kalman A., and Philip H. Highfill, Jr. *John Bell, Patron of British Theatrical Portraiture: A Catalog of the Theatrical Portraits in his Editions of Bell's Shakespeare and Bell's British Theatre*. Carbondale: Southern Illinois UP, 1998.

Collier, Jeremy. *A Short View of the Profaneness and Immorality of the English Stage*. 5th ed. London, 1730.

Cooper, Elizabeth. *The Rival Widows, or Fair Libertine*. London, 1735.

Copeland, Nancy. *Staging Gender in Behn and Centlivre: Women's Comedy and the Theatre*. Burlington, VT: Ashgate, 2004.

Cotton, Nancy. *Women Playwrights in England 1363–1750*. Lewisburg: Bucknell UP, 1980.

Eger, Elizabeth. 'Fashioning a Female Canon: Eighteenth-century Women Poets and the Politics of the Anthology'. *Women's Poetry of the Enlightenment: The Making of a Canon, 1730–1820*. Ed. Isobel Armstrong and Virginia Blain. London: Macmillan, 1998. 201–15.

Ellis, Frank H. *Sentimental Comedy: Theory and Practice*. Cambridge: Cambridge UP, 1991.

Fielding, Henry. *The History of Tom Jones: A Foundling*. 1749. Ed. Fredson Bowers. Middletown, CT: Wesleyan UP, 1975.

———. 'On the Knowledge of the Characters of Men'. *Miscellanies by Henry Fielding Volume One*. 1743. Ed. Henry Knight Miller. Oxford: Clarendon, 1972.

Genest, John, ed. *Some Account of the English Stage from the Restoration in 1660 to 1830*. 10 vols. Bath, 1832.

Goring, Paul. *The Rhetoric of Sensibility in Eighteenth-century Culture*. Cambridge: Cambridge UP, 2005.

Hammond, Brean. *Professional Imaginative Writing in England, 1670–1740: Hackney for Bread.* Oxford: Clarendon Press, 1989.

Highfill, Philip H. Jr., Kalman A. Burnim, and Edward A. Langhans. *A Biographical Dictionary of Actors, Actresses, Musicians, Dancers, Managers, and Other Stage Personnel in London, 1660–1800.* 16 vols. Carbondale: Southern Illinois UP, 1973–93.

Hobbes, Thomas. *Leviathan, or The Matter, Form and Power of a Common-Wealth Ecclesiastical and Civil* (1651). Ed. C.B. Macpherson. Harmondsworth: Penguin, 1968.

Hume, Robert D., ed. *The London Theatre World, 1660–1800.* Carbondale and Edwardsville: Southern Illinois UP, 1980.

———. *The Rakish Stage: Studies in English Drama, 1660–1800.* Carbondale and Edwardsville: Southern Illinois UP, 1983.

Hunt, Margaret. *The Middling Sort: Commerce, Gender, and the Family in England 1680–1780.* Berkeley: U of California P, 1996.

Kavenik, Frances M. *British Drama, 1660–1779: A Critical History.* New York: Twaye, 1995.

Keymer, Thomas. *Richardson's 'Clarissa' and the Eighteenth-Century Reader.* Cambridge: Cambridge UP, 1992.

Kreis-Schinck, Annette. *Women, Writing, and the Theatre in the Early Modern Period: The Plays of Aphra Behn and Susanne Centlivre.* London: Association University Presses, 2001.

Loftis, John. *Comedy and Society from Congreve to Fielding.* Stanford: Stanford UP, 1959.

Maclaughlan, Daniel. *An Essay Upon Improving and Adding to the Strength of Great Britain and Ireland, by Fornication, Justifying the Same from Reason and Scripture.* London, 1735.

Mandeville, Bernard. *The Fable of the* Bees. 1714. Ed. Phillip Harth. Harmondsworth: Penguin, 1989.

Montagu, Lady Mary Wortley. *The Complete Letters of Lady Mary Wortley Montagu.* 3 vols. Ed. Robert Halsband. Oxford: Oxford UP, 1966.

Nicoll, Allardyce. *A History of Eighteenth-century Drama 1700–1750.* Cambridge: Cambridge UP, 1925.

Noble, Yvonne. 'Cooper, Elizabeth,' *Oxford Dictionary of National Biography*, Oxford: Oxford UP, 2004.

Pearson, Jacqueline. *The Prostituted Muse: Images of Women and Women Dramatists 1642–1737.* New York: St. Martin's Press, 1988.

Potter, Tiffany. '"A Certain Sign that He is One of *Us*": *Clarissa*'s Other Libertines'. *Eighteenth-Century Fiction* 11.4 (1999): 403–20.

———. 'The Female Libertine of Sensibility: Elizabeth Cooper's *The Rival Widows'. Restoration and Eighteenth-century Theatre Research* 17.2 (Winter 2002): 2–38.

———. *Honest Sins: Georgian Libertinism in the Plays and Novels of Henry Fielding.* Montreal and Kingston: McGill–Queen's UP, 1999.

Rubik, Margaret. *Early Women Dramatists 1550–1800.* London: Macmillan, 1998.

Shaftesbury, Anthony Ashley Cooper, Earl of. *Characteristicks. An Inquiry Concerning Virtue and Merit.* 4 vols. London, 1758.

Sherbo, Arthur. *English Sentimental Drama.* East Lansing: State UP, 1957.

Steele, Sir Richard. *The Conscious Lovers.* London, 1722.

Stephens, Frederick George. *Catalogue of Political and Personal Satires Preserved in the Department of Prints and Drawings in the British Museum, Volume III.1 (1734–1750).* 11 vols. London: British Museum, 1870–1954.

Stone, George Winchester, Jr. 'Sentimental Comedy: Introduction'. *British Dramatists from Dryden to Sheridan.* Ed. George H. Nettleton, Arthur E. Case, and George Winchester Stone, Jr. Carbondale and Edwardsville: Southern Illinois UP, 1969.

Stone, Lawrence. *The Family, Sex, and Marriage in England 1500–1800.* London: Weidenfeld and Nicholson, 1977.

Todd, Janet. *Sensibility: An Introduction.* London and New York: Methuen, 1986.

Turner, James. *Libertines and Radicals in Early Modern London, 1630–1685.* Cambridge: Cambridge UP, 2002.

———. 'Properties of Libertinism'. *Eighteenth-Century Life* 9.3 (1985): 75–87.

Turner, John. *A Discourse on Fornication: Shewing the Greatness of that Sin.* London, 1698.

Ward, Edward (Ned). *The Libertine's Choice; or, the Mistaken Happiness of the Fool in Fashion.* London, 1704.

Index